· 中英双语 ·

外国专家讲科普

Science Classes from Foreign Experts

科学技术部国外人才研究中心 ◎ 编

Edited by Foreign Talent Research Center, Ministry of Science and Technology, China

科学技术文献出版社
SCIENTIFIC AND TECHNICAL DOCUMENTATION PRESS

· 北京 ·

图书在版编目（CIP）数据

外国专家讲科普：汉文，英文 / 科学技术部国外人才研究中心编. —北京：科学技术文献出版社，2020.12（2022.1重印）

ISBN 978-7-5189-7551-8

Ⅰ.①外…　Ⅱ.①科…　Ⅲ.①科学知识—普及读物—汉、英　Ⅳ.① Z228

中国版本图书馆 CIP 数据核字（2020）第 266223 号

外国专家讲科普（中英双语）

策划编辑：魏宗梅	责任编辑：张 红 责任校对：张永霞 责任出版：张志平

出　版　者　科学技术文献出版社

地　　　址　北京市复兴路15号　　邮编　100038

编　务　部　（010）58882938，58882087（传真）

发　行　部　（010）58882868，58882870（传真）

邮　购　部　（010）58882873

官 方 网 址　www.stdp.com.cn

发　行　者　科学技术文献出版社发行　全国各地新华书店经销

印　刷　者　北京虎彩文化传播有限公司

版　　　次　2020 年 12 月第 1 版　2022 年 1 月第 2 次印刷

开　　　本　710×1000　1/16

字　　　数　216千

印　　　张　18.75

书　　　号　ISBN 978-7-5189-7551-8

定　　　价　58.00元

编 委 会

序

我与中国的"化学反应"

文／戴伟（英）　译／孙梦格

在我十一二岁时，有两大兴趣：化学和中国！我知道我对化学产生兴趣的原因，那是因为在花园里进行的激动人心的实验中，我看见了一抹新世界的神秘曙光。而我对中国的兴趣也缘于与此类似的好奇心。我在 1996 年加入了北京化工大学，自此就幸福地工作、生活在这里。 在大学的教学研究之外，我一直在寻找机会向中国的学生科普化学知识，激发他们对化学的兴趣，就像我小时候一样。春节期间，我会经常拜访中国乡村里的朋友并给孩子们做一些科普。我记得有一年，我从村子的商店里买到了一些醋和小苏打，给孩子们制作了"火山"，发射了口香糖"火箭"，度过了一段愉快的时光。

英国皇家化学学会，正式科普的机会

2011 年，我得到了很多更稳定、更正式的做科普的机会。那一年是联合国教科文组织的国际化学年。几年前，我在北京设立了英国皇家化学学会（RSC）的分支，RSC 运营着大量的书籍和学术出版业务，但作为一个非营利组织，也会用出版部门产生的盈余开展慈善活动，增加公众对化学的兴趣。当时 RSC 的主席大卫·菲利普教授迫切地感到，除了帮助组织国际化学年的一些活动外，RSC 也应该尝试开展一些属于自己的长期活动，扩大国际化学年的影响。他非常开明地决定，给每个地方的 RSC 分支机构（共有 100 多个）一笔 1000 英镑的资金，要求他们尝试一些此前从未做过的事情。

我在北京的英国朋友海伦·博伊尔成立了一家慈善组织"打工子弟基金会"（MCF），专门为在北京的务工人员子女学校的学生上课。基金会里有一群志愿者，他们会在周末给孩子们上课，主要教英语，也会教音乐和艺术。我决定去教孩子们化学。于是，我购买了一整套烧杯、试管、量筒和其他设备，还买了一些无毒的化学试剂、儿童尺寸的实验室外套，以及最重要的防护设备——护目镜。我把 4 个孩子和 1 个研究生分为一组，开始了化学试验，孩子们玩得很开心。我们继续和城市务工人员子女学校合作，并陆续收到了更多来自公立学校和其他组织的邀请，如北京科技教育促进会。

因为化学实验经常有火花和爆炸，所以我们不能让孩子们自己操作。我通常会先问学生，是否相信我可以通过在蜡烛上喷水的方式把蜡烛点燃，他们当然会说不相信，然后我会让孩子们一起用英语倒数"三、二、一"，接着就把"水"喷洒在蜡烛上，此时蜡烛就会迸发出火焰。300 多名学生兴奋地跳上跳下，并惊呼着"哇!"，给实验课堂开了个好头。当然，等孩子们冷静下来时，我会告诉他们，我到底是怎么做到的，而不是像魔术师那样保持神秘。我喷洒的"水"实际上是酒精，并且在演示之前，我在蜡烛上挖了一个小坑，在其中填充了一些红色的固体。接下来，我不用蜡烛，再次重复上述演示过程，孩子们就会看到，其实是红色固体和酒精引发了火苗，而红色固体燃烧后残留了绿色固体。在这个过程中，他们看到的就是化学的本质——将一种或多种材料（在这个实验中就是酒精和红色固体）转换为新的材料（绿色固体）。

北京化工大学，面向公众科普

除了皇家化学学会，我还得到了北京化工大学的大力支持。根据习近平总书记在全国科技创新大会、两院院士大会、中国科协第九次全国代表大会上的指示，要把科学普及放在与科技创新同等重要的位置，希望广大科技工作者以提高全民科学素质为己任，把普及科学知识、弘扬科学精神、传播科学思想、倡导科学方法作为义不容辞的责任。北京化工大学将我的大部分工作职责转换为面向公众的科普。例如，我每年都会在北京化工大学副校长和招生办公室主任的陪同下，访问全国 50~60 所顶级中学。在同事们介绍完北京化工大学之后，我会给学生们（通常是数百人，有时超过千人，一次在长沙学生人数超过了 2000 人）演示与过氧化氢有关的化学实验，与他们在中学课堂里学过的化学知识紧密相连，这些实验演示都大受欢迎。

我们也很高兴多次应邀参加全国科技活动周活动。除了一大批和我的团队一起做实验的孩子们之外，我们的实验室还迎来了几位特殊的嘉宾，其中包括原副总理刘延东、科技部原部长万钢、现任科技部部长王志刚、北京市原市委书记郭金龙与现任北京市委书记蔡奇。刘延东女士非常喜欢和孩子们一起做实验：我给了她一个装有黄色液体的烧瓶，她摇晃烧瓶后，液体变成了红色，再摇晃一次，液体又变成了绿色，然后她会请学生们猜想为什么会发生这种变化。刘延东女士说，做实验的经历激动人心，让她想到了 50 年前自己在清华大学化学工程系学习的时光。尽管 2020 年全国科技活动周受到了疫情的影响，但我仍旧给孩子们展示了化学实验，孩子们只能间隔坐开，但他们的欢笑声依然令人激动。

"戴博士实验室"上线

2018 年，我的助手索乐乐建议把一些化学实验的视频放到快手平台上。当时他半开玩笑地说："我觉得肯定没人会看！"我说，科学家们都是通过做实验来观测结果的，想知道怎么样，就必须亲自尝试一下。尝试之后，我们发现，真的有不少人观看我们的实验演示！我们的平台账号"戴博士实验室"在快手上有 370 多万粉丝，其中一些视频的播放量达到了 1500 万次。"戴博士实验室"在抖音和哔哩哔哩等其他平台上也有不少粉丝。这些平台除了吸引大量的观众之外，还有其他优势。它们为那些地处偏远小镇或山村、很少有机会参与科学探索的年轻人提供了亲近化学的机会。

我在全国各地讲课时发现，许多高中生进行化学实验的机会非常有限，只能从书本上学化学。造成这种现象的一部分原因是高考化学的局限性，还因为许多学校的班级中可能有 70 名或 80 名学生，一旦做实验，就需要大量的玻璃器皿和试剂溶液，所以很难组织。为了解决这个问题，我们目前正在开发"微型化学实验"项目，这个项目只需要简单的设备和几毫升的溶液，甚至可以在普通教室而不是实验室中进行。我们于 2019 年夏季在北京开展了试点，由皇家化学学会和快手共同赞助，30 名来自云南和湖北深度贫困地区的学生和老师在免费提供设施的北京王府学校的大力支持下参与了项目。这次活动取得成功之后，我们计划在不同的深度贫困地区展开更多的试点，然而因为疫情的暴发，我们不得不暂缓计划。

为什么科普如此重要？

很多人，有时甚至是其他科学家，经常问我为什么认为科普如此重要。当然，原因之一是我们希望激励学生成为中国未来所需要的科学家和工程师。此

目 录
Contents

contributed their efforts to the class, to the project team of the VIPKID Foreign Experts Science Classes, and to the editing and publishing team of this book. Any suggestion from readers is welcome.

Editors

Dec. 2020

This book is edited based on the 2019-2020 Foreign Experts Science Class. The publication of this book will expand the ecology of the Foreign Experts Science Class and realize the trinity of on-site classes, online video courses and publication of the book. This book has three chapters.

Chapter 1: Man and Nature. This chapter covers human senses, brain, female fertility, as well as dolphins and the animal migrations. As Jean-Marc Bovet, a Swiss expert working as Chief Technology Officer of Changfeng Pharmaceuticals, stated that we got knowledge by observing the material world and verifying it through experiments. Science is knowledge about the material and the natural world. Therefore, it is always important to maintain curiosity and to explore the unknown.

Chapter 2: Engineering. This chapter includes the selection of bridges, airplanes, building materials, and the application of bionics in architectural design. Engineering is a general term for the various disciplines formed by applying the theories of natural science to specific industrial and agricultural production sectors. Applying scientific knowledge to real life, using technology to build buildings, manufacture machines, and build bridges and roads, our lives are more comfortable and convenient.

Chapter 3: Amazing Science. This chapter constitutes topics related to robots, nanotechnology, astrophysics and black holes, and the theory of relativity. The macroscopic world involves the operation of celestial bodies and galaxy evolution while the microscopic world contains gene editing and particle structure, both of which are at the forefront of the current development of science and technology. In these areas, scientists continue to explore and experiment, trying to expand the boundaries of science.

On September 11, 2020, President Xi Jinping called on scientists to "continuously march into the breadth and depth of science and technology" at a symposium. May this book plant a seed of science in children's mind and inspire them to love science, explore the unknown, and climb to the top with courage.

We want to extend special thanks to the Department of Science and Technology Talent and Popularization, Ministry of Science and Technology of China for funding and supporting the publication of this book, to all the international experts who

Foreword

Chinese President Xi Jinping has pointed out that as the two wings of achieving innovative development, the innovation and popularization of science and technology must weigh the same. Without improvement of citizens' scientific literacy, it is difficult to establish high quality talent pool, thus hard to achieve rapid transformation of scientific and technological achievements into application. President Xi stressed that scientists can take the responsibility of popularizing science, fostering a social environment, in order to unleash the creative potential of hundreds of millions of people.

In early 2019, the Foreign Talent Research Center of the Ministry of Science and Technology of China and VIPKID jointly launched VIPKID Foreign Expert Public Science Classes, a project inviting foreign experts in science, technology, engineering, arts and mathematics to schools in China, especially schools in remote rural areas and urban schools for children of migrant workers, giving science classes. In this way, scientific knowledge can be more accessible to increasing numbers of children and their scientific interests can be stimulated. Until 2020, a total of 28 Classes have been organized, with 23 experts from 11 countries, including the United Kingdom, the United States, France, Germany, Canada and Italy taking part in. The courses they gave had a wide range from chemistry, physics, engineering, aviation, materials, pharmaceuticals to public health. The total number of students on site reached 4000. One of the prominent features of the project is high-calibre foreign experts offering the class. This project extended to elementary schools and middle schools in remote areas such as Dabie Mountain and Jinggang Mountain, bringing rare high-end resources there.

书出版三位一体。本书共分为 3 章，主要内容如下。

第一章：人与自然。本章包括人的感官、大脑、女性生育能力，以及海豚、动物大迁徙等内容。正如长风药业公司首席技术官、瑞士专家博江盟（Jean-Marc Bovet）所说，知识是我们通过对物质世界进行观察、通过实验进行验证而总结出来的，科学就是关于物质和自然世界的知识，所以，好奇心很重要，要永远追求对未知的探索。

第二章：工程世界。本章包括桥梁、飞机、建筑材料的选择，以及仿生学在建筑设计中的应用等内容。工程是将自然科学的理论应用到具体工农业生产部门中形成的各学科的总称。将科学知识应用到现实生活中，运用技术建造屋宇、制造机器、架桥修路，我们的生活才更舒适、更便捷。

第三章：科技魅力。本章包括机器人、纳米技术、天体物理学和黑洞、相对论等内容。宏观世界大至天体运行、星系演化，微观世界小至基因编辑、粒子结构，都是当前世界科技发展的最前沿。在这些前沿领域，科学家们不断探索，不断尝试，努力拓展科学的边界。

2020 年 9 月 11 日，习近平总书记在科学家座谈会上向广大科学家和科技工作者发出"不断向科学技术广度和深度进军"的号召。愿本书能在孩子们心里埋下一粒科学的种子，启发他们热爱科学，探索未知，勇攀高峰。

特别感谢科学技术部科技人才与科学普及司对本书出版的资助和支持，感谢所有参与课堂并付出心血的外国专家们，感谢"VIPKID 外国专家科普公益课堂"项目团队，感谢本书的编辑出版团队。不足之处，请读者批评指正。

编　者

2020 年 12 月

前　言

　　习近平总书记指出，科技创新、科学普及是实现创新发展的两翼，要把科学普及放在与科技创新同等重要的位置。没有全民科学素质普遍提高，就难以建立起宏大的高素质创新大军，难以实现科技成果快速转化。希望广大科技工作者以提高全民科学素质为己任，把普及科学知识、弘扬科学精神、传播科学思想、倡导科学方法作为义不容辞的责任，在全社会推动形成讲科学、爱科学、学科学、用科学的良好氛围，使蕴藏在亿万人民中间的创新智慧充分释放、创新力量充分涌流。

　　2019 年年初，科技部国外人才研究中心和 VIPKID 共同发起了"VIPKID 外国专家科普公益课堂"，邀请科学、技术、工程、艺术和数学等领域的外国专家走进学校，尤其是偏远乡村学校、城市务工子弟学校，开展科普课堂，传播科学知识，激发科学兴趣。截至 2020 年年底，共组织"VIPKID 外国专家科普公益课堂"28 节，共有来自英、美、法、德、加、意等 11 个国家的 23 位外国专家参与了科普课堂活动，主讲课程涉及化学、物理、工程、航空、材料、制药和公共卫生等领域，现场学生受众累计达 4000 人。外国专家科普公益课堂的最大特点，即高端外国专家做科普。科普公益课堂深入大别山、井冈山等偏远地区的小学、中学，为当地带来了难得的高端资源。

　　本书是在 2019—2020 年科普公益课堂的基础上编辑而成。本书的出版将拓展外国专家科普公益课堂项目的生态，实现学校实体课堂、线上视频课程、图

accurate amongst the vast amount of information that is fed to us every day.

I have been fortunate to be able to visit many places of China for one reason or another. Counting up the other day, I found that there are only two— Guangxi and Tibet—where I have not done a chemistry outreach lecture or class in a school or science museum. I hope to be able to complete my goal as soon as possible.

David G. Evans

Chinese Government Friendship Award Winner，Professor from Beijing University of Chemical Technology and Director of the Popular Science Experiment Center experiments on Kuaishou. Half joking, he said "I'm sure no one will watch them!" I said that since scientists must do the experiment to be sure of the result, we should have a go. And lo and behold, we found that people did watch them! Our site has over 3.7 million followers on Kuaishou and some of the videos have been watched over 15 million times. The site also has quite a few followers on other platforms such as Tik Tok and Bilibili. As well as reaching large numbers of people, these platforms have other benefits. They provide a way of bringing chemistry to young people in small towns or remote villages who have no, or very few, opportunities to take part in science activities.

I have found on my travels that many high school students have very limited opportunities to do practical chemistry, and when it becomes all bookwork they find chemistry very boring. This is partly because of the constraints imposed by the college entrance exam, but also because in many schools there can be 70 or 80 students in a class so that is difficult to organize practical activities, since large amounts of glassware and reagent solutions are required. To combat this problem, we have worked on developing a program, which only require simple apparatus and a few milliliters of solution, and can even be carried out in a normal classroom rather than a laboratory. We ran a pilot program in Beijing in summer 2019 for 30 students and teachers from regions in deep poverty from Yunnan and Hubei which was sponsored by RSC and Kuaishou, with strong support from Beijing Royal School who provided their facilities free of charge. Following the success of this event, we had planned to start rolling out the program in regions in deep poverty in different parts of the country this year, but of course the coronavirus epidemic means we have had to put our plans on hold for the moment.

Why Is Doing Outreach So Important?

People, even other scientists, often ask me why I think doing outreach is so important. One reason of course is that we hope to inspire students to become the scientists and engineers that China will need in the future. We try to help students develop a scientific way of thinking. This is an important skill, because when faced with all the rumors and fake news available these days. Everyone needs a scientific attitude to pick out what is true and

BUCT Strongly Supports Our Outreach Work

In addition to RSC, I have also received strong support from BUCT. Following the guidance of President Xi Jinping on the importance of popularizing science, the university converted most of my job description to involving outreach. For example, I visit each year has around 50 or 60 of the top high schools all over the country in the company of a BUCT Vice-President and the head of the Admissions Office. After my colleagues introduce BUCT, I give the students usually several hundred, but sometimes over 1000, or once in Changsha, as many as 2000 lecture demonstrations based around hydrogen peroxide which links exciting experiments with their high school curriculum. This usually receives a rapturous reception.

We have also been delighted to be invited on several occasions to take part in the National Science Week. In addition to the large numbers of enthusiastic children who have carried out chemistry experiments with myself and the team of BUCT postgraduates, we have welcomed several honored guests to our laboratory, including Liu Yandong—the former Vice Premier, Wan Gang—the former minister of the Ministry of Science and Technology (MOST) , Wang Zhigang—the minister of MOST, Guo Jinlong—the former Party Chief of Beijing, and Cai Qi—the Party Chief of Beijing. Madam Liu Yandong was particularly keen to do an experiment with the children: I gave her a flask containing a yellow liquid, which turned red when she shook it, and then green when she shook it again, and then she asked the students for their hypotheses about what was happening. Madam Liu Yandong was very excited, because she said it took her back 50 years to her time as a student in the Department of Chemical Engineering, Tsinghua University. Although 2020 National Science Week was constrained by the coronavirus outbreak, I was still able to give two lecture demonstrations to young children (sitting one meter apart). They were very excited to see the chemical reactions and generated a great atmosphere in the classroom.

Going Online: "Dr. Dai's Lab"

In 2018 my assistant Suo Lele suggested we should put videos of some chemistry book and academic publishing operation but, as a not-for-profit organization, uses the surplus generated by the publishing section to run charitable activities promoting interest in chemistry. The RSC President at the time, Professor David Phillips, felt strongly that as well as organizing activities during IYC itself, RSC should try to set up some longer-term activities to mark IYC in a more sustainable way. He had the inspired idea to give every local section and interest group (over 100 in all) one thousand pounds and challenged them to do something outside their normal remit.

Helen Boyle, my British friend in Beijing, who had set up a charity (MCF) to organize classes for children attending migrant schools in Beijing. Helen had a team of volunteers going into schools at weekends, mainly teaching English, but also some music and art. I bought a whole load of beakers, test tubes, measuring cylinders and other apparatus all plastic, rather than the traditional glass to avoid accidents, nontoxic chemicals, child-sized lab coats and— most importantly of all—safety glasses. We divided them into pairs with a postgraduate looking after a table of four pairs and the chemistry began,they had great fun. We have continued to work with the migrant schools, but also began to receive more and more invitations from state schools and other organizations.

Sometimes the postgraduates and I run hands-on practical classes at school science fairs, and at other times I go alone and do a lecture demonstration of experiments that we couldn't let the children do themselves, since they often involve fire and explosions. I usually start by asking the students if they think I can light a candle by spraying water on it. Of course they don't believe I can, but I ask them to help me by counting down "three, two, one" in English and then I spray "water" onto my candle which bursts into flame. The sight of 300 children jumping up and down shouting "Wow!" gets the lecture off to a good start. Of course, unilke a magician, when they calm down, I will tell them how I did the trick. The "water" is actually alcohol and before the lecture I dug a little pit in the candle and place some red solid in it. By repeating the process without the candle they can see that it is the red solid and alcohol which causes the fire, and afterwards we are left with a green solid. From this they can see the essence of chemistry—changing one or more materials, the alcohol and red solid in this case into a new material, the green solid.

Preface

My Chemical Reaction with China

By David G. Evans (Britain)

When I was around 11 or 12 years old, I had two main hobbies and interests. One was chemistry, and the other was China! I know where my interest in chemistry came from: it was doing lots of exciting experiments in our garden shed which began shining light on the mysteries of a new world. I think my interest in China was sparked by a similar sense of curiosity. I jumped at the chance to move to Beijing University of Chemical Technology (BUCT) in 1996 and have been there happily ever since. Apart from my university work, I was always looking for a chance to introduce Chinese children to chemistry, and see if it could inspire the same sort of interest in them that it had in me all those years ago. I did a few ad hoc sessions with the children of friends whose countryside home I regularly visited over the Spring Festival. I remember one year I were able to buy some vinegar and baking soda from the village shop and had a great time making "volcanos" and launching chewing gum bottle "rockets".

RSC Provides a Chance to Popularize Science

My chance to something more formal and substantial came in 2011, which was the UNESCO International Year of Chemistry (IYC). I had set up a Beijing Local Section of the Royal Society of Chemistry (RSC) a couple of years earlier. RSC has a substantial

外，除了教化学，我们还试图帮助培养学生科学的思维方式。这是一项很重要的技能，因为当今世界，我们面对着许许多多的谣言和"假新闻"，每个人都需要具备科学的态度，才能从每天接收的大量信息中挑选出真实且准确的信息。

我很幸运有各种机会能够访问中国的很多地方。在不久前的统计中，我发现还没有去广西和西藏讲过课或做过实验，我希望能够尽快完成这个目标。

戴伟（David G. Evans）

中国政府友谊奖获得者

北京化工大学教授、科普实验中心主任

第一章　人与自然

Man and Nature

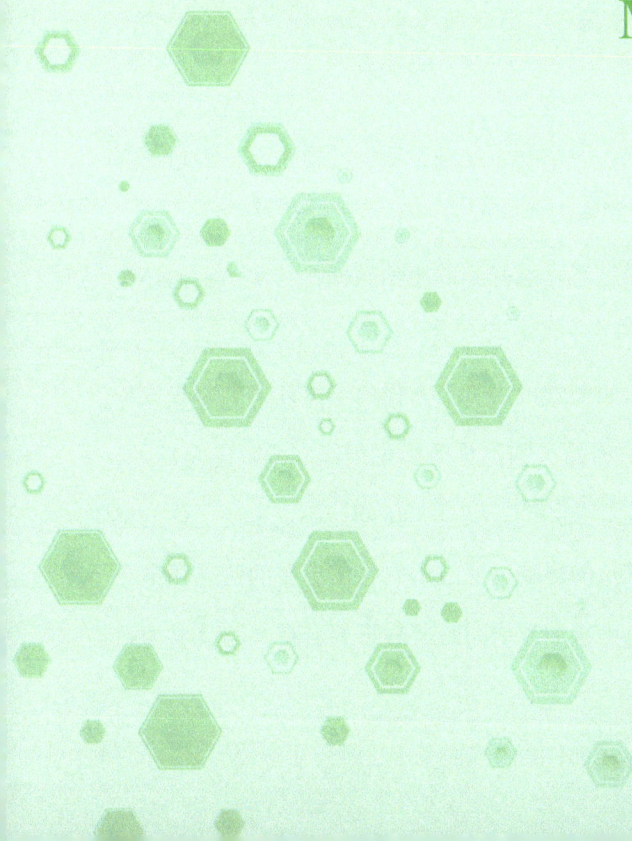

科学，我们如何知道我们所知道的？

文 / 博江盟（瑞士）　译 / 孙梦格

我是一名医药科学家。但今天我不打算谈论我的专业领域，而是希望聊聊这些年来我作为一个热爱科学的人的一些思考。具体来说，我想问问你：我们如何知道自己究竟知道些什么？

什么是知识？

让我们先从科学的定义谈起吧。科学知识是关于某一特定主题、经过"系统性组织"的"信息体系"。我们需要记住两点：首先，我们需要有信息输入，换句话说，我们的大脑先要收集通过感官感知到的原始数据；其次，我们还要把这些数据组织成一个"故事"，而这个故事我称其为科学知识。

信息的输入主要依赖于感官，如触觉或听觉。当你用手捧住雪的时候，你就会收集到关于雪的信息。然后，你的大脑把你的感觉组织起来：它是冷的，它融化了，它变成了水。这就形成了"故事"。这个"故事"不仅来源于你的感知，还可能受到你对雪的预设所带来的影响。通过观察收集更多的信息并把它们组织在一起，我们就能够讲出更丰富的故事。这些故事聚合在一起就成为科学理论。科学理论必须始终与物质世界保持一致。通过对物质世界进行观察，并经实验确认所得的想法，就形成了知识（图1）。

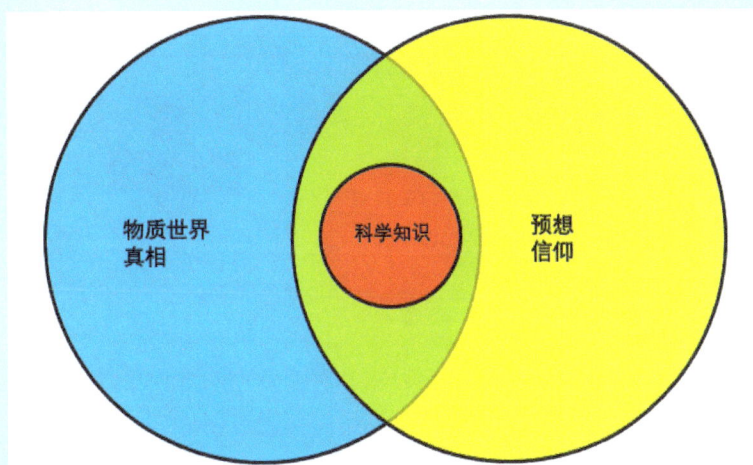

图1 科学知识是什么？

大脑的认知

我们的大脑可以看作是由两个回路构成，其中一个回路反应很快，主要依靠记忆的储备；而另一个则比较慢，靠的是思维和处理信息的能力。这两个回路共同作用，一起对接收到的信息做出判断。

让我们来做一个简单的测试（图2）。请问，图片 A 和图片 B 哪一个是瑞士国旗？

这个问题的要点在于记忆的调动。如果你已经率先掌握了相关记忆，那就应该能迅速做出回答，答案是 A（我的祖国！）。但如果你没有相关的记忆，那么你的大脑就会自动切换到思维模式。你的大脑会想：为什么这两面旗帜是如此相似？原来红十字会的发起人是瑞士诺贝尔和平奖获得者让－亨利·杜南，而他设计红十字会会旗的灵感来源正是反转过来的瑞士国旗。

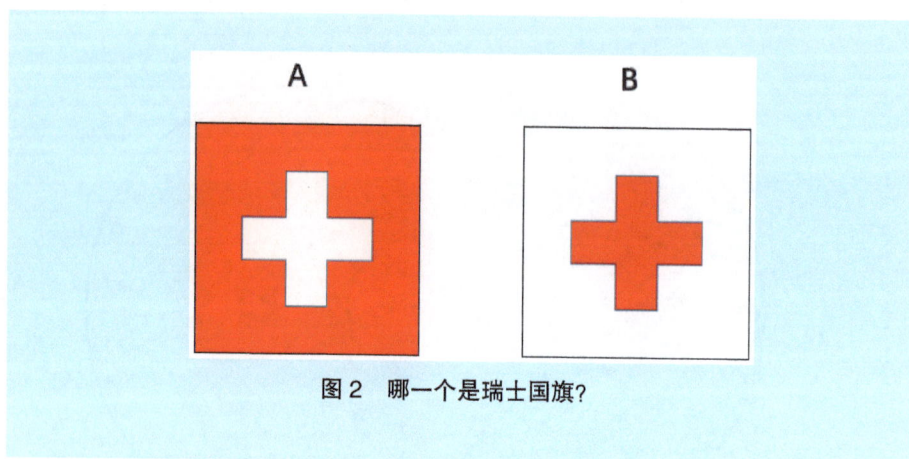

图2　哪一个是瑞士国旗?

人类的感官

　　人类只能接收到有限的信息,因为我们所知道的一切都来自以下五感:嗅觉、触觉、味觉、听觉和视觉。它们是人类收集到的所有信息的最初来源。

　　图3中的人叫作Homunculus先生。他的样子看上去是不是很有趣呢?Homunculus先生身体的某些部位大得不成比例,如手和嘴巴。为什么会这样?要回答这个问题,我们得首先看看图4。图4显示的是大脑中用于接收触摸感知的部分。我们可以看到,这部分大脑中分配给手的部分要比分配给手臂的大。所以,Homunculus先生的肢体其实是按照各部位的敏感程度来的。我们可以试

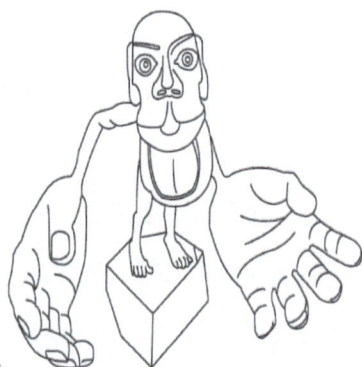

图3　Homunculus 先生

着触摸一下自己身体的不同部位，你会发现手掌内侧要比臂膀敏感得多，哪怕是很细小的东西也能感觉得到。

那么，听觉呢？人在发出声音时，其实是在空气中产生了一个声波，听者的耳朵捕捉到这个波，也就听到了声音。波有两个属性：振幅和波长。声调越小，振幅也就越小，反之振幅则越大；声调越低，波长越长，反之波长则越短。声音传播时，空气中的分子相互运动，而波的特点就由这些分子的压缩形态表现出来（图5）。

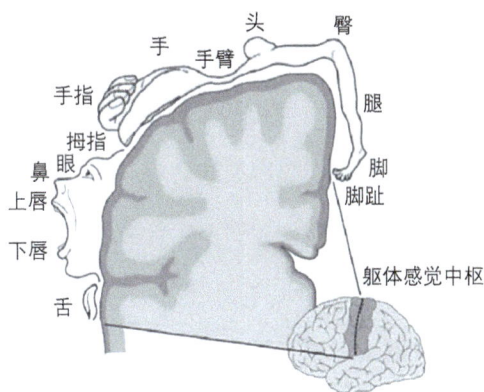

图4 大脑中负责触觉部分的比例

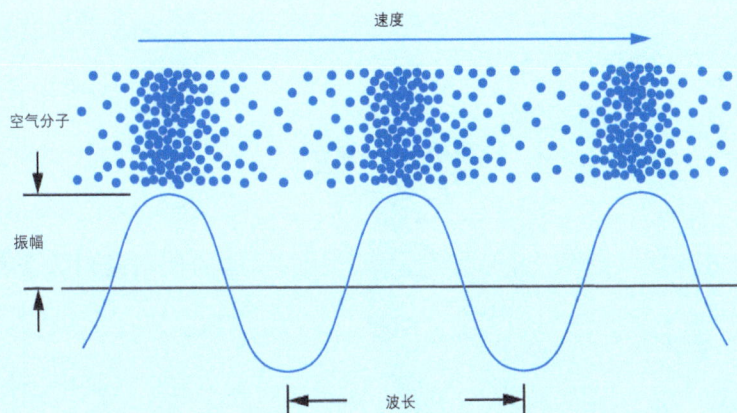

图5 声波

人的耳朵并不能听到所有声音。我们只能听到一小部分声音，音调太低或者太高都不行，即人类的听觉有一个频率范围。而狗能收听到的频率范围更大，能感知到更高的音调。这也是为什么你可以买到只有狗才能听到的哨子来驯犬而不用担心打扰到邻居。

很多动物对声音的接收范围都不一样。蝙蝠就非常特别，它们可以发出并收听到一种叫作超声波的高频声音。蝙蝠正是利用这种声音来"看"世界的——它们可以利用超声波回声定位周围环境，并且锁定猎物的位置。

那么，我们是如何看见东西的呢？这和周围的光有关。光也像波一样运动，有着振幅和波长的属性。但与声音不同的是，光是一种电磁波。

和听觉差不多，我们的视力也有局限。我们只能看到所谓的"可见光"，它只占到了电磁波谱的一部分。一个普通人的眼睛能感知到 400~700 nm 波长段的光线。

蜜蜂与人类不同，仅仅能看到波长极短的光线。蜜蜂的可见光波长在 300~600 nm。所以，对两个不同的物种来说，同一朵花可能看上去完全不同（图 6）。

由于感官的局限性，我们需要利用仪器设备来将自己无法感知到的信息转化为可以看到或听到的东西。仪器的使用是对人类感官的扩展。不过我想告诉你们的是，这个宇宙中每时每刻都发生着很多很多的事情，就算是用上所有的感官，我们仍然不能感知到全部这些事物的存在。

图 6　对两个不同的物种来说，同一
朵花的颜色可能看上去完全不同

思考的作用

思考能力是我们大脑的另一个重要作用。我们用大脑来理解收集到的所有信息。一种理解的方式是演绎：从理论到假设，再到观察，通过观察最后确认假设。历史上，亚里士多德等哲学家提出过这种思维方式。另一种思维方式则更像福尔摩斯：我们首先像一个侦探一样观察，然后从中发现一个模式，形成一个假设，最后浓缩出一个理论。

柏拉图的洞穴之喻

洞穴之喻是柏拉图著名理论之一。故事中苏格拉底描述了这样一个人：他的一生都被锁链锁住，只能面对着山洞里的一面空白墙壁。这个人的身后有一股燃烧着的火焰。他日日夜夜看到的都是从他身后的火堆前经过的物体投射在墙上的影子，并为这些影子命名，而他却认为，自己看到的影子就是现实。实际上却并非如此。

在某种程度上，由于感官的局限，我们就像这个山洞里的囚徒，只能依赖自己的感知，并不能确切地掌握发生的一切。真实的世界存在于远方和山洞之外。

大脑对信息的解读

我们用眼睛来观察世界。人类眼睛的底部有一个叫作视网膜的器官，它可以捕捉外界的图像。但视网膜上的图像是上下颠倒的。接收了图像后，大脑便想：这不是世界真实的样子。于是，大脑就帮我们把图像再正过来，否则我们就没办法看到我们现在所看到的东西了。

看到图 7 里的这些人了吗？你的大脑正试图弄清楚发生了什么。他们是要上楼吗？还是在下楼？我们的大脑不喜欢这样的不确定性，因为这个图像在物理学上是不可能的，所以大脑分析起来可能会有点困难。

图 7　埃舍尔的错觉

再来看看另外一张图。请大家仔细观察图 8 里的这个蓝色十字架。这个十字架是在立方体的外面还是里面？是一直都在外面还是一直都在里面？不管是哪种情况，我们的大脑都无法彻底地全盘接受。事实上，这幅图提供了两种可能性，但我们的大脑似乎必须坚持要做出一个决定。

所以，虽然大脑非常强大，但它也会遇到一些问题。你不能总是相信你的大脑，

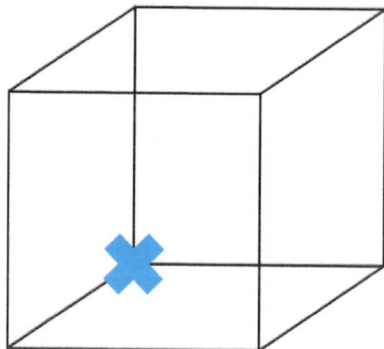

图 8　内克尔立方体

也要对看到的东西多加思索。你对事物的看法不同，事情本身就会随之变得不同。你可能已经听过了盲人摸象的故事：如果找来6个盲人，让他们各自试着描述一头大象，那么一共就会有6幅截然不同的画面。有人认为大象是一把扇子，有人觉得是一条蛇，还有人说是一堵墙。他们每个人都有自己的观点。科学家要做的就是把大家从不同角度得到的信息都收集起来，从而描绘出一个更接近真相的全貌。其实，我们在某一时间点所掌握的信息从来都只是真相的一部分，但我们却总以为自己已经知道了所有的真相。这就是为什么人类必须对周围的一切事物、每一条新的信息都保持开放的态度，因为只有这样才能不断地提高我们对世界的认识。

科学和技术

科学与技术有什么区别？科学是关于物质和自然世界的知识，科学规律则被假定为永不改变的定律。技术则不同，技术是对科学知识的利用，能够创造出许多有用的东西。在科学世界中，科学家着重探索的是事物的基本性质。例如，当谈到空气时，科学家们会去研究空气怎样流动、空气的温度、气压和空气密度等。就其本身而言，这些概念有时看起来很有挑战性，甚至难以理解。但是如果我们面临工程建设的考验，要试图做出一些既实际又好用的东西时，科学知识的基础就是重中之重。如果你想成为一名杰出的工程师的话，你就必须勤奋学习，了解非常丰富的科学知识。

将科学应用到现实生活中、创造出一个能够真正良好运转的东西是一个复杂的过程。工程方案可能会多种多样，任何微小的设计变化都会对其性能产生不同的影响。就拿折纸飞机来举例吧。假设我们用相同的纸来制作飞机，在同一个房间里试飞，所有测试条件都非常相似，但每个人折出来的纸飞机都不一定一模一样。有的纸飞机设计不同，而有的设计相同的纸飞机又在折叠的方式上有出入。因此，它们在飞行中的表现也各有千秋。如果你想成为一个优秀的纸飞机工程师，制作出最好的飞行纸飞机，那么首先就必须了解纸飞机能够飞起来的科学原理。所以，你必须学习掌握丰富的科学知识。

好奇心和好习惯都很重要

现在让我们来聊聊好奇心。随着年龄的增长，人的好奇心通常会变得愈发枯竭。你们还很年轻，对这个世界充满了好奇。等上了年纪以后，你们也一定要尽可能地珍惜和保留这种品质。

图9　2012年8月成功登陆火星的好奇号火星车
由华裔美国女孩马天琪命名

再告诉你们一件有趣的事。图9中的这个美国女孩曾赢得了美国宇航局为火星探测器取名的大赛——她为它取名"好奇号"，就是被送到火星上的好奇号火星车。这个女孩在当时只有12岁。她不仅赢得了命名比赛，还为我们留下了这样一句话："好奇心是一种永恒的火焰，燃烧在我们每个人的心中……它是一种强大的力量。没有它，就不会有今天的我们。好奇心是推动我们在日常生活中前进的激情所在。在好奇心的驱动下，在提高和探索中，我们成为探险家和科学家。"这话说得再好不过了。

除了好奇心之外，其他方面的技能同样需要得到培养。想在一门学科有所建树，我们不能只依靠好奇心，还需要保持专注并持续努力。这是一种叫作"坚韧"的人类品质。要做到这一点有个诀窍，叫作"习惯"。在习惯的帮助下，所有的工作和任务都不再是一种负担。如果你每天都有作业要做，那么你要做的就是把完成作业变成一种习惯，这样一来你就不会再去为它烦恼，而只是去做就可以了。当一件事成为一种习惯的时候，你对它的好恶也就不复存在。你只是在遵从一项习惯罢了。

所以，你们要尽早地养成一些好习惯，如完成作业、锻炼身体、先工作后玩耍、勇于承担责任、在机会面前积极主动。除此之外，还别忘了要劳逸结合，好好吃饭。不要害怕思考那些经常让你感到困惑的事。永远记得，要保持积极主动，思想开放！

作者简介

我 叫 Jean-Marc Bovet，中文名是博江盟。我出生于 1955 年，来自美丽富饶的瑞士。我的父母都在瑞士从事纺织业的生意。1993 年，我在密歇根大学攻读完了自己的博士学位，随后又在北卡罗来纳大学完成了博士后的研究。此外，我还是两家公司的联合创始人之一。一家叫作 Cirrus Pharmaceuticals，是一家研发多种不同药品的合同研究组织；另一家是

Kalliste Systems，专门为医药监管环境提供灵活平台软件服务。在 2016 年，我加入了长风药业股份有限公司。公司的中国同事们还给我起了个小名，他们都亲切地叫我老马。现在，我在江苏省工作和生活。

我是吸入式药品研发和信息科学方面的专家，目前于长风药业股份有限公司任首席技术官一职。在中国，很多人都不幸患有哮喘和慢性阻塞性肺病，而我正是致力于为这些呼吸系统疾病患者提供质量可靠且价格合理的药物。一款药物的开发通常需要耗费大量的时间和资源，利用信息科学技术有助于加速药物的研发。与此同时，我也常常为中国的科技、教育和产业发展建言献策，贡献自己的一分力量。

扫描收看
本文视频课程

Science, How Do We Know What We Know?

By Jean-Marc Bovet (Switzerland)

Today, I'm not going to talk about my profession as a pharmaceutical scientist. Instead, I'm going to talk about some reflections I have had over the years as a person who loves science, to be specific, how do we know what we know.

What Is Knowledge?

Let's begin with the definition of science. We can define scientific knowledge as a "systematically organized body of information" on a particular subject. There are two things to remember here. Firstly, there is the body of information, or in other words, our brain gathering raw data we perceive through our senses. Secondly, there is the way to organize the data to create a "story" that I would call scientific knowledge. The primary information comes from senses, such as touching or hearing. For example, you will gather the information about snow when you have the chance of holding it in your hands. Then your brain organizes the sensation you have had: it is cold, it melts and it changes into water into the "story". That "story" is not only based on your perceptions but may also influenced by your preconceptions of what snow is like. The more information you gather through observation, the bigger the stories will be after you organize them, which forms scientific theories. The scientific theories must always be consistent with the physical world so that knowledge is what we believe filtered by observation and experimentation of the physical world (Image 1).

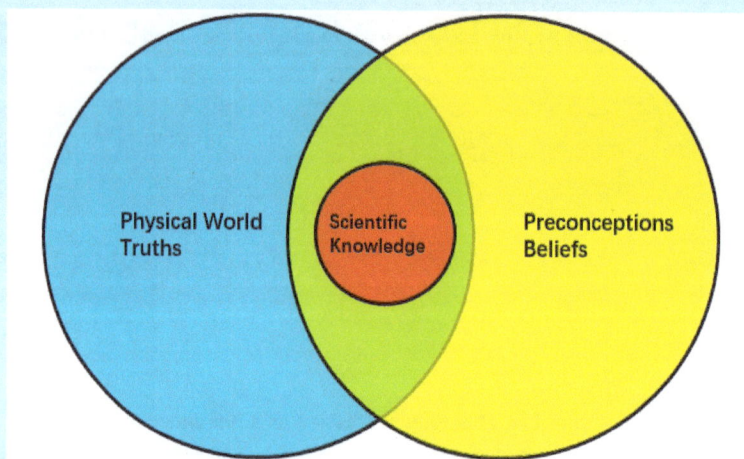

Image 1   What is scientific knowledge?

How Does Our Brain Help Us?

We can see our brain as having two circuits that differentiate what is true from what is false. One circuit is very fast and relies on memory. while the other one is slower and relies on your thinking and your processing of information. Now, I'll give you a simple test and let's see how you're doing.

Between Picture A and Picture B, which one is the Swiss flag (Image 2)?

What I'm asking you to do here is to go to your memory so if you know the answer already you should be able to provide a quick answer. The answer is actually A (And that's my country). If you could not answer it based on your memory, then you are automatically switching to a thinking mode. Now, why is this flag so similar to that one? Funny story here: it turned out that the person who started the red cross was Swiss Nobel Peace Prize laureate named Jean-Henri Dunant. And he saw the Swiss flag and thought to himself "I cannot use this one, so I'll change it just a little bit by inverting the colors".

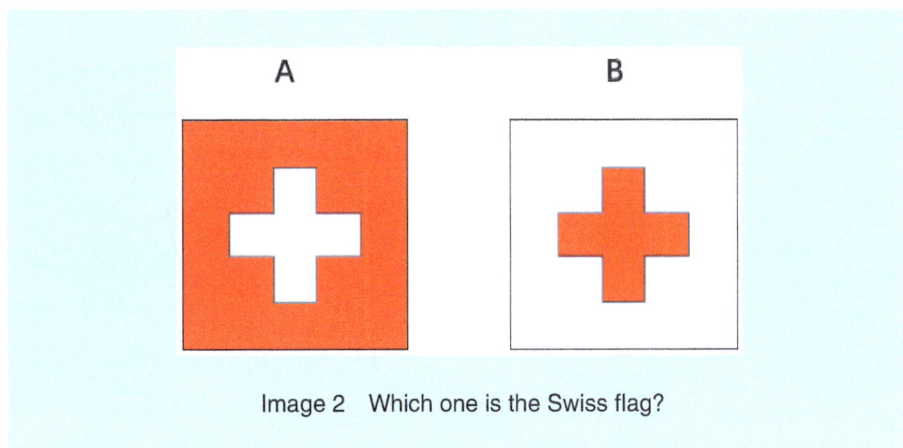

Image 2   Which one is the Swiss flag?

Our Senses

As human beings, we are limited because everything we know comes from the following five aspects: the smell, the touch, the taste, the hearing and the sight. All the information we gather, originally comes from these five senses.

Now I'm going to introduce you a guy whose name is Mr. Homunculus, as shown in Image 3. He looks like a funny person, doesn't he? We can notice that some parts of his body are disproportionately larger than some other parts. For example, his hands and his mouth. How come? To answer this, let's pay attention to Image 4. It shows the proportion of brain dedicated to touch. As you can see, the part of the brain dedicated to, let's say, the hand, is larger than that for the arm. Therefore, this person here, actually is made in such a way that the part of his body which is very sensitive are bigger in proportion to the sensitivity of the part. We can also try this for ourselves, try to touch different parts of your body and you can find out

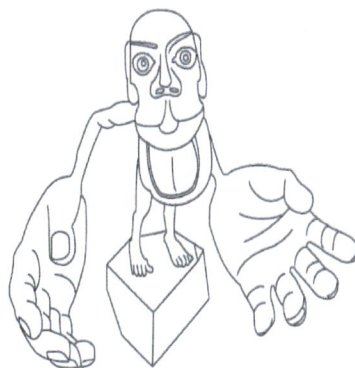

Image 3   Mr. Homunculus

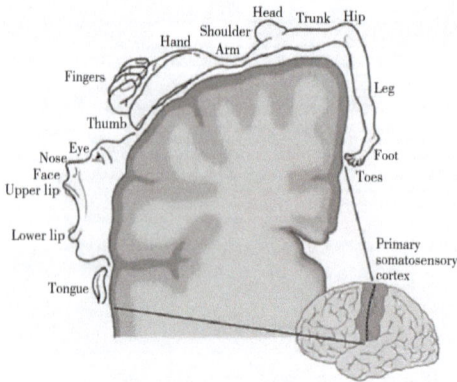

Image 4   The proportion of brain dedicated to touch

that, for example, the inside of your hands is much more sensitive than your arm. You can feel even the very small things. And you cannot feel the same things on your arm.

So how about our hearing ability? What is hearing? When making noise, one is actually producing a wave in the air that goes toward one's ear. Then others can perceive that sound as catching that wave. A wave has two main features: amplitude and wavelength. A small sound has a small amplitude and a loud sound has a high amplitude while a low-pitch sound has a long wavelength and a high-pitch sound has a short wavelength. It is the molecules in the air that actually move with each other. These characteristics can be shown in the compression pattern of molecules in the air, as shown in the Image 5.

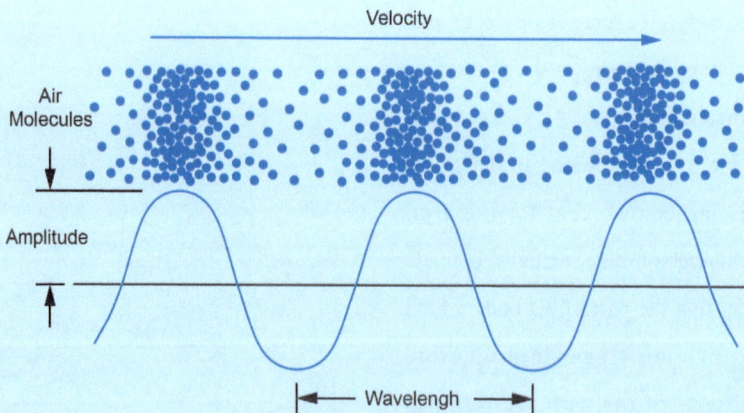

Image 5 What is sound?

Human ears can't hear all sounds. We can actually hear a small fraction of sound in the human pitch range and can't hear the sound either too high or too low. there is 9 window of pitches of sound where one can actually hear. While human ears have their preferred frequencies, dogs have a larger range. Dogs can perceive sounds of much higher pitch than humans do. You can buy whistles that only dogs can hear and use it to train them without disturbing the neighbors.

You see, many animals have different frequencies in terms of sound reception. For example, bats can produce and hear a kind of high frequency sound called ultrasound. Bats use this sound to "see" the world. They can echolocate their environment and find where their prey is.

Now I'm going to talk about what we see. Take light as an example. Light also acts like a wave featuring amplitude and wavelength. However, it is different from sound because it is electromagnetic.

And the same is true as before, we have limitations on our sight, that is, we only see what is called "visible light", which only consists of a portion of the electromagnetic spectrum. A typical human eye will respond to wavelengths from about 400 to 700 nanometers.

Bees, unlike human beings, can see very short wavelengths. For example, a bee's visible wavelength ranges from 300 to 600 nanometers, compared to human's 400 to 700 nanometers. That is why the same flower may appear very different to two different species (Image 6). We don't see the same thing.

Since our senses have limitations, we are using machines to transform unperceivable

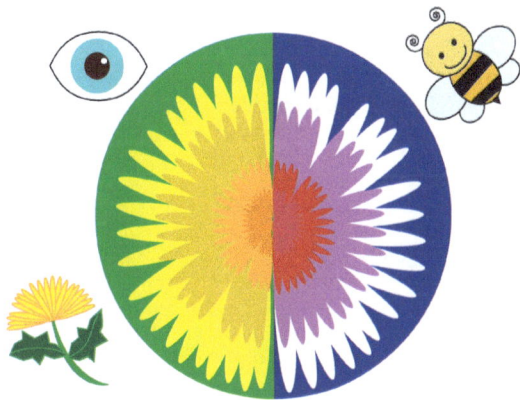

Image 6　The same flower may appear very different to two different species

information into something we can either see or hear. The use of instrumentation can expand on human senses. In conclusion, what I'm trying to say here is that there are many, many more things happening in this universe that even with all our senses we still can't see or hear.

The Role of Thinking

Another key is our ability to think. We use our brain to make sense of all the information we gathered. One way is deduction, which goes from theory to hypothesis, and then to observation, and finally to confirmation. This way of thinking is historically brought up by philosophers like Aristotle. Another way of thinking is like Sherlock Holmes. We go from observation like a detective, noticing a pattern, forming a hypothesis, and finally making a theory.

Plato's Cave Allegory

So now I'm going to talk about an allegory. Socrates describes a person who has lived chained facing a blank wall of a cave all of his life. The person watches shadows projected on the wall from objects passing in front of a fire behind him and give names to these shadows. The shadows are this prisoner's reality rather than accurate representations of the real world.

In some way, due to our limited senses we are like a prisoner in the cave. We don't know everything exactly because we only know our perceptions. The real thing is what happens far away and outside the cave.

Brain Interpretation of the Information

We have eyes to see the world. At the back of the eye there is a retina to capture the image. But inside the eye on the retina, the image is received upside down. The brain is saying, no, this is not correct and then it flips the image right-side up. Otherwise, we will not be seeing what we are really seeing.

Take Image 7 as an instance. When you see these people, your brain is simultaneously

Image 7　Escher's illusion

trying to figure out what they are doing in the image. Are they going upstairs? Or are they going downstairs? Our brains don't like that these uncertainties very much, for this image is not physically possible and we may feel a little difficult analyzing it.

Another question for you. Please look at this blue cross (Image 8) carefully. Is the cross outside or inside the cube? Is it always outside or inside? Our brain can't accept both situations. In fact, the picture provides two solutions, but it is our brain that has to make a decision.

The point is that though the brain is very powerful, it does have some problems. You can't always trust your brain, and you also have to reflect a little bit more on what you see. You probably have already heard about this story before: if you take six blind people and ask them to describe an elephant, then they will all have six different descriptions. Some of them think the elephant is a fan, or a snake, or even a wall. Each one of them has their own perspective. What we scientists are doing is to take all of that information from everybody's different perspectives to come up with a picture that is closer to the truth. What we actually know at a point in time is only part of the truth, yet we always think we know all of

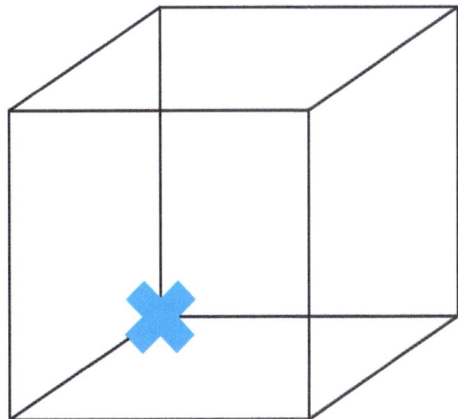

Image 8　Necke's cub

the truth. That's why it is imperative for us to stay open to everything around us, every new piece of information, in order to always improve our understanding of the world.

Science and Technology

What is the difference between science and technology? Science is knowledge about the physical and natural world whose laws are assumed to never change, that they stay the same whenever and wherever. Technology is a different matter; it uses scientific knowledge to create something useful. In science we will focus on understanding some fundamental properties such as air flow, air temperature, air pressure or air density, etc. By themselves, these concepts sometimes seem challenging to understand. However, when we are faced with engineering challenges to make something that actually works well, the scientific knowledge will be very useful. If you want to be an effective engineer, you will have to study diligently and know a lot about science.

Applying science to create a thing that actually works well in the real world is a complex process. There are many engineering solutions available but only one physical world where this object will perform. Any small design changes will have an impact on its performance. For example, let's make a few paper airplanes and have them fly in the same room. We use identical sheet of paper to make the airplanes and because we are test-flying them in the same room, the testing conditions are very similar. The paper airplanes that were produced are not all identical, some of which were made with different designs and others with the same design were not folded exactly the same way. Consequently, they do not fly the same way. Hence, to be a talented paper airplane engineer and produce the best flying paper airplane, you really need to understand the science of why something can fly. That's why you have to learn a lot about science.

Curiosity and Habits Both Matter

Now let me talk a little bit about curiosity. Given my age, all of you are all much better than me in this because as people grow older, they usually get less curious. But you guys here are still very young and curious about the world and that is a quality that you must cherish and preserve as much as possible as you get older. There is a very interesting story. This American girl in Image 9 has won the contest to name the rover that was actually sent to Mars by NASA: "Rover Curiosity". This girl was only 12 years old at that time, and not only did she win the competition to name the rover, but has also left us with this inspirational remark: "Curiosity is an everlasting flame that burns in everyone's mind...[It] is such a powerful force. Without it, we wouldn't be who we are today. Curiosity is the passion that drives us through our everyday lives. We have become explorers and scientists with our need to ask questions and to wonder." I think I could not do a better job to put this in other words.

Curiosity is very important but to be effective one has to also develop other skills. You can be curious about one subject, but to be good at it you will need to keep focused and work hard. You can call this resilience. There is a trick for that, actually, which is called habit. Habits will help you by not having to decide every time to work hard at something. For example, if you have to do your homework every day, what you need to do is to make it a habit, then you won't think about it anymore as you just do it. When it becomes a habit, your liking or disliking doesn't exist anymore. You just do it.

Image 9   Clara Ma, a Chinese American girl won the contest to name the rover that was actually sent to Mars by NASA: "Rover Curiosity"

As young people, it is important for you to have a few good habits, such as doing your homework, practicing your sport but also working before playing or taking responsibility and initiative. Don't forget to live a balanced life by eating well and exercising often, and don't be afraid of thinking over things that have confused you. Always remember to be proactive and have an open mind!

(Sun Mengge contributed to this article)

About the Author

I am Jean-Marc Bovet, my Chinese name is Bo Jiangmeng. I was born in 1955 in a beautiful and affluent country, Switzerland, where my parents were engaged in the home textile business. I received my PhD from the University of Michigan in 1993 and completed my postdoctoral research at the University of North Carolina (UNC). I was also a co-founder of two companies Cirrus Pharmaceuticals, a contract research organization (CRO) developing a number of different pharmaceutical products, and Kalliste Systems, a software company with a flexible platform dedicated to the pharmaceutical regulated environment. After I joined CF Pharmtech, Inc. in 2016, my Chinese colleagues gave me a nick name so they affectionately called me Lao Ma. Currently, I live and work in Jiangsu Province, China.

I am an expert in inhalation product development and information science. I am currently the Chief Technical Officer of CF Pharmtech, Inc. Many people in China are suffering from asthma and COPD (chronic obstructive pulmonary disease), so I am committed to providing high-quality and affordable medicines to those with respiratory diseases. Drug development usually takes a large amount of time and resources, so I implemented information science technology to facilitate drug development. I actively offer suggestions for China's science, technology, education and industrial development.

为人类健康服务的光学技术

文 / 储扎克（美） 译 / 杨云舟

什么是科学研究？科学研究有其遵循的一定流程。首先，我们需要提出一个想法来构成初步的假设；其次，我们需要制定一个研究方案来验证假设，精心设计并开展试验；最后，通过分析试验得出的数据，我们能够揭示最初的假设是否正确。如果假设错误，我们就必须回到第一步，修改假设，进行"再研究"，再将流程循环到底。其实，科学研究的方法可以越过纯粹科学的边界，应用到生活中的许多方面。它实际上是帮助我们应对和解决生活难题的一个视角。正因如此，我们发现，有着严谨诚实的态度并且秉持以公众利益为重的科学，掌握着世间所有问题的答案，也拥有能够改变世界的力量。

那做科学家又是什么样的呢？他 / 她是一个像谢尔顿·库珀（美剧《生活大爆炸》中主角之一）那样的人，还是一个整天做实验的实验室小白鼠？其实，医院里的医生也是科学家，他们采集样本，进行测试，以验证他们的假设——医疗诊断——是否正确。某些政府领导人也是科学家，他们在不同研究领域都有着各自的科研成就，科学训练帮助他们更好地领导、治理我们的社会。

我和我的研究团队将目光定格在了一个特殊的领域：生物医学光子学。这一方向研究的基本思路是利用光子的力量来解决生物和医药领域的核心问题。目前，我们的研究主要有 3 个分支：无标记显微技术、纳米尺度拉曼光谱和成像，以及资源匮乏地区专用的医疗诊断技术。

无标记显微技术

我们首先来看无标记显微技术。当低头看向自己的双手时，我们可以分辨出它们的颜色和背景是不一样的。这种颜色的区别使我们能够将特定事物与附近的东西区分开来。但一个自然状态下的细胞是无色的，导致研究人员要想对它直接进行观测会十分困难。所以，如果我们想锁定某个分子并对其进行观察，就要首先赋予它一种颜色——一种荧光标记——使它变得易于区分。举个例子，科学家可以给艾滋病毒打上荧光标记。感染了艾滋病毒的细胞会和健康的细胞进行信息交换，为病毒创造一条通道，让它能够移动到正常细胞内并感染正常细胞。如果成功地给病毒贴上了一个荧光标记，研究人员就可以顺利观测到艾滋病毒在细胞间的移动现象，并进一步对其进行研究。

从这个例子中我们可以看出，荧光标记是一个非常有用的工具。通过这项技术，我们能够看到很多以前无法看到的东西。那么，为什么科学家们还要研究一种"无标记"的显微技术呢？原因在于，首先，给细胞打上荧光标记本身就是一项挑战。这一步骤很可能会直接杀死细胞。其次，即使有了荧光标记，要观察细胞仍然不是一件容易的事。为了捕捉到更好的图像，研究人员必须用强大的激光束照射被标记的细胞。这可能使得细胞过热，或者释放出有毒的自由基。最后，即使研究人员既成功地给细胞打上了标记，又让细胞存活了下来，他们在观察细胞时仍然会面临关键性的困难。这是因为荧光标记可能会"破损"，这个过程被称为"光漂白"，即随着时间的推移，我们接收到的信号会越来越弱。因此，第 1 张图像的质量通常会非常好，但第 10 张或第 20 张图像可能会变得无法识别。解决这个问题的方法之一是使用较温和的激光。较温和的激光生成的细胞图像质量较差，但我们可以利用计算机算法来帮助我们提高这些照片的成像质量，从而在保护细胞的同时获得相对更清晰的图像。但是，这种方法仍然有其局限性，科学家们还是需要寻找其他的方法来观察细胞。

为了能够在没有荧光标记的情况下观察细胞，科学家们选用了弗里茨·泽尔尼克发明的相衬显微镜（泽尔尼克也因此获得了诺贝尔奖），并根据需要对其进行了一些改进。一束光在穿过细胞时的速度会比穿过细胞周围的液体时要慢，这种速度差异会影响到光的一种被称为"相位"的属性。利用速度差，相衬显微镜可以让观测者看到原本难以看见的无色细胞（图 1）。然而，相衬显微镜只能呈现有限分辨率的图像，而且，这些图像都是"定性"信息。也就是说，图像上细胞某些部位的明暗并不能准确反映出细胞内部的真实结构。科学家们需要更适合的技术来更全面、深入地观察细胞的内部结构，并使测量出的数据变得"定量"。

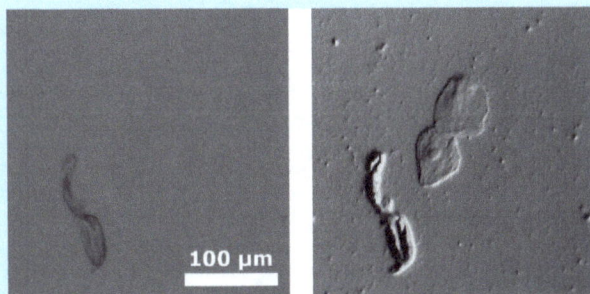

图 1 在相衬显微镜下（右），我们能看见在普通显微镜（左）下难以看到的细胞

　　超斜照明高分辨率相衬显微镜技术的出炉使得我们掌握了观测活体正常细胞的全新角度。有了这项技术，科学家可以清晰地看到细胞内部的大部分结构，包括脂滴、细胞核、线粒体、液泡，以及一种非常微小的网状结构——内质网（图2）。我们还得以注意到从前没有被发现过的东西。例如，我们发现在某些细胞内，许多线粒体总是在不停旋转，就像跳舞一样。这种运动会消耗细胞的能量，但细胞通常都十分节约，不喜欢浪费任何能量。因此，线粒体的这种"舞蹈"背后一定有着重要的原因。我们需要用科学的方法，提出一个假设，通过实验来检验，由此发现这个问题的答案。又如，内质网存在着一种不间断的摇摆运动。由于新的显微技术不存在"光漂白"效应，也不会伤害细胞，所以科学家们现在有充分的时间去观察内质网不停摇摆背后的生物功能。

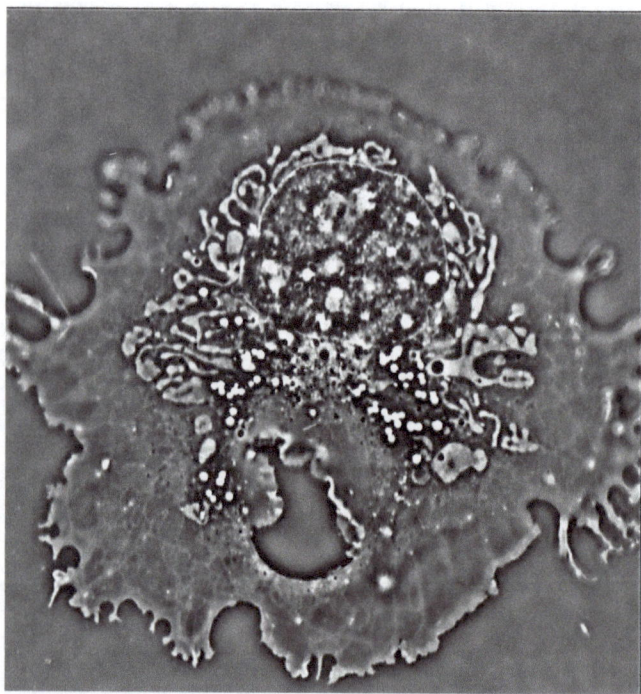

图2　运用新的技术，我们能够清晰地看到细胞的内部结构

拉曼光谱与成像

既然已经能够对细胞内部进行更清晰地观察，科学家们便开始设想，是否可以进一步观察出这些内部结构之间在化学成分上的差异？要满足这个雄心壮志，科学家们需要一种名为拉曼光谱的技术。简单来讲，科学家会将一种颜色的光照射向细胞，而由于光线与不同化学成分之间的相互作用，许多不同颜色的光束会从细胞里折射出来。在光谱仪的帮助下，这些不同的颜色可以被分离成被我们称为"光谱"的信号，它可以告诉我们每种颜色各占多少（图3）。每个分子都有自己独特的拉曼信号。而运用拉曼光谱，我们可以分析出在细胞的每个部分存在着什么样的化学分子。这项技术有着多种多样的应用。例如，通过观察一个脂滴，科学家可以判断出里面有什么，以及它是否由健康的脂肪构成。通过进一步分离并辨别细胞摄入的脂肪，我们甚至可以判断出它是一个健康的细胞还是癌细胞。

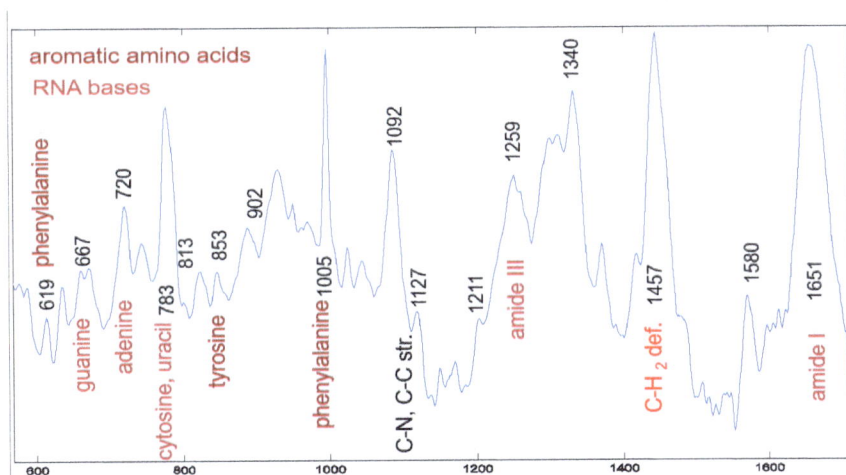

图3 通过光谱仪，我们能够得出这样的图像

　　这项技术还可以从其他角度对癌症进行诊断。目前,"细胞外小体"的研究是生物学中的一个新兴领域,其中最受关注的是"外泌体"。外泌体是一种纳米级大小的信使,它的功能类似细胞之间沟通时所发送的"信件"。外泌体包含蛋白质和核酸,可以向附近的细胞发出指令。但是,不仅正常细胞会释放外泌体,癌细胞也会,而且数量往往比正常细胞多得多。事实上,癌细胞可以利用外泌体发送虚假信息,来欺骗本应消灭它们的白细胞。在拉曼光谱仪下,我们能够研究每一个外泌体的化学成分,并分析它们之间的微小差异。针对这一点,科学家们使用一种叫作"光镊"的工具,挑选出单个的外泌体进行深入研究。我们用这种方法发现,癌细胞和健康细胞的外泌体有着不同结构的表面蛋白。这无疑将为癌症的研究、诊断及可能的新治疗手段提供参考。

适于资源匮乏地区的医疗诊断技术

　　除了解决分子层面的生物学问题,光学科学还可以为组织层面的医学问题做出贡献。人们生病了会去"看医生",但其实是"医生在看你"——医生通过显微镜观察你的组织或血液样本。值得一提的是,近一个世纪以来,医生使用的显微技术几乎没有根本性的变革。也许,科学家们在相关领域通力合作,如让显微镜变得更小、更智能,也能推动医用显微技术的进步。

　　人们希望无论何时何地都能获得高质量的医疗服务。但在现实生活中,患者必须去到特定的地方——医院——才能顺利就诊。医院配备有所有可能需要的专业设备和仪器,它们将帮助医生进行测试,做出可靠、准确的诊断。但这些设备往往体积庞大、价格昂贵,而且需要经过大量的培训才能操作。如果你居住在一个发达国家的城市,这样的资源对你来说可能唾手可得。但那些生活在贫困(如非洲农村)或偏远地区(如西藏地区)的人所面临的情况就大不相同了,在那里资源稀缺且十分昂贵，患者往往需要几天甚至几周的时间才能就医。

为了让医疗服务更方便、便捷，科学家们考虑将我们的日常工具改造成医疗设备。手机是否能够承担这样的工作？它有摄像头、麦克风，内置电脑和网络模块。如果再加上一个镜头，它基本上就能变成一台显微镜，足以用来进行疾病观察、细胞计数，甚至成为一台光谱仪。当我们制造出这样一个简单的手机显微镜时，我们发现它的确可以达到很好的显微效果，观察到细胞核和疟疾寄生虫（图4）。然而，我们随后发现，尽管手机显微镜具有成为便捷医疗工具的潜力，但它只适合那些具备专业操作技术的人。在手机显微镜的成像方面，由训练有素的实验室研究人员操作出的图像和由医院工作人员或其他没有接受过使用培训的人操作出的图像可能在质量上差异很大。为了更适应医疗卫生从业的需要，我们的低成本显微镜必须更智

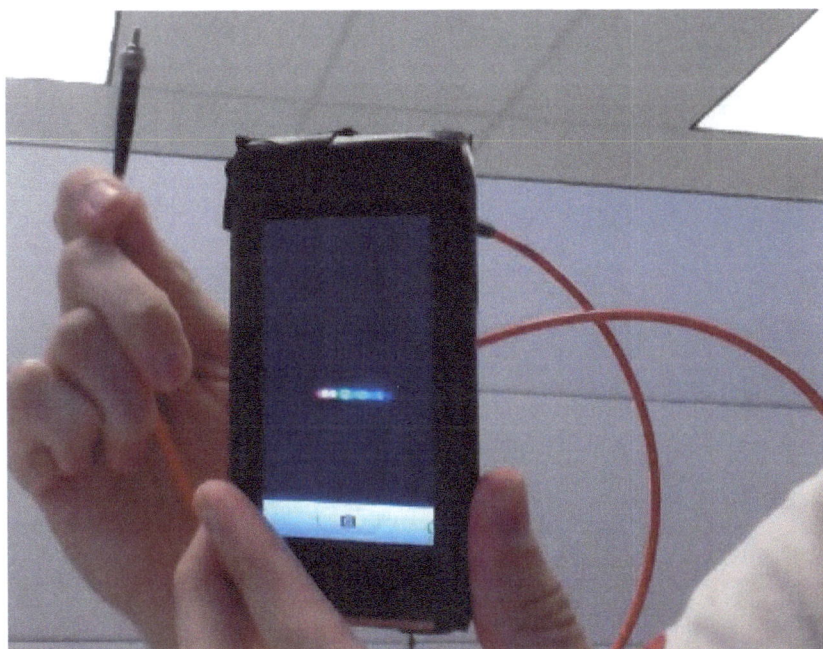

图 4　简易手机显微镜

能，必须对那些不十分熟悉光学科学的人更加友好。于是，我们研发出了一种新型"全自动"显微镜（图5）。它可以自动聚焦和扫描微小的微观样品，体积小，便于携带，操作也不需要经过额外培训，还能观察从血液、粪便到组织样品的多种类型的样品。相比之下，虽然普通的自动显微镜可以生成质量稍好的图像，但价格要比我们的显微镜贵很多倍。此外，新型显微镜非常便于组装，材料在网上很容易就能买到，基本上就像一套乐高玩具一样。

图5　低成本、全自动的显微平台

我们的自动显微镜可以应用于许多不同的医疗场景。它可以协助进行动物诊疗。众所周知，山羊是杂食动物，因此很容易遭到寄生虫的感染。在对山羊进行寄生虫检查时，兽医通常会先从山羊的粪便中取样，与水混合，然后再放在显微镜下分辨并归类样品中的寄生虫卵。如果采取纯手工操作的方法，这套流程会非常累人。医生一般需要花20~30分钟的时间来仔细研究样本。而我们的自动显微镜可以自主对动物的大便样本进行细节拍照，随后利用深度学习技术，自动从图像中挑出虫卵，进行计数，并分辨出这些虫卵是来自蛔虫、壮虫还是其他寄生虫。这样一来，既节省了医生的时间，又可以帮助动物尽快得到正确的药物治疗，减少它们的痛苦。

新型显微镜在人类体检中也有用处。当我们去看病时，医生通常会先抽取一小瓶血。通过统计血液中红细胞、白细胞和血小板的数量，医生能够掌握我们的健康状况。对于老年人，尤其是对罹患癌症的老年人来说，定期查血是很重要的一项检查。治疗癌症的药物不仅会杀死癌细胞，还会伤害到身体其他健康的部位，所以医生要时刻监测患者血液中的白细胞水平，避免其降低到临界水平以下。目前，患者只能去医院查血，而每个月可能只查一两次。这就造成了医生在信息掌握上的滞后。一种理想的情况是患者每天在家里就能自己验血。我们的新型、便捷、适合家庭使用的显微镜或许能够为他们提供帮助。患者可以将血液样本与一种特殊液体混合，然后放在我们的显微镜下。显微镜会自动扫描样品，进行分析，然后计数。不同种类的细胞——如红细胞或白细胞——在输出图像中会显示为不同的颜色或亮度。整个系统完全自动，所以即使是由业余的爸爸妈妈们来操作，得出的检测结果也可以和专业的研究人员一样准确、可靠。

即使是要给动物抽血，我们的显微镜也能帮上忙。动物并不了解健康检查的重要性，所以，为了抽血这一过程不刺激到它们或让它们不安，医务人员会尽可能轻柔地从它们身上抽取尽可能少量的血。我们的系统只需要几微升（不到一滴）的血液就足以得到准确的检测结果，因此能够非常好地适应这项工作的特殊条件。

最后，我们的技术还可以在另一个重要领域——贫血诊断——中发挥作用。贫血是全球公共卫生面临的一大严重威胁，影响着全球约1/3的人口，尤其是那些医疗资源稀缺地区的人。中国有10%~20%的儿童患有缺铁性贫血，通常与营养不良有关；有4300万儿童患有地中海贫血，这是一种遗传性贫血，常见于泰国、越南及中国的广东和广西。这两种不同的疾病对治疗方法有着不同的要求。对于缺铁性贫血，治疗方法可以非常简单——提高铁质摄入量；然而，对于地中海贫血的患者来说则相反，铁的摄入对他们非常危险。正因如此，我们希望能够对社会中的每个公民进行贫血检测。但让全国人民都去医院看病检测是一件不可能的事，所以我们需要研发一种仪器，可以在医院外使用，价格便宜，每个城市都可以有几个这样的仪器。在贫血筛查过程中，第一项任务是找到那些贫血的人；第二项任务是诊断出患者所患的是哪种贫血。人体内红细胞的形状和大小不尽相同，而健康人、缺铁性贫血患者和地中海贫血患者之间的红细胞也不一样。但是，由于缺铁性贫血患者和地中海贫血患者的红细胞大小及形状的差异非常微小，所以，通常需要大型昂贵的设备才能成功区分。这些设备在医院以外的地方很难操作，所以我们采用了一种低成本的光学散射系统来测量红细胞的大小、形状或血红蛋白浓度等参数。通过我们这套系统产生的数据，医生几乎可以 100% 准确地区分贫血患者和健康人。在缺铁性贫血患者和地中海贫血患者的区分上，这套系统能达到超过 90% 的准确率。我们希望在未来，这样的技术可以顺利应用于大范围、全人口的贫血筛查。

光的力量可以帮助我们解决许多生物和医学上的问题，助力我们改善现在所处的社会。光学科学的发展是许多杰出科学家努力的结果。每一位科学家都是"站在巨人的肩膀上"贡献自己的微薄之力。在他们的共同贡献下，世界可以变得更加美好。

作者简介

储扎克的教育起步于罗切斯特。除了如画的风景、寒冷的冬雪和奇特的本地美食"垃圾盘"，这里还以光学科学研究而闻名。他在罗切斯特大学获得了光学专业学士和博士学位。随后，他告别了寒冷的天气，前往阳光明媚的加州大学戴维斯分校生物光子学中心继续从事博士后研究。2015年，储扎克离开美国来到中国科学技术大学，成为精密机械与精密仪器系的教授和博士生导师。

现在，在妻子和两只爱猫的陪伴下，储扎克渴望运用他的光学知识，为人类和动物同伴们做出贡献，让世界变得更加美好。

扫描收看
本文视频课程

Using Light for Human Health

By Zachary J. Smith (America)

What is scientific research? It has its own internal cycle where the first step is to bring forward an idea, which will constitute your hypothesis. To examine this hypothesis you will need to come up with a research protocol and carry out well-designed experiments. Experiments produce data to be analyzed, thus revealing if the initial hypothesis is correct or not. And if not, we must return to the first step, revise our hypothesis, and "re-research" until the whole cycle is completed. This method of scientific research can also be applied to many other aspects in life beyond the boundaries of strict science. The scientific method is actually a perspective through which to look at any problem we are faced with in life. It is with this idea we can see that science, carried out faithfully and in the public interest, possesses the answer to all our worldly problems and has the power to change the world.

And what does it mean to be a scientist? Does it mean someone like "Sheldon Cooper", or a lab rat spending all day carrying out experiments? It can also be a doctor in a hospital, who runs tests on collected samples to see if their hypothesis – their diagnosis- is correct or not. It can also be one of our government leaders, among whom there are many accomplished scientists specialized in different areas of studies. Scientific training has helped them become more proficient as leaders of our society.

As for me and my team, our research fixes the eyes on one particular field: biomedical optics. The basic idea of this study is utilizing the power of light to solve problems crucial to our society that have risen in the realm of biology and medicine. Our research has three major branches, which are namely label-free microscopy, nanoscale Raman spectroscopy and imaging, and point of care technologies for resource-limited settings.

The Label-free Microscopy Technology

The first is the label-free microscopy technology. Looking down at our hands, we can tell they have a different color than the background, which enables us to tell them apart from things nearby. But a cell in its natural form is colorless, difficult for researchers to observe. So, should we wish to find a certain molecule and look at it, we first have to give it a color - a fluorescent label - thus making it discernible. For example, we can give a fluorescent label to an HIV virus. A cell infected with HIV will exchange information with a healthy cell, creating a tunnel for the virus to move to and infect the normal cell. If labeled with fluorescence, the cell-to-cell movement of the HIV virus will become observable for researchers.

As we can see from the example above, a fluorescent label is a powerful tool that allows us to see many things that have eluded our eyes before. Then why are scientists researching a "label-free" microscopy technology? First, the addition of a fluorescent label to a cell is challenging in itself - in fact, it might just kill the cell in the first place. Second, it is still not an easy task to observe the cell even with a fluorescent label. In order to capture better images, researchers will have to hit the labeled cell with a powerful laser beam, which will possibly overheat the cell or make it release toxic free radicals. Finally, even if researchers have succeeded in both labeling and keeping the cell alive, they still will face critical difficulty in observing it, since fluorescent labels can "break", a process we call "photo-bleaching", where the signal we receive gets weaker and weaker over time. Thus, the first image is very high quality, but the 10th or 20th image may be impossible to recognize. One of the solutions to this problem is to use a gentler laser, producing a poorer image of cells. Then we can take these poor-quality images and use a computer algorithm to help us enhance the quality, thus obtaining a relatively clearer image while protecting the cell.

However, this method still has its limitations, and we nevertheless need to find other ways to observe the cell.

To observe cells without fluorescent labels, scientists chose to utilize the outstanding work of Frits Zernike, the phase contrast microscope, (for which Zernike earned the Nobel Prize) and modify it to our demands. Beams of light that go through the cell move slower than those that move through the water surrounding the cell. This speed difference changes a property of light called its "phase". Making use of this speed difference, the phase contrast microscope allows us to see colorless cells that are otherwise invisible (Image 1). Yet the resolution of images coming from a phase contrast microscope is limited, and the information is "qualitative", meaning that the brightness or dimness of certain parts of the cell cannot be exactly mapped to the cell's real structure. Scientists need more to see better and as well deeper into a cell's internal structure, and to make the measurement "quantitative".

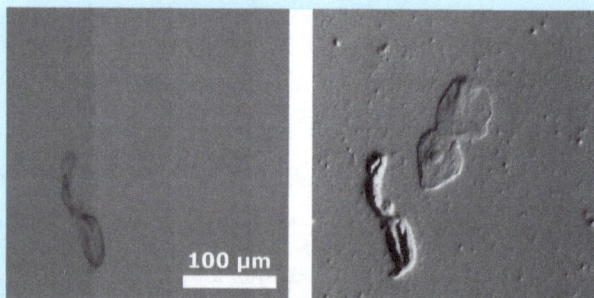

100 μm

Image 1   Under a phase contrast microscope (right), we can see cells that are difficult to see with an ordinary microscope (left)

The devising of the ultra-oblique illumination high resolution phase contrast microscope technology affords us with new insights into cells that are alive and functioning. We can now clearly visualize most of the cell's internal structure, including lipid droplets, nucleus, mitochondria, vesicles, and a very tiny web-like structure called the endoplasmic reticulum (Image 2). We can also notice many things that haven't yet to be found up to this moment. For example, with this new technology, we have found out that many of the

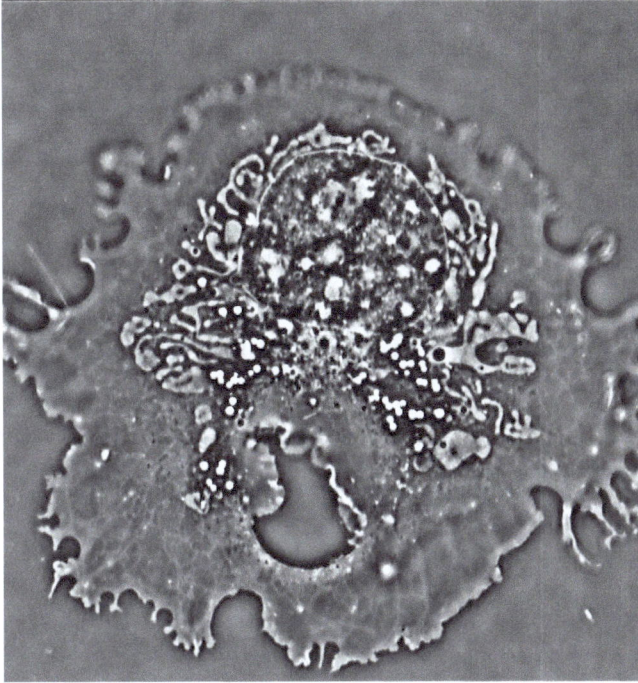

Image 2　We can see the internal structure of cells clearly using new technology

mitochondria within certain cells are always spinning, as if the mitochondria are dancing. This movement costs the cell energy, but cells are very conservative and don't like to waste any energy. Therefore, this mitochondrial dancing must have an important reason behind it. Now we need to use the scientific method, and devise a hypothesis we can test through experiment to discover the answer to this question. Since the phase image does not "photobleach", and the imaging does not hurt the cell, scientists now also have all the time in the world to look at the endoplasmic reticulum, an important organelle, and study the biological function behind its incessant shaking motion.

Raman Spectroscopy and Imaging

With a clearer vision looking inside the cell, scientists also want to know, what are the chemical differences between these internal structures? The technique required for this ambition is called Raman spectroscopy. Basically, scientists shine one color of light onto a cell. Many different colors will come out from it due to the interaction of the light with different chemical components. With the help of a spectrometer, these colors can be separated into a signal we call a "spectrum", which tells us how much of each color is present(Image 3). The Raman spectrum can tell us what kind of chemicals are present within each point of the cell, because each molecule has its own unique Raman signal. Therefore, scientists, for example, can look at a lipid droplet and tell what's inside and if it's made of healthy fat or not. By separating the fat intake of a cell, we can even tell if it's a healthy one or a cancer cell.

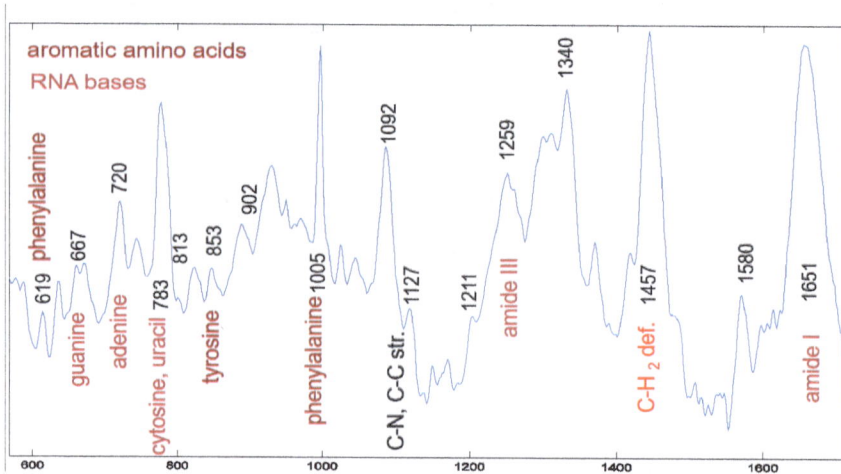

Image 3   With a spectrometer, we are able to translate colors of light into this kind of graphs

This technology can take on cancer diagnosis from other perspectives. A new topic in biology is the study of "extracellular vesicles", among which one of the most studied is called an "exosome". The exosome is a nanoscale messenger. It functions like a letter sent between cells for communication purposes. It contains proteins and nucleic acids that can give instructions to nearby cells. Not only do normal cells release these exosomes, but cancer cells also release them, often in much higher numbers than normal cells. In fact, cancer cells can use exosomes to send false information to trick the white blood cells that are supposed to eliminate them. Using Raman spectroscopy, we can study the chemical composition of each individual exosome and see that every exosome is a little bit different from one another. Regarding this, scientists use a tool called optical tweezers to pick up each single exosome and examine them closely. We found that the surface protein of the exosome is different between a cancer cell and a healthy one, which can provide new information for cancer studies, cancer diagnosis, and possibly cancer treatments.

Care Technologies for Resource-limited Settings

Besides biological questions at the molecular level, optical science can also contribute to medical questions at a tissue level. When we are sick, it is natural for us to "see a doctor". What really happens is "the doctor sees you" - the doctor looks at the tissue or blood sample of yours through a microscope. The microscopic technology used by doctors, in fact, hasn't really changed in almost a century. Maybe through the coordinated efforts of scientists, we can improve medical microscopes, for instance, by making them smaller and smarter.

It is a universal dream to have access to high quality medical care whenever and wherever we want, which is in stark contrast to the reality where patients must go to certain places - hospitals - for that is where all the professional equipment and machines are. These machines help doctors run tests and make solid diagnoses. But they tend to be large, expensive, and require extensive training to operate. If you are an urban citizen in a developed country, such resources might be not so difficult to get. Things are very different for those live in poorer areas where such resources are scarce and exorbitantly priced, like rural Africa, or a remote district - like Tibet - where it takes days, even weeks, to reach a hospital.

To make medical services more convenient and accessible, scientists are thinking to turn everyday gadgets into medical devices. Can cellphone take up such a job? It has a camera, a microphone, a built-in computer and network modules. With a lens added on, a cellphone can be essentially modified into a microscope that can be used to look at diseases, count cells, and even become a spectrograph. When we developed a simple cellphone microscope, we found we could achieve excellent results, being able to see cell nuclei and malaria parasites (Image 4). Yet for all the potential it has to become a convenient medical tool, we found out that it only suits those with specialized know-how, as images produced using a cellphone microscope can vary a great deal between those operated by trained lab researchers and those operated by hospital staff or others who have not been trained in the cellphone microscope's use. In order to truly impact health care, our low-cost microscope must be made smarter and more friendly to those who are not so familiar with optical science. A new type of microscope was then made to satisfy this demand (Image 5). It is a "fully-automated" microscope that can automatically focus and scan tiny microscopic samples, has a portable size, requires no additional training, and can look at many types of samples, from blood to feces to tissue samples. In comparison, a normal automated microscope can produce slightly better images, but is many times more expensive than our microscope. Ours is easy to put together, basically like a Lego set, and can be set up with materials that can be easily purchased online.

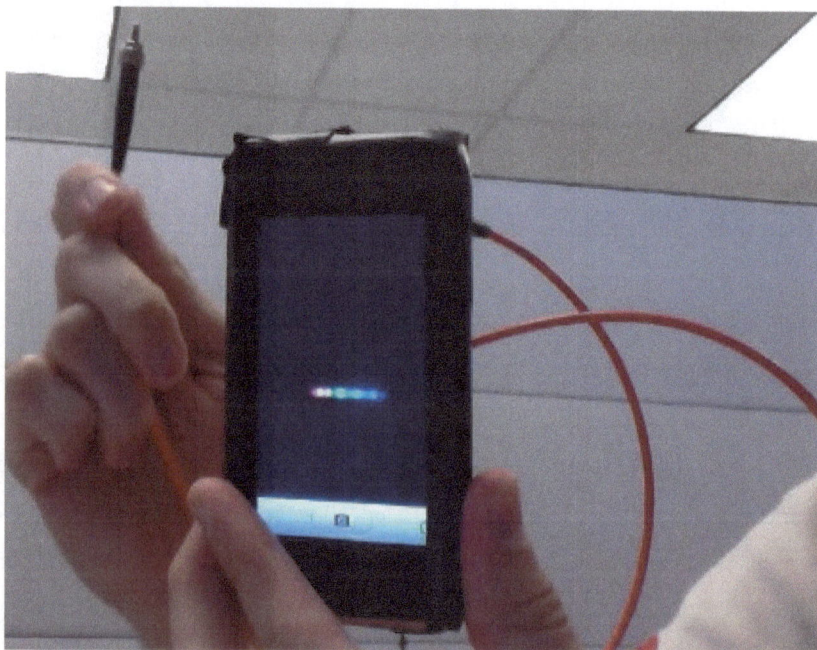

Image 4　A cellphone microscope

Image 5　A low cost, fully-automated microscope

Our automated microscope can find application in many different medical scenarios. As one example, we have shown how it can help treat animals. Goats are known to be messy eaters, and are consequently very easily infected by parasites like parasitic worms. The usual procedure for a vet to perform a parasite check on a goat is first taking a sample from its feces, mixing it with water, then putting it under a microscope to tell apart and classify the parasite eggs in the sample. This can be exhausting if done manually. It usually takes 20-30 minutes of the doctor's careful study. Our automated microscope can take a detailed pictures of a large sample of the animal's feces and, subsequently, using deep learning technology, pick out eggs from the image automatically, count them, and tell us if they are from ascarids, strongyles or other parasites. This can save the doctor's time, and help the animal to get the correct drug as soon as possible, reducing its suffering.

This can also be applied to the medical examination for human beings. When seeing a doctor, it is a common practice to have a vial of blood taken. By counting the number of red blood cells, white blood cells and platelets, our blood serves as a window of our health status in the eyes of a doctor. Regular blood check-ups are important for the elderly, especially those who have cancer. Drugs used in cancer treatment will not only kill the cancer cells but also hurt the healthy body parts, so doctors will want to monitor the white blood cell level in the patient's blood to avoid it reducing beyond a critical level. Using current technology, patients have their blood tested only when going to a hospital, which probably only happens once or twice a month. This creates a time-lag of information on the doctor's side. The ideal for us is to enable the patient to have his or her blood tested right at their own homes on a daily basis. Our new, convenient, household friendly microscope is qualified to help. Blood samples from patients will be mixed with a special liquid that prepares the sample and put under our microscope. Samples will be automatically scanned, analyzed and counted. Different kinds of cells, like red cells or different types of white blood cells in the output image will have different colors or brightness. Because the system is totally automatic, in our experiments the test results obtained by amateur moms and dads can be just as accurate and reliable as those of professional researchers.

And even when it comes to draw blood from animals, our microscope can get the job done. Animals don't understand the importance of health check-ups. To not irritate or upset them, medical practitioners would wish to take as little blood as possible from them, and in the most gentle manner. Our system requires only a few microliters (less than one drop) of blood, and it's sufficient to get an accurate test result.

Last but not least, there is one more application where our technology can pitch in - the diagnosis of anemia. Anemia is a serious threat to public health globally as it's affecting around one third of the world's population, especially plaguing those who have the least access to competent medical resources. 10%~20% percent of children in China have iron deficiency anemia, which is related to malnutrition; 43 million in China have thalassemia, a genetic type of anemia, which is commonly found in Thailand, Vietnam, Guangdong and Guangxi in china. These two different diseases should be countered with different treatments. For iron deficiency anemia, the solution can be as simple as boosting up one's iron intake. Yet on the contrary, iron intake is dangerous for patients with thalassemia. Because of this, we would like to test every citizen for anemia, but it's not possible to have the whole country go to the doctor to get tested. We need to make an instrument which can be taken outside of the hospital, and is inexpensive enough that every town can have several such instruments. In this screening process the first job is to find those with anemia and the second job is to tell which kind of anemia it is. Blood cells are not the same in shapes and sizes, and they are different among a healthy person, an iron deficiency anemia patient and a thalassemia patient. However, because the size and shape differences are very tiny in iron deficiency and thalassemia, to differentiate blood cells according to their sizes normally requires large and expensive devices that are not easy to operate outside of a hospital. So we have come up with a low cost optical scattering system that can be used to measure parameters of red blood cells like size, shape, or hemoglobin concentration. With data produced from our system, doctors can tell an anemic patient from healthy people with nearly 100% accuracy, and separate iron deficiency anemia patients and thalassemia patients with an accuracy over 90%. We hope in the future such a technology could be used for widespread, whole population screening of anemia.

The power of light can help solve many biological and medical questions, tackle challenges, and change the society we are now living in. The development of optical science is the results of effort from many outstanding scientists. Each scientist "stands on the shoulders of giants", and tries to add their own small contribution to the greater good. Thanks to their combined contributions, the world can be a better place for all of us.

(Yang Yunzhou contributed to this article)

About the Author

Zachary J. Smith got his educational start in Rochester, a place not only known for its picturesque scenery, snowy cold winters, and a strange local cuisine called the "garbage plate", it is also famous for the study of optical science. It is at the University of Rochester that Zach has finished his bachelor and doctoral degrees in optics. Then, he left cold weather behind and pursued his postdoctoral research at Center for Biophotonics at the University of California, Davis, where every day is warm and sunny. In 2015, Zach left the U.S. for the University of Science and Technology of China to become a professor and doctoral supervisor at the Department of Precision Machinery and Precision Instrumentation.

Together with his wife and two cats, Zach has been desiring to turn his knowledge in optics into contributions to both human races and fellow animals.

脑机接口浅谈

文 / 兰尼斯·梅里诺（哥伦比亚）　译 / 朱晟泼

脑电图简介

在我们的大脑中，密集的神经元团转化为强大的脑信号，帮助我们完成一系列人类活动，如交谈。利用脑信号，我们开发出了脑电图（Electroencephalography），英文简称为 EEG。

我们利用传感器的原理，发明了一种装置——脑电图头戴式耳机（以下简称耳机）。传感器的种类很多，有些非常复杂，有些非常简单。我们实验室中使用两种耳机：一种是干式；另一种是湿式。它们都可以帮助我们收集并记录大脑语言。例如，医生可以通过将电极放在患者的胸部，以测量患者的心脏状况，得到心电图。同理，我们也可以通过脑电图耳机感测大脑的语言。两种头戴式耳机的区别在于：干式接触头皮并直接感测大脑活动；而湿式则需要液体以增加电导率。

此外，还有一些国际惯例规定了将电极放在耳机的具体哪一部分。有一种常见的惯例，被称作 10-20 国际体系（图 1）。具体来说，它将我们的头部划分为多个区域，顶部是鼻子，侧面是耳朵。图中展示的是头部的顶视图。我们通常会在被测者头皮上放置最少 8 个、最多 256 个电极，通过脑电图做研究。脑电图被广泛应用在医院和高校等地。脑电图揭开了大脑的内部运作原理，人们更加明白人脑是如何运作的。现在，神经学家们也可以利用它来诊断治疗脑部疾病。

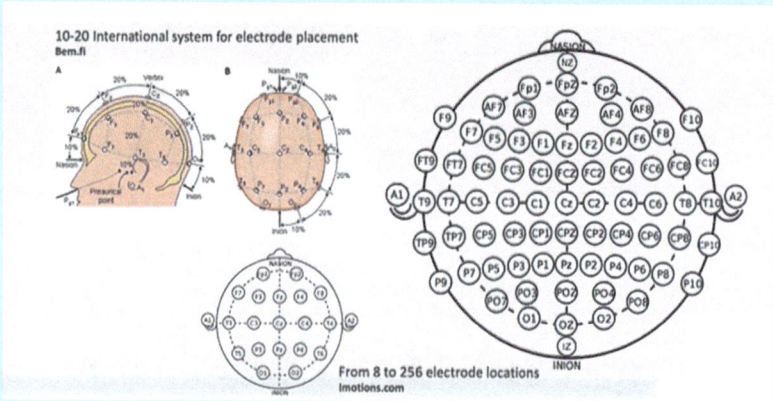

图 1　怎么戴耳机？

尽管如此，脑电图仍有两个主要的缺点：第 1 个是临近的传感器记录的信号类似，导致使得我们很难精确地知道大脑活动来自哪个部分；第 2 个是脑信号思维任务负荷和人员的不同表现出的高度可变性，这是指不同的人之间脑信号的差异很大。因此，这个领域需要各行各业人们的合作，如医生、神经学家及计算机科学家等。

脑电图研究概述

现在介绍几个脑电图研究的例子。第一个实验运用了一种被称为快速串行视觉演示的技术（Rapid Serial Visual Presentation，RSVP）。该实验给予参与者一项任务，即在计算机上查看快速图像——城市航拍图，并需要注意其中是否包含飞机。

此类研究的目的就是确定参与者看到目标图片时会发生什么，这被称为事件表征。这个过程有助于我们理解与兴趣事件有关的大脑活动。

实验结束后，我们可以找出与兴趣有关的大脑活动来自头部何处。此外，我们可以确定这个大脑活动的时间和频率，以及活动的模式。

结果显示，额叶和视觉皮层是人们看到图像时的大脑活动来源（图2）。在实际应用中，这些图像对于医生很有用，因为他们可以更好地诊断和分析患有精神疾病的人。

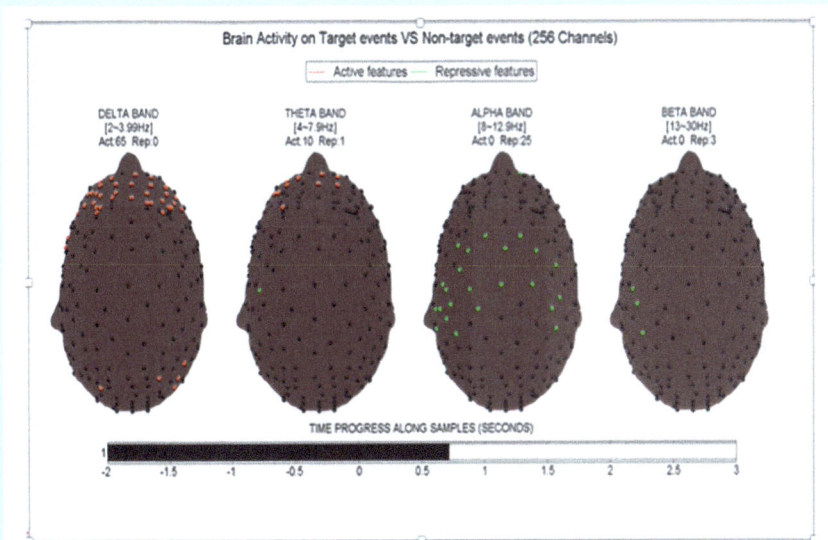

图2 RSVP 研究发现的动画

在另一项研究中，我们在美国招募了资深军人以进行更复杂的实验。我们设计了一个电脑模拟实验，实验期间，士兵们的任务是进入城市中并与恐怖分子战斗。士兵们同时是驾驶员，他们需要一边驾车，一边战斗。总而言之，他们会进行许多非常复杂的活动。

这项模拟的时间大约为 20 分钟。在 20 分钟内，士兵们从基地驶入城市，快速穿过并回到基地。只开车的这部分任务属于低负荷任务，而当穿过城市的时候，士兵们参与到了更多的活动中，他们需要注意力非常集中，保持警惕。这一部分就属于高负荷任务，因此，我们就要研究负荷不同时大脑活动的差异。

同样，实验过程还是确认这些信号的位置并发现其不同。如此多次进行实验，我们的实验目标就是确定活动模式、来自哪里、持续多久等。通常，做此类研究是有一个固定的程序的。我们首先要确定要使用哪种耳机、多少个电极、设置和记录条件等；其次要执行数据分析，使用的工具会根据实验的不同而不同；最后要将数据可视化，这样就可以展示并分享我们的成果。

除了出版研究，许多实验室的研究成果会经历产业化过程，也就是从试验品到产品，从产品再到商品。最近，越来越多的公司正尝试着基于脑电图研究来开发新产品，提高人们的生活质量。例如，有些公司开发了可以帮助解决睡眠问题的产品，还有些产品可以帮助人们集中注意力并放松。

脑机接口及其研究概述

脑电研究最重要的领域之一就是脑机接口。在这个领域中，我们尝试着开发一个体系，它可以将脑信号作为输入源，处理并生成命令，以与人或其他机器进行交互。

这套程序与之前提到的基本相同。识别信号之后，我们会提取对我们有用的信息。我们需要阐释解读这些信息，并将其转换输出，以便我们可以控制脑海中的事物，并用大脑来发送消息。

脑机接口这一领域已经活跃了几十年。例如，患有闭锁综合征的患者不能说话，也不能动。然而，脑机接口给予了这类患者一个与外界交流的窗口。他们可以用大脑去拼写——用脑和眼睛去选择键盘上的字母，这样就可以给他人传递信息。

其他常见的应用如控制轮椅、手臂、腿等。还有针对注意力障碍患者的应用，也可以通过脑机接口系统治疗改善认知功能障碍等一些精神疾病。

另一种常见的脑机接口技术被称为"想象中的运动"（Imagined Motion）。事实证明，如果我摆动手臂，那么我的大脑也随之产生信号。但是，如果我只是想象我在摆动手臂，而没有真的摆动，那么产生的信号应该是与前者相似的。在进行分析后，我们可以区分开想象的运动和真实的运动，然后建立脑机接口。

另一个例子叫作 SSEVP（图 3）。这个技术是基于视觉闪烁的大脑自然反应而构建的。其工作原理是：当你看到在一定频率下闪烁的光源时，大脑从视觉皮层（负责处理我们的大部分视觉刺激的区域）发出信号，其响应频率与视觉刺激相似。

在实验过程中，参与者看着白色的屏幕，白屏每秒钟闪烁 10 次。而后在大脑活动中，我们可以看到来自视

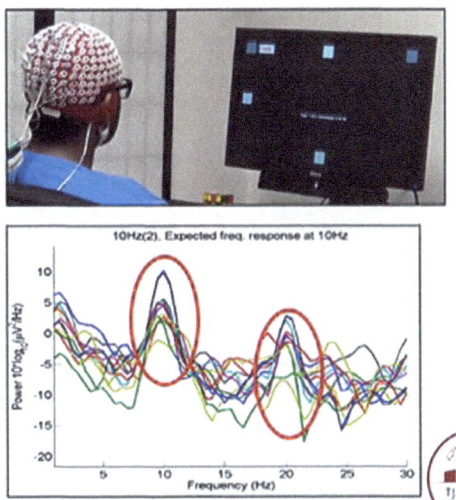

图 3 SSEVP 的工作原理

觉皮层的强烈的信号，且频率相同。重点在于，我们可以仅通过查看闪烁的刺激来构建系统，在检测到刺激之后将其转换为命令来实现控制或创建消息。

我们还做了另一个项目，就是用脑机接口技术来操控无人机。对此，我们记录了来自 42 个参与者的数据。具体来说，我们在屏幕上给了他们 6 次闪烁，每次闪烁代表一个不同的指令：前、后、左、右、上、下。下一步是开发一个

程序，并利用它发现参与者在该时间段内正在查看哪些闪烁。同时，我们也能检测到他们现在是否正在看。

最终结果如图 4 所示，参与者在看着视频，并与我们的镜头交谈。并且我们的系统知道参与者何时在看、何时不在看某个闪烁。第二个视频中，他需要选择一个闪烁的方块，看着它并给出指令，然后他可以再去看无人机。他的任务是绕过障碍物，且最终成功完成了任务。

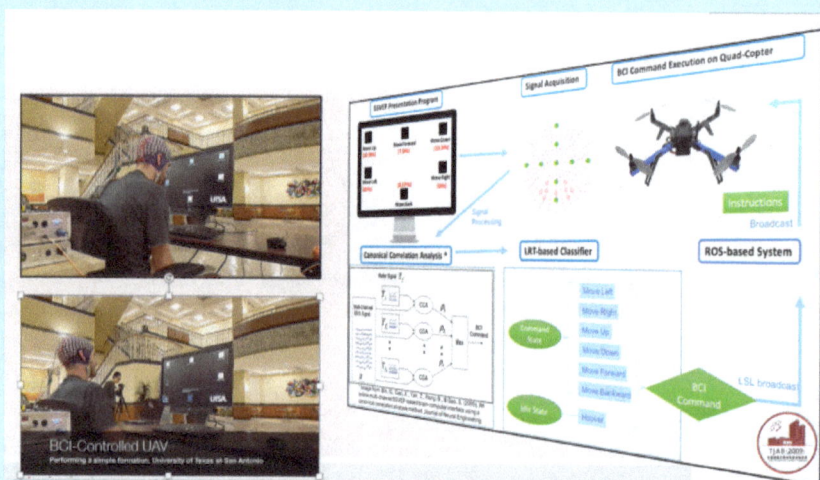

图 4　脑机接口研究：控制无人机和 UAVS

简而言之，你必须选择一个闪烁的正方形。系统会识别你正在查看的是哪一个，然后将其转换为无人机指令。这就是脑机接口的基本含义，即将大脑活动转化为指令。

我们也从游戏的运用中达成了同样的效果。例如，一个简单的迷宫小游戏，我们用同样的技术来控制角色，并让他移动到某个空间，也就是只运用大脑活动来玩游戏。

除了游戏，我们也在探索运用虚拟现实技术（Virtual Reality，VR），因为虚拟现实可以使人们获得更为沉浸式的体验及更自然真实的反应。这是一个应用虚拟现实技术的示例，当人集中注意力时，树木将长大，而当人放松时，花朵会生长。因此，这是一个以交互为基础的应用程序，可以与大脑活动进行互动。不过，现代的游戏需要更复杂的控件，我们也在开发更复杂的游戏来获得实验数据，使得我们的结果更完善。

以上是对于脑机接口领域的简单引入，希望为大家打开新的大门，发现更多科学乐趣。

作者简介

兰尼斯·梅里诺是天津国际生物医药联合研究院脑电产研平台研究员，主要研究方向为脑机接口研究、脑电信号处理。他曾在美国得克萨斯大学圣安东尼奥分校黄宇飞教授脑机实验室担任研究员，设计并主导了大型脑机接口实验的脑控无人机项目，设计并开发了脑电采集设备的数据采集、传输通信的软件等。

扫描收看
本文视频课程

Introduction to Brain-Computer Interface

By Lenis Mauricio Meriño (Columbia)

Introduction to Electroencephalography (EEG)

In our brains, dense clusters of neurons translate into powerful brain signals that help us perform a range of human activities, such as talking. Using these brain signals, we have developed Electroencephalography, or EEG for short.

We've created a device called EEG headset. As we know, there are many kinds of sensors. Some of them are very sophisticated, and some of them are very simple. We use both the dry and the wet headsets in our lab, which help us collect and record the brain sayings. The way this headset works is very similar to electrocardiogram in the hospital. To measure the patients' heart activity, people put the electrodes on the chest so that they are able to know how the patients' hearts are. This is an analogy that we can also listen to the brain sayings through the EEG headset.

The difference between dry and wet sensor-based headsets was that dry ones touch the scalp and measure the brain activities directly while the wet ones require liquid in order to increase the electrical conductivity (between the sensor and the scalp).

And there are also a few International conventions that suggest where to put the electrodes on an EEG headset, a common one is called 10-20 International system(Image 1). Basically, it divides your head into regions. On the top is the nose and on the side are the ears. This is a top view of the head. To make studies based on EEG, usually at least 8 and up to 256 electrodes are located on the scalp. EEG is widely used in hospitals, clinical research, universities and so on. Neurologists can utilize it to diagnose and treat brain disorders. Brain's inner mechanisms are revealed to neuroscientists to better understand how our brain works.

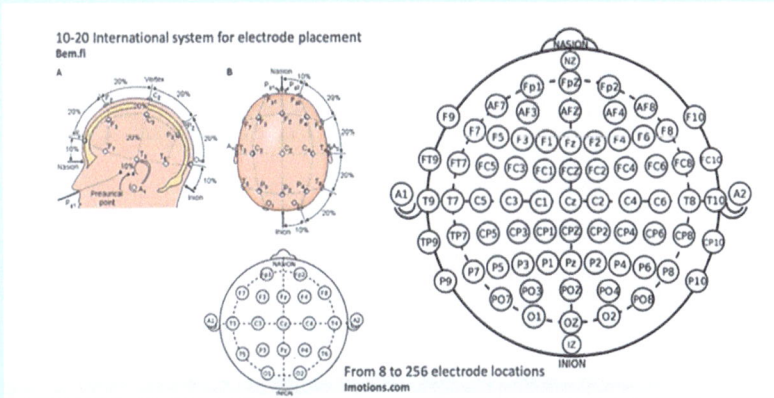

Image 1　How to wear the headset?

There are, however, two important disadvantages for EEG. The first is that nearby sensors record similar signals. In other words, it is difficult to know the exact source of the activity that we are listening to. The second is the high variability across mind task-loads and persons. This means that the signals change a lot, whatever men or women, the young or the old. That's why these areas require the collaboration of many people such as doctors, neurologist and also computer scientists.

Overview of EEG Research

This is one of the examples of the EEG studies which uses a technique called Rapid Serial Visual Presentation (RSVP). What happens on this experiment is that when the participants look at the fast images on the computer, some interesting activities in their brains are taking place. For these examples, the images are aerial pictures of a city and the participants were given a task: to watch short sequences of images and pay attention if any of them contained an airplane.

And one of the resources we want to get from this kind of study is to identify what happens when the participants see the target image, that is, the image they are looking for. This is called Event Characterization. This process helps us to obtain brain activity related to event of interests. After the experiment, we can find out where in the head this activity is coming from. Also, we can identify time and frequencies locations of the shape(pattern) of this activity.

The animation shows that the frontal lobe and the visual cortex are the source of activity that people report when they see the images (Image 2). In real life applications, these images are useful for doctors, for they can better diagnose and analyze those who suffered mental illness.

Another research recruited veteran military soldiers in the United States to perform

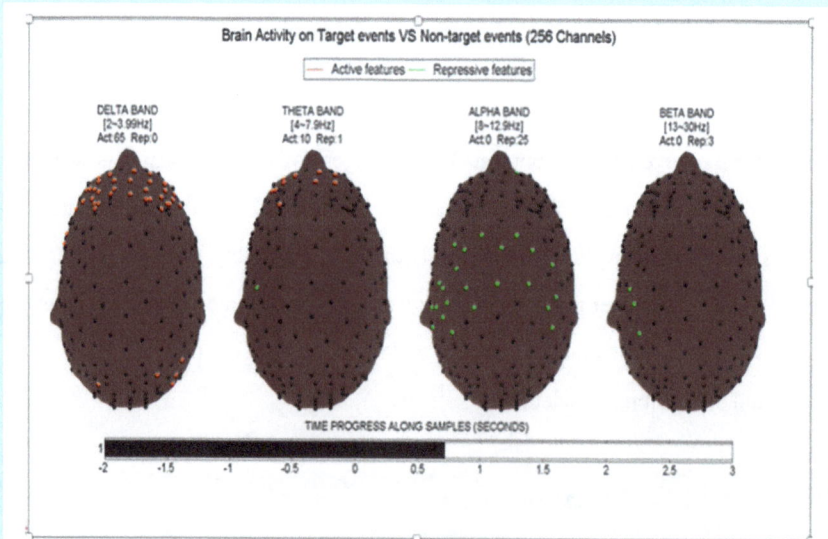

Image 2　The animation of RSVP research findings

a more complicated experiment. This is a computer simulation where the soldiers were required to complete a mission. The mission is that they will travel to a city and meet some terrorists on their way. Therefore, they should fight them. Soldiers play the role of the driver. He should drive the car and simultaneously fight. In general, he would be doing a lot of very complex activities.

This simulation was about 20 minutes. In these 20 minutes, the soldier drives from the base to the city, goes quickly through the city and then return to the base. Those sections of just driving contain a low intensity task load. But when going through the city, the participant is engaged in many activities. He must be very focus, and alert. Then these parts contain high-intensity task loads. Thus, what we are going to do is to study the differences between the two kinds of sections.

Again, we go through the procedure to which we can find the presentation of these signals and find the differences. So many times, when we conduct a research, this is our goal to identify what is the pattern, where does it come from, how long does it last, so on and so forth.

In general, there is a procedure to perform this research. We begin by deciding what kind of headset to use, how many electrodes, the setup and recordings conditions, etc. The next stage is to perform data analysis, here different things are used depending on the experiment, after there is the important stage of visualization that allow us to display and share results.

Besides research publications, many findings from the lab are used to create products and commercialize them. Recently there has been a growing number of companies which are trying to create products based on EEG research to improve people's life. For example, some of them have created a product using EEG to help solve some problems of sleep. Some have created a product to help people focus and navigate for concentration and relaxation.

Introduction to Brain-Computer Interface (BCI) and Overview of Past Research

One of the most important field of EEG research is the Brain Computer Interface (BCI). This is an area in which people are trying to create a system that receives brain signal as input, processed and generated commands as output for interaction with humans or other machines.

The procedure is almost the same. After recognizing the signals, we extract the information that would be useful for us. We need to interpret this information and convert it into an output so that we can control stuff in our mind and send messages with our mind.

This area of BCI has been active for a couple of decades. For instance, there's a patient there who is suffering from locked-down syndrome. He cannot speak and move. However, BCI allows a system for patients like him in which they could use a brain spelling. He can use his brain and eyesight to select a letter on the keyboard so that he can convey messages to other people.

Other common applications are, for example, to control wheelchairs, arms or legs. There's also application for people who have problems with attention disorders, some mental problems related to dysfunctional cognitive ability can be treated or improved with the usage of BCI systems.

Another common BCI technique is called Imagined Motion. It turns out to be that if I move my arm, my brain is generating some signals. But if I imagine that I am moving my arm, but I am not moving it, the generated signals can be similar.

The image here, the participant is moving their hand, shows that is how the signals look like. On the right the participant is imagining that he is moving his hand. Apparently, not very similar, but it can be used. By applying the procedures of the analysis, we can find a way in which we can separate imagining from the actual movement. For example, after performing the analysis, the movement and the imagination of the movement is more similar. Then it can be used to construct BCI.

Another example is called SSVEP (Image 3). This technique is built based on a natural brain response to a visual flickering. It works like this: when you look at a source of light that is flickering at a certain frequency, the brain signals from the visual cortex(an area of the brain responsible for processing most of our visual stimulus), gets excited and produces a response with similar frequency to the visual stimuli.

During the experiment, the participant looks at the white screen, which is flickering 10 times per second. Then in his brain activity, the signals from the visual cortex,

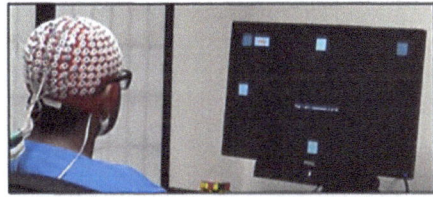

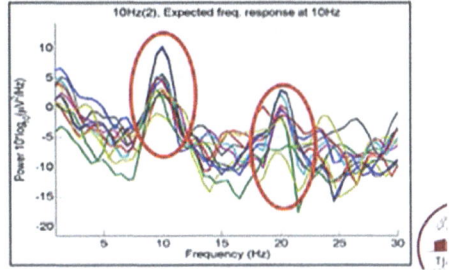

Image 3　How SSVEP works

we can see a strong response at the same frequency, which is also 10 times per second. The point of this is that we can build a system just by looking at the flickering stimuli, can detect it and translate it into a command in order to control something or create messages.

We also worked on another program in which we want to control the drones by using this technique (Image 4). We've recorded data from 42 participants. Specifically, we gave them six flickers on the screen. Each one represents a different command: forward, back,

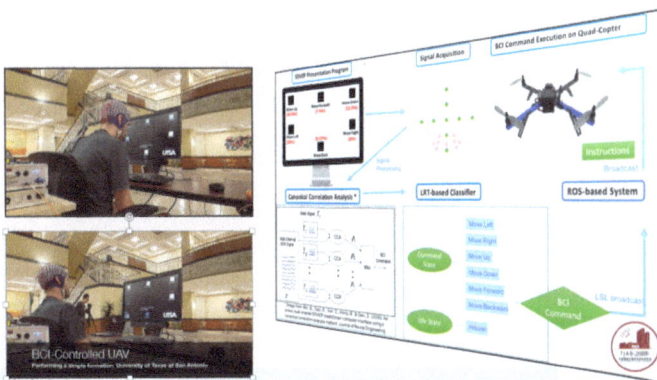

Image 4　BCI Research: controlling drones and UAVS

left, right, up and down. The next step is to find a procedure in which you can find out which of the flickers the participants are looking at during that period of time. At the same time, we are able to detect whether they are looking or not.

The final results look like this: the participant is working on the video and talking to the camera, and the system knows when the participant is looking or not to one of the six flickers (idle detection). In the second video, he has to choose one of the flickering squares, look at it to give a command and then he can look outside to see the drones in this process. He has a task of avoiding these obstacles and he completed it successfully.

In short, you have to select one of the flickering squares. The system comes to recognize which one you are looking at, and then translates it into the command for the drones. This is a basic meaning of BCI-to convert a brain activity into a command.

We also realize the same thing from the use of a game. This simple game is a maze game. We use the same technique to control the character and move to the space so that we can play the game by using our brain activity.

In addition to games, we explored using Virtual Reality because it increases the immersion and therefore evoked response by the participants. This is another example of Virtual Reality. When the person is concentrating, the trees are going to grow. When the person is relaxing, flowers will grow. So, this is an interaction-based application that can interact with brain activities. But as we know, modern games require more complex controls. We also hope to incorporate this. Currently we are exploring more complex games, which you can also incorporate data activities.

This is a basic introduction to this area, the Brain-Computer Interface. I hope you find it interesting.

(Zhu Shengyue contributed to this article)

About the Author

Lenis Mauricio Meriño is a researcher of the Tianjin International Joint Academy of Biomedicine (TJAB) at their recently created BCI platform. He completed studies on Telecommunication Engineering and has a background on electrical engineering, signals and systems as well as software development. He joined Brain-Computer Interface Lab at The University of Texas at San Antonio directed by Professor Yufei Huang as a research assistant, where he got exposure to machine learning, designed and conducted experiment to obtain brain recordings with multiple devices, and developed software and tools to analyzing EEG data and then getting it visualized.

女性的生育能力

文 / 阿尔弗雷德·奥托·缪克（德国） 译 / 李扬璐

　　我们是如何来到这个世界上的呢？在我的祖国德国有个传说，孩子是大鸟衔来的。

　　实际上，孩子是来自爸爸的精子和来自妈妈的卵子的结合。卵子和精子结合受精便形成受精卵，即一个新生命的开始。

　　每一个卵子小公主都披着漂亮的衣裳（颗粒细胞），卵子与颗粒细胞共同称为卵泡，她们都是乖巧的好孩子，她们平时静静地待在卵巢里等候指令，听到"发育"的指令

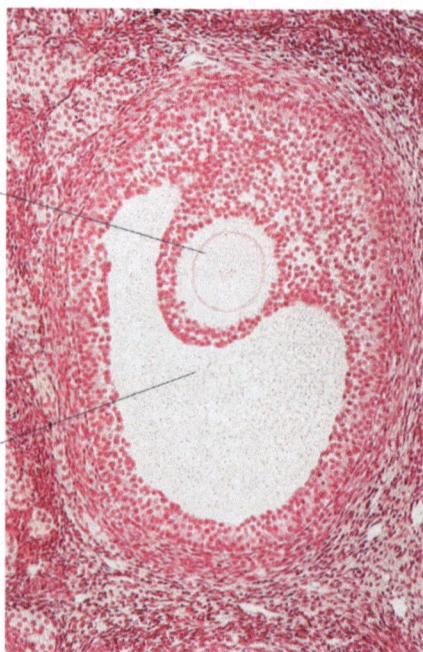

图 1　一颗美丽的"成熟卵泡"（排卵前卵泡）

卵细胞

卵泡液

下达以后，她们才茁壮成长。随着时间的推移，卵子公主不但会增加自己的外衣（图1），还会携带足够的干粮（卵泡液等），使自己由一颗小卵泡（始基卵泡）长成一个亭亭玉立的大姑娘（排卵前卵泡）。

每个生理周期内（一般为21~35天），卵巢里会有一小队卵泡（3~11个）一起发育，它们"竞争上岗"去争夺唯一的一个"优势卵泡"名额，经过复杂的竞赛程序和激烈的角逐，一枚又大又圆、健康美丽的成熟卵泡成功脱颖而出，脱掉美丽的外衣，排出卵子，成为产生生命的母细胞，羞涩地期盼与精子小王子的相遇。

在卵泡发育和排出过程中，会产生大量的雌激素和孕激素，它们作用于女性的全身，使女性变得身材窈窕、皮肤细腻，而当女性逐渐衰老的时候，卵泡产生雌激素和孕激素的能力下降，女性开始出现皱纹，皮肤变得粗糙，身体逐渐发胖，睡眠质量变差，脾气逐渐暴躁……出现一系列衰老的迹象。

每个女性一生里所能拥有的卵泡数量是一定的，一般只有400~500个卵泡发育成熟并排卵，如果没有成为优势卵泡，它们自行启动凋亡程序，退化闭锁。

卵泡也是美丽而脆弱的，当女性不幸患了癌症需要化学药物治疗或者放射治疗杀死癌细胞的时候，化学药物进入体内及盆腔（卵巢所在的位置）受到放射线照射后，许多卵泡也会同癌细胞一起"阵亡"。

显微镜下一个个闪闪发光的圆点（图2a）代表着卵巢组织中的一个个卵泡，这一片星光璀璨就意味着卵泡很多，产生卵子的机会特别大。相反，如图2b所示，这是经过放射线照射和化学药物治疗的卵巢，卵泡数量大幅减少，就意味着几乎没有卵子产生，从而导致这名女性不能怀孕生宝宝，甚至早早地开始衰老。

2012年，北京妇产医院妇科内分泌科主任阮祥燕教授来德国学习交流（图3），我请她去观摩一台手术。患者是一位年轻的患有乳腺癌的女孩，我们要为

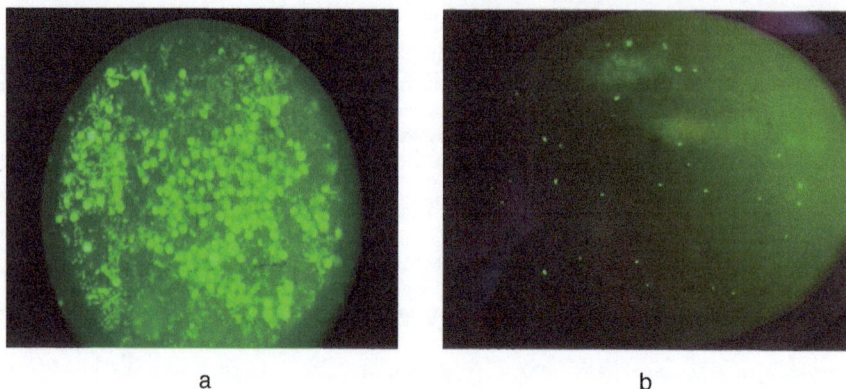

图2 荧光显微镜下的卵泡

她做卵巢组织活检，阮教授当时满怀疑惑与好奇，乳腺癌患者为什么要做卵巢组织活检？

图3 阮祥燕教授在德国跟随 Mueck 教授学习

原来，这个女孩确诊了乳腺癌，将要进行放射治疗和化学药物治疗（我们常称为放化疗），化疗药中的环磷酰胺对卵巢的损伤非常大，放射治疗如果波及卵巢也会造成不可逆的损伤，导致患者在放化疗后卵巢功能减退甚至衰竭，出现潮热、盗汗、失眠、骨质疏松、心血管疾病的风险明显增高，所以要在放化疗前将卵巢组织取出，经 4~8 ℃低温运输到生育力保护实验室，应用低温处理和冷冻技术将其冻存起来，当患者癌症临床痊愈后再自体回植，重新让卵巢发挥内分泌和排卵功能（图 4）。

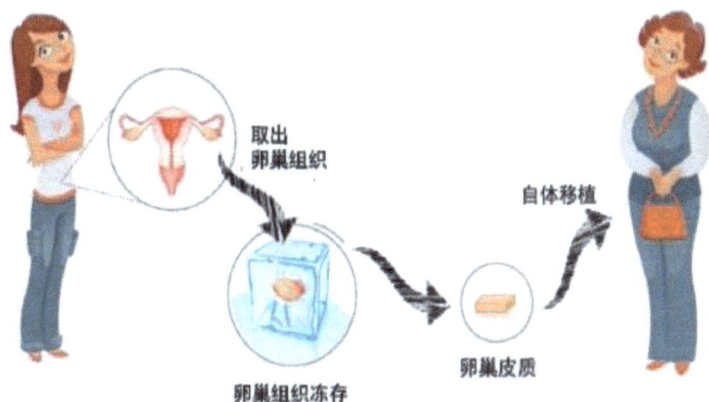

图 4 卵巢组织冻存示意

阮祥燕教授是妇科内分泌领域的著名专家，她深知，年轻女孩们一旦被诊断为"早发性卵巢功能不全"（俗称卵巢早衰），无异于被判了妇科内分泌领域的不治之症。近年来，因为患乳腺癌、血液病等多次放化疗后闭经的女性越来越多。在她的门诊里，因为各种原因导致早发性卵巢功能不全而四处求医的年轻姑娘比比皆是。她们满怀希望而来，却被告知除了激素补充治疗，没有其他更好的办法。她们饱受卵巢早衰后潮热、失眠、焦虑、浑身不适等日常生活的折磨，即使有生育意愿者妊娠率也仅有 5%~10%。

中国人口基数众多，每年新发癌症患者 400 多万人，阮祥燕教授认为这项技术在中国处于空白，中国女性太需要这项技术了！我们二人一拍即合，2012 年，我组织德国生育力保护领域顶尖专家 Markus Montag 教授和 Jana Liebenthron 教授，将此技术引入首都医科大学附属北京妇产医院。经过近 3 年的筹备，

2015 年 1 月，中国首个人卵巢组织冻存库——国际生育力保护实验室正式成立，实验室建立了一整套完善的标准化操作规范，内容包括卵巢组织取材、处理、冻存和复苏。大到卵巢组织冻存相关的各项操作、仪器的维修维护，小到生物安全柜的无菌程度、冻存管的排列顺序、更衣间是否整洁，实验室都有极其严格的质量控制。迄今为止，北京妇产医院生育力保护中心已冻存卵巢组织 300 余例，疾病种类 20 余种，移植 10 例，所有移植患者卵巢功能全部恢复，随访期内卵巢功能均良好。国内许多肿瘤科医生也意识到了女性生育力保护的重要意义，与该生育力保护中心开展合作的医院达数十家，均为大型三级甲等医院。

2015 年，我们为一名 34 岁因宫颈癌进行了全子宫切除术的女性实施了冻存卵巢组织移植手术，术后 3 个月激素水平完全恢复正常，截至发稿日（随访 4 年多），该患者的卵巢功能仍处于正常水平。她回忆说："在得知患了癌症后，我惶惶不可终日，每天都沉浸在沮丧、哀怨的负能量里，术后周期性放化疗的不良反应，以及提早绝经的症状如潮热出汗、腰背疼痛、失眠焦虑加重着我对癌症的恐惧，求生的欲望与身体的折磨不停地碰撞交织……直到我的卵巢重新移回体内，我的身体里就像移植了一个'小太阳'，让我的身体充满了能量。东西还是'原装'的好啊！"

作者简介

阿尔弗雷德·奥托·缪克，德国图宾根大学教授，德国绝经学会主席，医学博士、药理学博士、生物化学博士。德国图宾根大学绝经内分泌及妇女健康中心主任，德国南部妇女健康中心主任。首都医科大学附属北京妇产医院荣誉教授及内分泌科名誉主任，首都医科大学客座教授。主持超过 25 项国际 / 国内 I～IV 期临床试验，发表论文 600 余篇，主编 / 参编论著 14 部。荣获中国政府友谊奖、长城友谊奖等诸多荣誉。

扫描收看
本文视频课程

德国生育力保护团队与北京妇产医院临床专家团队移植术前共同访视患者
（左二为 Mueck 教授，左四为阮祥燕教授）

Mueck 教授受邀参加"一带一路"国际合作高峰论坛

Fertility of Women

By Alfred Otto Mueck (Germany)

How did we come into this world? In my home country, Germany, some fairy tales say that a baby is carried to us by a big bird. In reality, a child is a combination of the sperm from the father and the egg from the mother. The egg and the sperm meet together and fertilize, forming a fertilized egg, an oosperm, thus the beginning of a new life.

Each little egg princess is beautifully clothed with granulosa, together they are called follicles. Follicles are well-behaved children who stay quietly in the ovaries, waiting for instructions to "grow". Over time, the egg princess not only adds to her

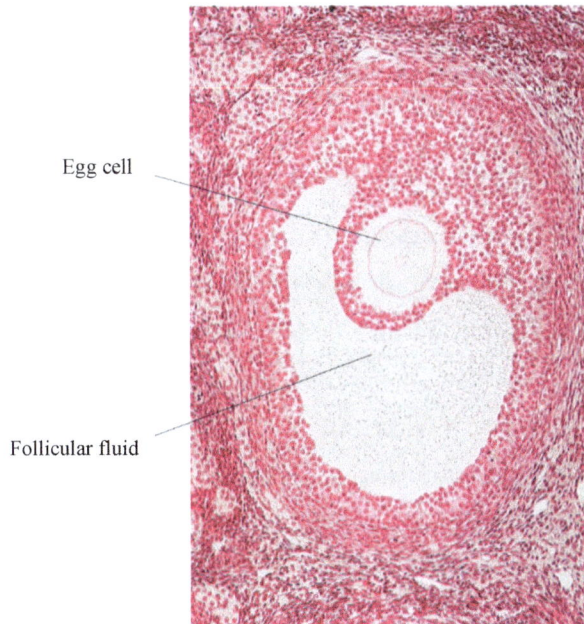

Egg cell

Follicular fluid

Image 1　A beautiful "mature follicle" (pre–ovulatory follicle)

coat（Image 1）, but also starts preparing enough food supplies with her (follicular fluid, etc.). From a small follicle (primordial follicle) she grows into a big girl (pre-ovulatory follicle).

During each physiological cycle (usually 21-35 days), a small group of follicles (about 3-11) will grow up together in the ovaries and compete for becoming the one and only "dominant follicle". A long and intensified competition will produce one large, round, healthy and beautiful mature follicle. This one will shed its beautiful coat, releases an egg that finally becomes a life-generating mother cell, expecting the sperm prince in all her shyness.

During the process of a follicle's development and release, a large number of estrogen and progesterone are produced. These chemicals have their effects on the whole body of a woman. They can keep a woman's figure slim and skin tender. When a one gradually ages, the ability of the follicle to produce estrogen decreases, so as she begins to grow wrinkles, the skin becomes less radiant, the body less in shape, the quality of sleep poorer and the temper more irritable... As such, to show a series of signs of aging.

Each woman can produce a certain number of follicles in her lifetime. If not becoming the dominant one, follicles will engage in the process of apoptosis themselves and degenerate into atresia.

A follicle is beautiful, but also fragile. When a woman unfortunately falls ill to cancer and needs chemotherapy or radiotherapy to kill the cancer cells, many follicles will "die" along with the cancer cells when the chemicals are administered into the body, especially when the pelvic cavity (where the ovaries are located) is exposed to radiation.

As shown in Image 2a, each shiny dot under the microscope represents a single follicle in the ovarian tissue. The starry patch on the left means that there are many follicles and exists a particularly good chance of producing a healthy egg. Conversely, as shown in Image 2b, this is an ovary that has been irradiated with radiation and treated with chemicals, resulting in a large reduction in the number of follicles, meaning that little or no eggs are produced. Sadly, this woman may experience difficulty to conceive a baby, or even an early onset of aging.

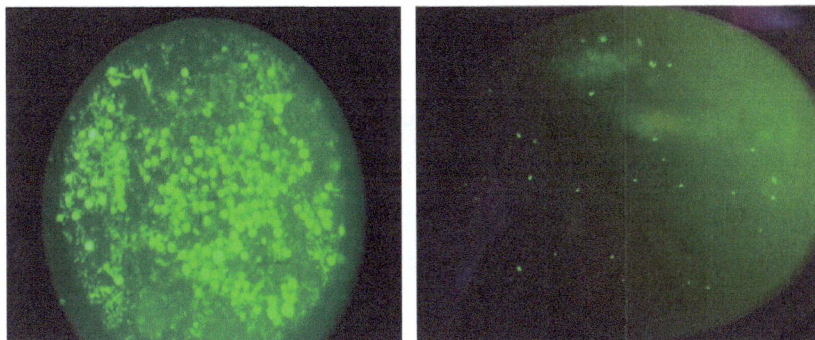

a   b

Image 2   Ovarian follicle under fluorescence microscope

In 2012, Prof. Xiangyan Ruan, Director of Endocrinology Department of Gynecology and Obstetrics Hospital, came to Germany (Image 3). I invited her to observe an operation where the patient was a young girl with breast cancer, and we were going to operate an ovarian tissue biopsy on her. Prof. Ruan was full of questions, also immensely curious about it: why does a breast cancer patient need an ovarian biopsy?

The reason lies with the cyclophosphamide in chemotherapy drugs. It can deal great damage to the ovaries, and if the ovaries are affected by radiation therapy, it will result in

Image 3   Prof. Xiangyan Ruan studying under Prof. Mueck in Germany

irreversible damage of a reduced ovarian function, or even ovary failure, after radiotherapy and chemotherapy, which will lead to hot flashes, night sweats, insomnia, osteoporosis, and a significantly higher risk of cardiovascular disease. As such, the ovarian tissue should be taken before radiotherapy and chemotherapy, transported to a fertility protection laboratory via 4-8 °C cryogenic transport, preserved with cryoprocessing and freezing techniques, and then autologously reimplanted when the patient's cancer is clinically healed that the bodily environment re-allows the ovary to perform endocrine and ovulatory functions (Image 4).

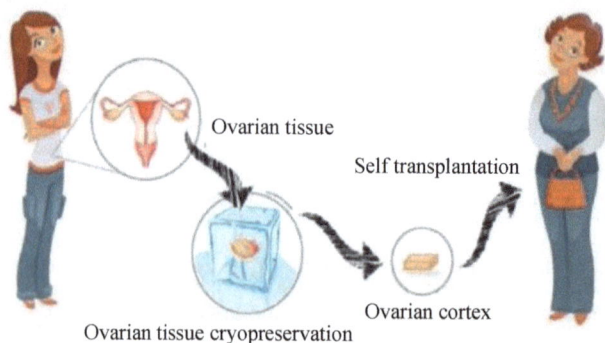

Ovarian tissue

Self transplantation

Ovarian cortex

Ovarian tissue cryopreservation

Image 4　Diagram of preserving an ovarian tissue

Professor Xiangyan Ruan, a renowned expert in the field of gynecological endocrinology, knows that once young girls are diagnosed with "premature ovarian insufficiency" (commonly known as premature ovarian failure), they are likely as well being condemned to an incurable condition in the field of gynecological endocrinology. In recent years, more and more girls have been agonizing over amenorrhea after multiple radiation and chemotherapy for breast cancer and blood disorder treatments. Ruan Xiangyan's clinic is crowed with young females who are seeking a solution to cure their premature ovarian insufficiency, which is caused by various reasons. They often come to her clinic full of hope, only to be told that there is no better option than a hormone replacement therapy, that they suffer from hot flashes, insomnia, anxiety, discomfort, and other daily life problems associated with premature ovarian failure. If, in future, they want to have children, they will find their dreams dampened by a pregnancy rate that is only about 5%~10%.

With China's enormous population and more than 4 million newly diagnosed cancer patients each year, Professor Xiangyan Ruan believes that this is the technology, which is currently not available domestically, that Chinese women need badly. The two of us hit it off right away. In 2012, I had the fortune to invite Prof. Markus Montag and Jana Liebenthron, Germany's leading experts in the field of fertility protection, to introduce this technology into the Beijing Obstetrics and Gynecology Hospital, Capital Medical University. After nearly 3 years of preparation, the first ovarian tissue cryo-preservation bank in China - the International Fertility Preservation Laboratory - was established in January 2015, which has erected a set of standardized and complete operating specifications, including procedures over ovarian tissue harvesting, processing, freezing, storaging and recovering. This laboratory has strict quality control over all operations and equipment maintenance related to ovarian tissue freezing and storage, as well as the sterility of the bio-safety cabinet, the procedures of frozen storage tubes, and the cleanliness of the dressing room. So far, the Fertility Protection Center of Beijing Obstetrics and Gynecology Hospital has handled more than 300 cases of ovarian tissue storage and 10 cases of transplants. Of all transplanted patients, their ovarian functions have recovered. Many oncologists in China have also realized the importance of female fertility protection, and there are dozens of hospitals cooperating with the Fertility Protection Center, all of which are large tertiary hospitals.

In 2015, we performed a frozen ovarian tissue transplant on a 34-year-old woman who had undergone a total hysterectomy for cervical cancer. Her hormone levels were completely back to normal three months after the surgery, and as of the date of publication (more than four years of follow-up), the patient's ovaries were still functioning at normal levels. She recalls: "After I learned that I had cancer, I was terrified, and every day I was shrouded in a negative energy of depression and grief. The side effects of cyclical radiotherapy and chemotherapy after surgery, as well as the symptoms of early menopause, such as hot flashes and sweating, back pain, insomnia and anxiety, aggravated my fear of cancer....Things were bad until my ovaries were moved back into my body. It was like a 'little sun' and filled me with energy. Things are back as they were!"

(Li Yanglu contributed to this article)

About the Author

Professor Alfred Otto Mueck, Doctor of Medicine, Doctor of Pharmacology and Doctor of Biochemistry; Professor at the University of Tübingen, President of the German Menopause Society. Director of the Centre for Menopausal Endocrindogy and Women's Health, University of Tubingen, Germany; Honorary Professor and Honorary Chief of Endocrinology Department at Beijing Obstetrics and Gynecology Hospital, Capital Medical University; Visiting Professor at Capital Medical University. Professor Mueck has conducted more than 25 international and domestic phase I-IV clinical trials, published more than 600 papers, and overseen editing of 14 books. Professor Mueck has received numerous honors, including the Friendship Award from the Chinese government, the Great Wall Friendship Award.

The team of German fertility protection and the team of clinical experts from Beijing OBGYN Hospital

Professor Mueck attended the Belt and Road Forum for International Cooperation

动物大迁徙

文 / 苏平（美国）　译 / 唐庆超

　　每年春节，中国到处都挤满了拎着大包小包的人群，春运期间，超过 3.85 亿人参与了这场世界上最大规模的人口迁徙，放眼望去，到处都是人山人海。

　　人类的迁徙尚且如此壮观，动物界的迁徙更是不遑多让。"迁徙"指的是许多人或动物从一个地方到另一个地方的大规模迁移。我曾经 4 次前往广袤的非洲大草原，亲自拍下了许多珍贵的动物大迁徙的影像资料。

为了食物而迁徙

　　这次，我带来了这些神奇的照片，将给小朋友们展现一幅广阔的非洲大草原画卷。在非洲众多动物群的迁徙里，最为典型的就是坦桑尼亚和肯尼亚两国之间的东非野生动物大迁徙了，其中，数以百万计的角马群便是这场一直处于进行时的大迁徙中当之无愧的主角（图 1）。

　　每年 1—3 月，角马群悠闲地生活在塞伦盖蒂国家公园的保护区内，4 月开始向塞伦盖蒂的西北面迁徙，7 月，它们继续北上，途中穿越马拉河，8—9 月停留在马赛马拉国家保护区。

图 1　迁徙中的动物

10 月，角马群又开始从东线南迁到塞伦盖蒂，终于，在 12 月，它们回到了家园，开始繁衍后代、休养生息，第二年的迁徙也即将到来。

每年 6 月是非洲动物们的哺乳期，这个时候，大量的小角马会诞生在迁徙路上，迁徙可给这些小生命的到来造成了一定难度。而迁徙路上也并非一帆风顺，马拉河中凶猛的鳄鱼和河马正潜伏着伺机偷袭。

是什么让角马们即便面对这些困难与危险也要不停迁徙呢？答案只有一个，那就是食物。对于角马这类动物而言，它们的食物是草；而对于草原上的食肉动物而言，它们追逐的就是这些不停迁徙的食草动物。

非洲大草原的气候有明显的旱季和雨季，大致每年 5—10 月大陆低气压北移，这时北半球热带草原上盛行西南季风，带来丰沛的降水，形成雨季。

11 月至次年 4 月，大陆低气压南移，北半球热带草原盛行来自副热带高气压带的信风，十分干燥，形成旱季。每到雨季，草木葱绿，万象更新；每到旱季，万物凋零，一片枯黄。

由于非洲大草原上的旱雨季变化，食草动物们不能定居一处，它们需要不停地追赶青草和水源，以满足它们的生存所需。因此，浩浩荡荡的大迁徙每年都在非洲大草原上演着。

食草动物 VS 食肉动物

先让我们来认识一下大草原上的食草动物们吧！在这场动物大迁徙中打头阵的是最喜欢吃高层新草的斑马们，紧随其后的是这场大迁徙的主角——角马，角马又称牛羚，是大迁徙的代表物种，每年有超过 150 万头的角马参与到这场动物大迁徙之中，它们喜食的是中层嫩草。

跟随在后的食草动物们还有大象、长颈鹿、非洲水牛、黑斑羚和羚羊，它们也纷纷加入迁徙行列当中。

然而，食草动物们需要应对的不仅是食物的难题。在这些迁徙食草动物群的末尾，它们的天敌也紧随其后——食肉动物对它们虎视眈眈。

大象、长颈鹿和水牛体型健壮，肉食动物对它们兴致不高，角牛有时捕猎起来也颇具难度，捕食者们通常会选择结伴对它们发动攻击。黑斑羚和羚羊则常常成为肉食动物们的盘中餐。

图 2　睡觉的狮子

但对于狮子而言，作为非洲大草原上的百兽之王，它们敢于对任何动物发起袭击，是食肉动物当之无愧的代表。大草原上的狮子们每天几乎要睡 20 个小时，不睡觉时便躲在树荫下百无聊赖，表现得极为懒洋洋，有恃无恐似的。面对镜头，它们也一点儿不害怕，任人拍摄，颇有王者风范（图 2）。

食肉动物的代表还有草原上的猎豹和豹子。虽然都是豹，但它们可不一样，猎豹奔跑速度极快，瘦长的身体在奔跑中显得轻盈灵动，而豹子相比猎豹则更加强壮。此外，

图 3 我拍摄到的趴在树上的豹子

豹子喜欢待在树上，它们在狩猎后会将食物拖拽上树后再进食，这能有效地防止狮子和猎豹前来抢食——毕竟猎豹和狮子可不会上树（图 3）。

拍摄豹子可不是一件简单的事情，它们天性害羞，不喜见人。我去过 4 次大草原，猎豹和狮子都多次拍到，豹子却还是头一次，可见它们有多害羞了。

河马被认为是最危险的哺乳动物

虽然猎豹速度很快，豹子极为强壮，狮子是草原百兽之王，然而，对于这些迁徙中的食草动物们来说，最危险的动物却并不是它们，而是河马！

河马被称为最危险的哺乳动物，它们昼伏夜出，潜水本领极高，脾气极为

图4　看似憨厚的河马

凶残，而且极易主动攻击其他动物，加上它们巨大的体型和在水中极快的移动速度，即便是鳄鱼和狮子也时常成为它们的猎物（图4）。

而在食草动物群每年需要穿越的马拉河里，就遍布着河马的身影，数以万计的动物丧生在河马的利齿之下。它们才是最危险的动物。

每年7—9月是东非动物大迁徙的高潮，数以百万计的角马和其他食草动物来到马拉河边，准备跨越马拉河。这是动物们的"天河之渡"。

渡河前，斑马、角马、羚羊……上百万只食草动物站在岸上，只待时机成熟，便倾巢出动，以超快的速度渡河。而河里的鳄鱼早已张着嘴，以尖锐的牙齿伺候送上门来的食物。

成千上万的角马、斑马、羚羊，为了生存，不顾猛兽的围捕，不顾马拉河鳄鱼的袭击，一波又一波前仆后继地跃入马拉河中。幸运者游向了对岸的天国，而不幸者则成为猛兽的盘中餐。

河马也加入了这一场混战，它们虽然以草食为主，脾气却十分暴躁，对侵入自己领地的动物一概不放过。不仅食草动物会命丧它们的利齿之下，鳄鱼和尾随而来的捕食者们也会被误伤，数万动物的生命将葬送在马拉河中。

在这场轰轰烈烈的动物大迁徙里，既存在食草动物，也存在食肉动物；既存在捕食者，也存在被捕食者。它们彼此之间交织成了一张大迁徙食物网。

食物网的最底层是众多的食草动物们——牛羚、非洲水牛、长颈鹿、羚羊和斑马。猎豹以牛羚、羚羊和斑马为食，有时它们会许多只一起出动来捕食，但非洲水牛和长颈鹿的体型太大，猎豹们并不爱去打扰它们。

狮子通常不以水牛为食，但有时食物缺乏，也会捕猎水牛。它们通常的食物是斑马、羚羊和牛羚。而豹子因为在树上进食，因此体型太大的动物并不在它们的捕食范围内。

因此，草原食物链最顶端的王者非狮子莫属。它们敢于猎杀所有的食草动物，小象、水牛也会成为它们的猎物，猎豹和豹子望尘莫及。

草原的旱雨季交替带来了食草动物们的大迁徙，追逐着食物而来的捕猎者们也参与到迁徙之中。弱肉强食，适者生存，大自然既残酷也公平。

希望通过我的讲解，会有更多的小朋友对美丽的非洲大草原产生兴趣，一起来探讨大自然的奥秘！

作者简介

苏平，来自美国的教育家、艺术家和摄影师，在中国生活和工作了 15 年，目前工作于中国苏州。除了在苏州外国语学校担任行政职务外，他还教授中学生物。在苏州期间，因教育工作出色、热心慈善事业，被授予苏州荣誉市民和江苏友谊奖。他对学习、教育和创作充满热情，其作品曾在中国和美国的 40 多个展览和项目中展出。

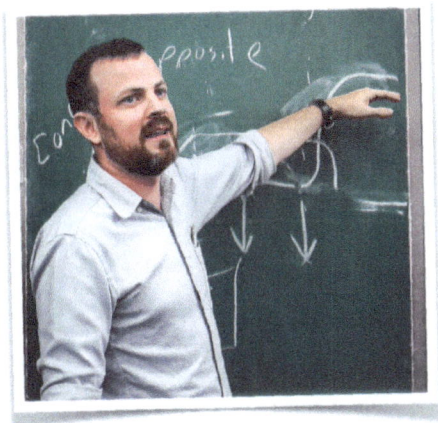

The Great Migration of Animals

By Nathan Pelton (America)

Every Spring Festival, the transportation in China is crowded with people carrying large and small bags. During the travel rush of the Spring Festival, more than 385 million people will participate in the world's largest population migration. As far as the eyes can see, there are crowds of people everywhere.

With the migration of human beings being so spectacular, the migration of the animal kingdom is even more impressive. Migration refers to the large movement of many people or animals from one place to another. I've been to the vast African savannah four times, and has taken many rare images of animal migrations.

Migration for Food

This time, I have brought these amazing photos to show the children a picture of the vast African savannah. Among many animal migrations in Africa, the most typical one is the great migration of East African wild animals between Tanzania and Kenya. Wildebeest herds numbering in the millions are the well-deserved protagonists of this ongoing migration (Image 1).

From January to March each year, wildebeest herds live leisurely in the protected area of Serengeti National Park. In April, they begin to migrate to the northwest of Serengeti. In

Image 1　Animals in the great migration

July, they continue northward, crossing the Mara River, and stop at the Masai Mara National Reserve from August to September.

In October, the wildebeest herds began to move south from the Eastern Front to Serengeti. Finally, in December, they returned to their original homes and began to reproduce and rest as they prepare for next year's migration.

June is the breastfeeding period for African animals. At this time, a large number of small wildebeests will be born on the migratory road, which makes the arrival of these small lives quite difficult. In addition, the migratory road is not all smooth sailing. The ferocious crocodiles and hippos in the Mara River are lurking for an opportunity to attack.

What fuels the wildebeests on-going migration, despite the difficulties and dangers they face? Food is the sole reason for the migration. Grass is the food for animals like wildebeests. In order for Wildebeests and other similar animals to have enough of a supply of grass, herbivores need to migrate constantly. In turn the herbivores are the food for the carnivores on the African savannah. For the sake of food, these animals also join the Great

Migration.

The climate of the African savannah has clear-cut dry and rainy seasons. Generally, the continental depression moves northward from May to October each year. At this time, the southwest monsoon prevails on the tropical grasslands of the northern hemisphere, bringing abundant precipitation and forming the rainy season.

From November to April of the following year, the continental depression moved southward, and trade winds from the subtropical high pressure zone prevailed in the tropical grasslands of the northern hemisphere, which was very dry, forming the dry season. In the rainy season, the vegetation is lush and green, and everything is renewed; in the dry season, everything withers and becomes yellow.

Due to the changes in the dry and rainy seasons on the African savannah, herbivores cannot settle in one place. They need to keep chasing grass and water sources to meet their survival needs. Therefore, the mighty migration takes place on the African savannah every year.

Herbivores VS Carnivores

Let us first get to know the herbivores on the African savannah! The first in this animal migration are the zebras who like to eat high-rise new grass, followed by the wildebeests who are the protagonist of this migration. Wildebeest is one of the representative species of the Great Migration. Every year, more than 1.5 million wildebeests, who like to eat mid-rise tender grass, participate in this animal migration.

Herbivores that follow are elephants, giraffes, buffaloes, gazelles and impalas. They also join the migration.

Elephants migrate in herds. Some people describe the migration of elephants as a convoy of heavy trucks. The feeling is extremely shocking when these herds of elephants each weighing several tons stomp and march collectively.

Giraffes are very gentle and socialble animals. In the African grasslands, they not only live in groups by themselves, but also like to live with ostriches, wildebeest and zebras, as they help to guard and protect each other.

However, even though the herbivores are so united, they still have to face more than food problems on their migration. At the end of these migrating herbivore groups, their natural enemies are also close behind-carnivores are stocking and hunting them.

Carnivores lack interest in elephants, giraffes, and buffaloes because they are too strong. Wildebeests are sometimes difficult to hunt, too. Predators usually choose to attack them in pairs. As for impala and antelope, they often turn out to be a delicacy for carnivores.

Lions, as the king of beasts on the African savannah and the well-deserved representative of carnivores, they will dare to attack any animal if the conditions are right. Lions on the African savannah sleep almost 20 hours a day, acting extremely lazy but also confident. Even if they are not sleeping, you can find them lazily napping in the shade, too. I have photographed lions many times. They are not afraid of the camera at all. This may be the king's style (Image 2).

Cheetahs and leopards are representatives of carnivores, too. Although at first glance may seem similar, they are not the same. Cheetahs run extremely fast, as their

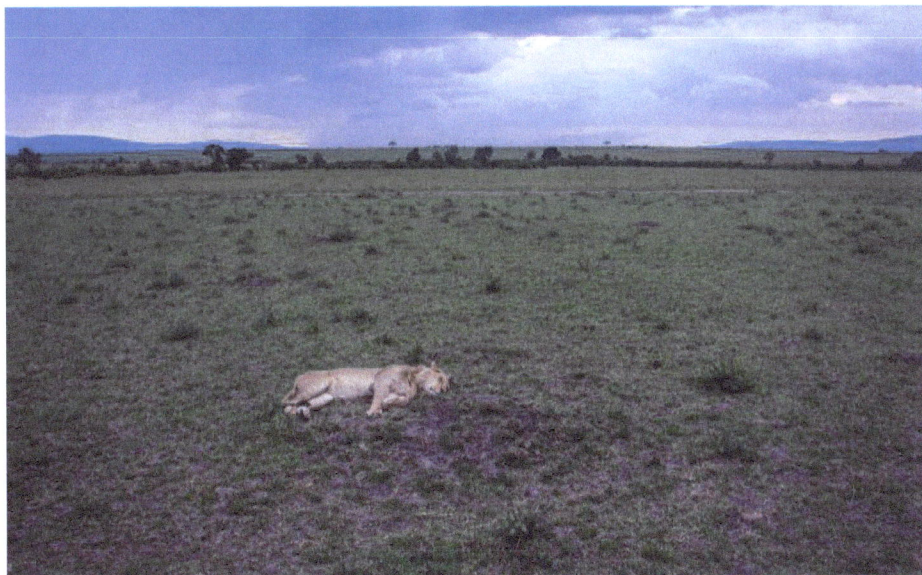

Image 2 A sleeping lion

Image 3　I photographed a leopard in a tree

slender body is light and agile designed for running, while leopards are stronger than cheetahs. In addition, leopards like to stay in trees. After hunting, they will drag food up the tree before eating. This can effectively prevent lions and cheetahs from coming to grab food. After all, cheetahs and lions cannot climb trees (Image 3).

Photographing leopards is not an easy task. I have been to the African savannah four times and taken many photos of lions and cheetahs, but this is the first time for leopards. They are shy by nature and don't like meeting people. It was a surprise to see this one this time.

Hipposare Known as the Most Dangerous Mammals

The cheetah is fast, the leopard is extremely strong, and the lion is the king of the grassland beasts. However, for the migrating herbivores, the most dangerous animal is not the carnivores, but the hippopotamus!

Hippos hide by day and come out by night, and are known as the most dangerous mammals. They are extremely capable of diving, but have a very cruel temper - they are prone to actively attack other animals. The huge size and the extremely fast speed makes them masters in the water, even crocodiles and lions are often killed by them (Image 4).

From July to September each year is the climax of the East African animal migration. Millions of wildebeests and other herbivores come to the Mara River and prepare to cross the river. This is called the "Crossing of the sky river" .

Before crossing the river, zebras, wildebeests, antelopes... millions of herbivores will stand on the bank, and then rush out to cross the river at super fast speeds when the time is right. At the same time, the crocodiles in the river have already opened their mouths, waiting for food to be delivered.

In order to survive, thousands of wildebeests, zebras, and antelopes, jump into the Mara River one by one, regardless of the rounding up of beasts and the attacks of the Mara River crocodiles. The lucky ones swim to the safety on the other side, and the unfortunate ones become the dinner for the river beasts.

Image 4　The hippos seemingly simple and honest

Hippos have also joined this melee. They will not spare any animals that invade their territory because of their violent temper, although they are mainly herbivorous. Not only will the migrating herbivores be killed by their razor sharp teeth, crocodiles and trailing predators may also be accidentally injured.

Tens of thousands of animals have lost their lives to the teeth of hippos. Indeed, they are the most dangerous animals in the savanna.

In this vigorous animal migration, there are both herbivores and carnivores, both predators and prey, which intertwining into a large migration food web.

At the bottom of the food web are numerous herbivores—wildebeests, buffaloes, giraffes, antelopes and zebras. Cheetahs feed on wildebeests, antelopes and zebras.

Sometimes many of them will come together to hunt. Buffaloes and giraffes are too big, cheetahs do not like to hunt them.

Lions usually do not feed on buffaloes unless food is lacking. Their usual diet including zebras, antelopes and wildebeests. Because leopards eat in trees, animals that are too big are not in their prey.

Therefore, the lions are the kings of the food chain. They dare to hunt all herbivores, elephants and buffaloes. In this respect, cheetahs and leopards are far inferior to them.

The dry and rainy seasons of the African savannah have brought about a great migration of herbivores, and hunters who are chasing for food also participate in the migration. The weak become meat and the strong eat. The survival of the fittest. Nature is cruel and fair.

Hoping that through my explanation, more children will become interested in the beautiful African savannah and explore the mysteries of nature together!

(Tang Qingchao contributed to this article)

About the Author

Nathan Pelton is an educator, artist, and photographer from the USA who has been living and working in China for 15 years. He currently lives and works in Suzhou, China. Along with administrative responsibilities at Suzhou Foreign Language School, he also teaches middle school Biology. While in Suzhou, for his work in education and with charity, he has been awarded as a Suzhou Honorary Citizen and the Jiangsu Friendship Award. He is deeply passionate about learning, educating, and creating. His artwork has been included in more than 40 exhibitions and projects throughout China and the USA.

闻声识海豚

文 / 萨拉·普拉托（意大利）　　译 / 杨云舟

与动物相伴的人生

　　我从小就十分喜爱小动物，身边一直有小动物陪伴。长大之后，这份对动物的亲昵之情自然而然地让我萌生了从事兽医职业的想法。不过，我的父母一开始对此表示反对，他们始终希望我能去攻读像法学一类的实用学位。但凭借着坚持不懈的努力，我最终说服了父母。也正是因为这份坚持，我最终说服了兽医学教授允许我前去加纳利群岛旅行。在研究兽医学的日子里，海豚这种动物引起了我极大的兴趣，而加纳利群岛广阔的海岸能为我带来与海豚亲密接触的丰富机会。

　　在海岛上，我花了很多时间来研究动物们的行为，时不时还会向它们提供一些帮助。不过我知道，自己想要的不仅是这些。我希望能够了解动物之间的交流方式。当还只有 5 岁的时候，我就有了第一次与动物交流的经验。通过模仿母猫的声音，我成功地把小猫从藏身处哄出来一起玩耍。于是，在一位德国教授的帮助下，当时还是学生的我从加纳利群岛搬到了以色列，继续进行着海豚研究。海豚和海豚之间——以及海豚与人类之间——究竟是如何互动的？它们用什么方法来交流？它们又是如何传达自己需求的呢？

与此同时，我一直没有忘记自己的另一个追求：为那些需要照料的动物提供帮助。我曾前往美国和加拿大的多家机构，与那里的工作人员一起为海洋动物和其他动物朋友们提供医疗和保护上的援助。

在这之后，2007 年，我来到了中国，开始着手进行博士后研究。自 2017 年开始到现在，我一直在江汉大学任教。

奇妙的海豚和奇妙的声音

海豚和人类都是社会性哺乳动物，都有着非常相似的社会结构，即"裂变－融合社会"。什么叫裂变－融合社会呢？这其实指的是由不同个体组成的小家庭作为社会单位又组成了社会。一个裂变－融合社会中的家庭成员在各自的日常生活中都会有很多事情要分头处理。例如，人类要上班，海豚则要出去捕食。我们每个人都会离开家庭去做各自的事情，但是到了最后，大家又会聚在一起。但人类和海豚又大有不同。我们生活在不同的环境中，也因此进化出了不同的感官系统来适应环境。生活在坚实的陆地上的我们有着独特的大脑构成，海豚的大脑则与我们的不同。不过，尽管有这样那样的差异，人类和海豚在小社会或大社会中却都有着共同的交流需求。

像海豚一样在海底生活和交流可能会面临着不少的挑战。其中一个挑战就是视觉能力。深海环境中的海水模糊不清，四周一片漆黑，几乎没有任何光线能到达这里。而就算在海水尚还清澈的地方，可见光也只能到达海平面以下100 米处的深度。更何况，大海里还常常有海浪的干扰和海草等障碍物的阻挡。所以，我们在海面下很有可能只能看到几米，甚至几厘米开外的东西。这样一看，视觉感官似乎对于海洋动物来说并没有那么大的作用。但是，如果海豚的视力如此之差，它们又是怎么能够如此自在地游来游去，和其他海豚交朋友，还要躲避其他捕食者的呢？它们要利用什么感官呢？答案就是——声音！

声音在海水中的传播速度受到多种因素的影响。由于水和空气的密度不同，声音在海平面以下的传播速度是在海平面以上时的 4.5 倍。除此之外，声音的传播速度还与海水的温度和盐度有关。水温越高、海水越咸，声音的传播速度就越快。还有，海洋深处的水压明显高于海面，而此时声音的传播速度也会相应加快。

海豚和声音

我们在水里也能听到声音。但海豚的听力和我们一样吗？遗憾的是，由于人类耳朵的形状和结构，我们在水中只能接收到有限的声音频率范围。出于同样的原因，我们在游泳时双耳也无法辨别声音的方向。那海豚呢？它们在水中的听觉能力要先进得多，因为它们不像人类——人类只能接收 20 Hz ～ 15 kHz 的频率，而海豚可以接收 75 Hz ～ 150 kHz 的所有声音频率。

那么，海豚是如何发声的？我们人类用声带来发声，而海豚则采用了另一种方法——它们通过自己鼻腔的器官发声，这个鼻腔器官位于额隆部位（海豚头顶的圆形部分）。空气会通过海豚的呼吸孔进入一个类似口袋状的结构中，一旦这个口袋状的结构发生震动，就会产生声音。但除了这一部分的器官，海豚还有另外的非常重要的发声装置——它们体内的两套唇状器官。这两个声唇使它们能够同时发出两种声音：既可以发出用来交流的哨声，也可以发出用来扫描环境的定位回声。

这些声音在发出来后是怎么被海豚听到的呢？海豚额隆里的脂肪组织和水的密度是一样的。这些组织的功能就像一个透镜，可以通过改变形状来把声音传到各个不同的方向和角度。在海豚的下颚周围也存在着类似的脂肪组织。当声音传来时，颌骨内的脂肪组织就会感知到它们的震动，然后将声音传到海豚耳朵的内部，而海豚的耳朵也被同样的脂肪组织所包围。虽然它们有耳朵，也有耳道，但由于结构与人类不同，海豚在水面上的听力不如在水下时的好（图1）。

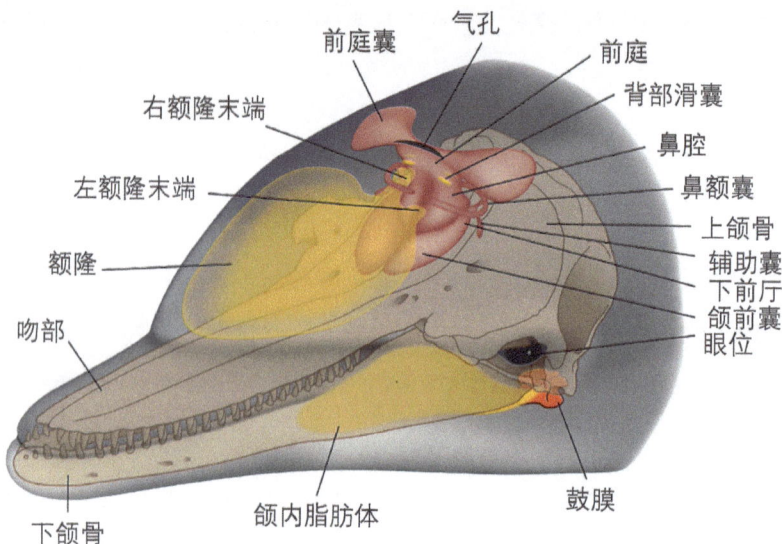

图1　瓶鼻海豚头部内声音发收结构示意（绘图：Vko Gorter）

海豚的"声音百宝箱"

为了能够更好地了解海豚所发出的声音，研究人员将几种不同模式的声像图分离了出来。从这些不同的声音模式中，科学家们能够辨别出这些声音发出时的场景，如当时海豚的心情怎样，或者当时它们是在赶路还是在做其他的事。

在海豚发出的不同声音里，有一种被称为"口哨"的声音，平均频率范围在

75 Hz ～ 24 kHz（有时候会超过 24 kHz）。哨声是全向的，这意味着很难根据它来辨别声音的源头。一声哨声由两个部分组成：基础频率，即主哨，以及以基础频率的整数倍频率传播的谐波，通常都达到了超声波（> 20 kHz）范围。同时含有非指向性和指向性成分的哨音被称为"混合指向"哨音。研究人员发现，哨声中的谐波其实可以用来进行方向追踪。因此，当海豚既要传达自己的信息，又要表达自己的位置时，就会同时释放出哨声和谐波。

人都有自己的名字，每个人都通过对方的名字来认识不同的人。海豚也有名字——这就是每只海豚的标志性哨音。海豚可以用特定的哨音给自己贴上标签——就像名字一样——每只海豚都有自己特有的哨音。这种标志性哨音也可以被其他海豚模仿，用来呼唤单独某一只海豚，就像我们叫一个人的名字一样。

除了口哨声外，海豚还有另一种声音，是用来回声定位的"滴答声"，听起来就像木棍互相撞击的声音。海豚用这种声音来扫描周围的环境，寻找食物或障碍物。每一次滴答声之后都有一个间隔，在这个间隔中，海豚会等待回声的返回，然后再发出下一次滴答声。通过测量这个时间间隔，海豚可以计算出自己与某个物体的距离，从而在脑海中绘制出一幅环境地图。

海豚还有第 3 种声音，叫作"脉冲声"。脉冲声包含了情感成分。当海豚感到不高兴或相互争吵时，它们就会发出这种声音。科学家们根据脉冲声的细微不同把这种声音分成好几类，如喊声、哭声、啜泣声。不同种类的海豚能够发出的声音其实不尽相同。例如，无鳍江豚就只能发出脉冲声，而发不出口哨声。

海豚的感知世界

人类主要通过视觉和语言来创造自己的现实。每当看到新的事物，我们就会忙不迭地给它命名，从而也就认识了它。一般来说，"自我"概念建立的根基是大脑对如以自我为中心的空间和时间轴等外部信息的处理，以及头部、身体的位置和方向等内部信息的定位。这些都是构建自我的要素。除此之外，记忆、期望、计划等只不过是一些附加要素。对于海豚来说，所有关于外部世界的信息都来自回声定位。

人类在交谈时会问："你看到我所看到的了吗？"或者"你看到我刚刚说的了吗？"海豚则不同，它们会问："你看到我刚刚听到的了吗？"每当海豚通过滴答声来回声定位、扫描周围的环境时，它们就能在大脑中构建出一种"全息图像"。令人惊奇的是，这些回声可以被附近的另一只海豚接收到，而它们则会收到完全相同的"全息图像"！当不同的人从不同的角度看同一个物体时，他们看到的画面也自然不一样。这取决于他们每个人如何感知他们的现实。回声定位有一个与人类语言截然不同的特征，即在此处，海豚大脑对现实的构建基于的其实是个体所产生的信号。在从回声定位构建现实的过程中，海豚可以彼此分享"原始"的感官信息。与我们用语言分享信息相比，这真是不同寻常。这些信息存在于听觉领域，它们所产生的"物体"图像就如同人类看到的画面一样真实。这是我们难以想象的。尽管这只是一种推测，但科学家认为，海豚之间存在一种社会性或者共同感知的可能性是存在的。事实上，一个由共享的原始数据构建的感知世界将赋予一个群体以不同寻常的凝聚力和个体概念。更有趣的是，海豚的感官共享有可能是一个主动的过程，而非纯粹被动地接收。这就像每个人都能够同样感知到某一个人所看到的世界的画面一样。感官共享的能力将大大改变"自我"的界限，"个体"的概念也将得到重新定义。

海豚大脑的特殊结构为这一假说提供了有力支持。人类的大脑可以划分出3重主要复合区：爬虫脑复合区、边缘系统和新皮层。然而，在鲸类身上，我们看到了一个彻底的进化跳跃——大脑结构中加入了第 4 段。这个部分被称为副边缘，位于边缘系统和新皮层之间，并突入新皮层之中。这种结构只存在于鲸类动物的大脑中。鲸类大脑的整个边缘系统是用于处理情绪和形成记忆的多个结构的组合，而副边缘额叶这一独特的进化则表明鲸类或许有能力处理更复杂的思想和情绪。由于鲸类的这一系统非常大，而且独特的副额叶又与新皮层双双合并，人们认为，它们的大脑中可能会产生出情绪和认知思维的混合。副边缘额叶也被认为是感觉区和运动区的延续。人类大脑中每个投射区之间的距离都很远，意味着我们从视觉、声音和本能中接收到的所有信息都必须沿着纤维道一点点传播到位。这一过程的时间和信息损失都非常大。鲸类的副边缘额叶则将所有感官反射集于一身，以我们无法理解的丰富性和迅速性处理着所有信息。副边缘系统的独特进化表明，在共同处理情绪和声音信息的背后，海豚之间有一些非常精密、复杂的交流机制。它们的大脑可能已经掌握了一种在动物王国中前所未有的社会共性。这将把所谓"社会性"的概念提升到一个完全不同的层次。而事实上，海豚在群体层面有着很强的凝聚力，当一两只海豚生病搁浅时，族群中所有其他的个体都会纷纷相随（图 2）。这在很大程度上可能是情感依恋的产物，这些动物可能有一种强烈的集体意识。一些科学家将海豚的这种凝聚力称为"集体灵魂"。

那么，海豚算得上聪明吗？它们必须要"像我们一样"才能称得上是智慧生物吗？虽然鲸类动物拥有包括人类在内的动物中最大的大脑，但这并不一定意味着它们比我们智力更高。不过，智力的定义其实是一个相当模糊的问题。到目前为止，我们还没有完全了解人类大脑的全部功能，也没有找到定义智力的准确标准。我们通常只会用我们的现实来定义其他动物的智力：因为我们会说话、会写字、做很多了不起的事情……所以我们把所有做不到我们能做的事

图 2　当一两只海豚生病搁浅时，族群中所有其他的个体都会纷纷相随

的动物都归类为不太聪明的物种。但是，在海豚的世界里，我们会表现得相当愚蠢：我们无法在水下听到声音，无法把自己的脑袋变成声呐发生器，也无法发出像海豚那样多种多样的声音。但即便如此，我们就不"聪明"了吗？不，我们和海豚只是不一样罢了。那么，海豚必须要"像人类一样"才能被人类视作平等的生物来对待吗？我们是否需要其他动物做到"像我们一样"，才能给予它们平等的待遇？

　　问题在于，人类不可能完全平等地对待任何与他们不同的生物。

作者简介

　　萨拉·普拉托（Sara Platto），
江汉大学生命科学学院副教授，
中国生物多样性保护与绿色发展
基金会生物与科学伦理秘书长。
普拉托博士曾在西班牙、美国和
加拿大的动物救助中心担任兽医，
与野生动物、海洋哺乳动物、爬
行动物和鸟类等不同物种打过交道。作为一名学者，普拉托博士的一大追求便
是通过在大学里开设相关课程，把动物保护和行为学的知识带给广大的中国青
年学生。普拉托博士在动物福利、动物行为、野生动物病理学和新冠肺炎疫情
等方面都有着研究贡献。

扫描收看
本文视频课程

How Does It Sound to Be a Dolphin

By Sara Platto (Italy)

A Journey around Animals

Growing up with pets around my house, I've found my fondness towards animals early in my life. I would tend to these lovely creatures with love and care that has naturally led myself to aspire after becoming a veterinarian in my future life. Yet, hoping me to get a "decent" degree in subjects like law, my parents were initially opposed to this idea. It was for my persistence that mom and dad finally let me have my way, and it was the same persistence that, when I was studying veterinarian, persuaded my professor to allow me on a travel to Canary Islands, where the sea presented profusion of intimacy with dolphins, my newly found passion.

Spending lots of time there studying animal behaviour and taking care of them, I knew that I wanted more than this. My ambition was to understand how animals communicate with each other. When I was only five, I have already had my first experience in animal communication. By mimicking the sound of the mother cat, I successfully coaxed the kittens out of their hiding place and played with them. With the help of a German professor, I moved to Israel to continue my study on dolphins. How they interact among themselves and with human beings? What methods they deploy to communicate? How do they convey their need?

All this time, I haven't forgot the other seeking of mine: helping animals. I have been to facilities and institutes in the U.S. and Canada, working with staff there to offer medical treatment and protection mainly to marine animals.

After this, in 2007, I came to China, where my post-doctoral research awaited. I have collaborated with several institutes. Since 2017, I have been working here at Jianghan University.

The Wonders of Dolphins and Sounds

Dolphins and humans are both social mammals. In fact, these two types of mammals share a very similar social structure, namely the fission-fusion society. What does this mean? A fission-fusion society is where individuals are grouped into small families. Each individual in one family will have many agendas to attend on a routine basis - for example, humans have to go to work, and dolphins have to go out and hunt - each of us will leave for our separate business, but we all come back together again at the end of the day. Yet, dolphins and humans are no doubt different. We live in different environments, thus we developed different sensory systems to adapt to and master these environments. We, living on firm lands, have our unique brain composition that are different to the brains of dolphins. Yet despite this difference, humans and dolphins share the need to communicate within their little or big societies.

Living and communicating undersea like dolphins may face quite a few challenges. One of the challenges is visual sight, for that a deep water environment can be dark and dense, the place where little light can reach. Even when the water is very clear, visible light can only travel 100 metres beneath the sea level. Actually, the sea water is hardly that clear, not to mention the disruption of waves and obstruction coming from seaweed and other things in the water. So it is far more likely that we can only see things metres, even centimetres away. In this, visual senses are not that useful for marine animals. But how can dolphins swim around, make friends with other dolphins, or hide away from predators with such poor eyesight? What senses are they going to utilize? The answer is sound!

The speed at which the sound travels in sea water is under multiple affecting factors. Because of the difference in density of water and air, sound can travel 4.5 times faster below the sea level than it does above. The transmission speed of sound also has to do with temperature and salinity. The warmer and saltier the water is, the faster the sound travels. More to this, in deeper areas of the ocean, where the water pressure is significantly higher than the surface, sound will accordingly travels at a faster speed .

Dolphins and Sounds

We can certainly hear sounds in the water, too. But are dolphins hearing the same as we do? Unfortunately, we can only receive a limited range of frequencies of sound in the water owing to the shapes and structures of our human ears. It is for the same reason that we are not able to discern what direction the sound is coming from when swimming. How about dolphins? They are lot more advanced in regard of hearing under the water, unlike human, who can only receive frequencies in the range between 20 Hz to 15 kHz, while dolphins can pick up sound frequencies all the way from 75 Hz to 150 kHz.

How do dolphins make sounds? We human beings use our vocal cords to produce sounds, whereas dolphins have taken up a different method — they make sounds through the nasal organs, which are located in the melon (the round part on top of their head). Air will enter through blowholes into a pocket-shaped structures which will vibrate, thus producing sounds. But the core of dolphin's sound-making are their two sets of lip-like organs. This dual-set of lips has allowed them to produce two types of sounds at the same time: whistles to communicate among individuals and echolocation to scan the environment.

Making sounds is just half of the equation. Now, how do dolphins hear these sounds? The fat tissue in the innerest part of the melon, it is of the same density of water. This tissue functions like a lens and can change its shape, transmitting the sound out in different directions. Around the jaws of a dolphin exists similar fat tissues. When the sound comes, fat tissues inside the jaw bones will perceive them, later transmit them to inner parts of dolphin ears that are also surrounded by the same fat tissues. Though they have ears, and also ear canals, but due to different structures from those of a human being, dolphins cannot hear as well out of water as they do under (Image 1).

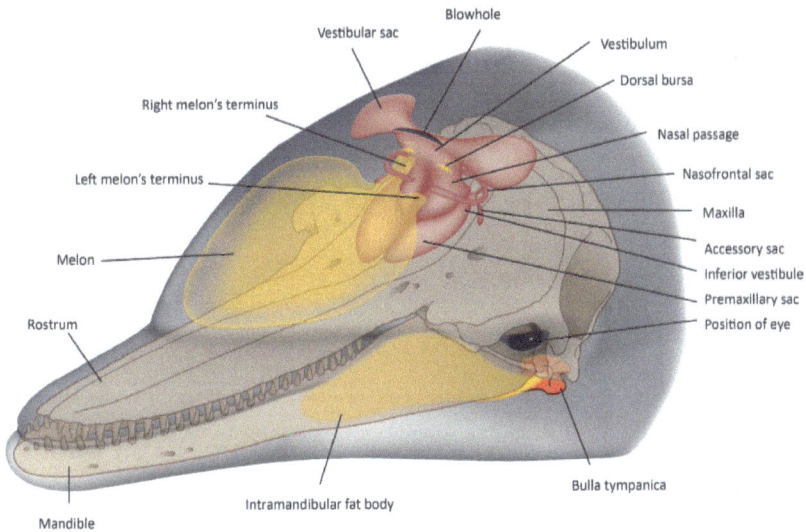

Image 1   Schematic representation of the structures related to sound production and
reception in the head of a bottlenose dolphin (Drawing by Vko Gorter)

Dolphins' Different Sounds

To understand sounds made by dolphins, researchers have separated out several
patterns of sonograms. From these different patterns of sounds, scientists are able to
identify the context where these sounds were made, what kind of emotions the dolphins are
experiencing, or whether the dolphins are moving or are engaged in other things.

Now we will discuss different types of sounds a dolphin can make. First, there are
sounds called "whistles", of which the average frequency range can be between 75 Hz to
24 kHz (with some whistles going above 24 kHz). Whistles are omnidirectional which
means it is difficult to identify which dolphin produces them. Whistles are composed by two
parts: the fundamental frequency which is the main whistle, and the harmonics which occur
at integer multiples of the fundamental frequency and usually extend into the ultrasonic
(>20 kHz) range. Whistles that contain both non-directional and directional components are
called "mixed directionality" sounds. In fact, researchers found out that the harmonics could
be used for direction-tracking. So when a dolphin is both conveying his or her message and

position, he or she will release both whistle sounds and harmonics(Image 5 and Image 6).

People have names, and we know each other by names. Dolphins have names, too - signature whistles. Each individual dolphin can label him or herself with a specific whistle tone - like a name - that is specific to each individual. The signature whistle can be also imitated by other dolphins to call upon the specific individual, just like we call the name of a person.

Besides whistling, dolphins have another type of sounds called echolocation clicks, which sounds like wooden sticks hitting each other. The dolphins use this type of sounds to scan their surroundings and look for food or obstacles. Each click sound is followed by an interval, in which dolphins are waiting for the echo of the click to come back and then to produce another click. Calculating this time lapse, dolphins can figure out how close they are to a certain object, thus mapping out the environment.

There is another type of sound called "burst pulse sound" which contains emotional components. This type of sounds are used by dolphins when they feel upset or argue with each others. Scientists would also describe this type of sounds with different names depending on how the sound goes: yelp, cry, weep. Different kinds of dolphins produce different kinds of sounds. For example, the finless porpoise, can only make pulse sounds but not whistles.

Dolphins' Perceptual World

Human beings mainly create their reality through visions and speeches. We see something new, we name it, therefore recognize it. In general, the concept of "self" is based on information processed by the brain such as external information about reference axis of space and time with the self at the centre, and internal information about the position and orientation of the head and the body. These are elements of construction of the self. Memories, expectations, plans and so on are just additional elements. For dolphins, all the information about the external world come with the echolocation.

While human would say, "do you see what I see" or "do you see what I am telling you?" (if the person is talking about something), dolphins put it in another way, "do you see what I hear". Every time a dolphin produces echolocation clicks to scan the surrounding environment, the echoes of the clicks will come back to the source, giving a sort of "holographic image" of what has been scanned. Here comes the amazing part: these echoes can be picked up by another dolphin in the vicinity who will receive the exact same type of "holographic image". When different humans see the same object, they will perceive it differently, that depends on how each of them perceive their reality. Echolocation shares an unusual structural feature with human language, namely, the construction of the reality by the brain, is based on a signal generated by an individual. In the construction of a reality from echolocation, dolphins could share "raw" sensory information with one another, which would be even more unusual than the way we share information with language. Since the information are in the auditory domain, the "objects" that they generate would be as real as human seen-objects rather than heard-objects, that are so difficult for us to imagine. Even though it is just a speculation, the possibility of a social or communal cognition is something can be seriously considered. In fact, a perceptual world constructed from shared raw data would permit unusual group cohesion and a different kind of individuation. The dolphins' social world could be an active rather than purely passive communal world. It would be as if humans were able to share the exact same image perceived by one individual. Therefore, the concept of an "individual" would be redefined where a communal experience might change the boundaries of the self to include several individuals.

This hypothesis could be supported by the special structure of the dolphins' brain. The human brain can be differentiated into three main complexes: the reptilian complex, the limbic system and the cortex. However, with cetaceans we see a radical evolutionary jump with the inclusion of a fourth segment. This segment, called the paralimbic, features between the limbic and cortex, and it erupts into the cortex. This structure is present only in cetaceans and not in any other animal on earth. This unique evolution of the cetacean's entire limbic system, which is a combination of multiple structures in the brain that deal with emotions and the formation of memories, suggests that cetaceans have the ability to process more complex thoughts and emotions. Since the system is so large in cetaceans, and the unique paralimbic lobe merges with the cortex, it is believed that the lobe may create a mixture of both emotional and cognitive thinking. The paralimbic lobe is also believed to be a continuation of the sensory and motor areas. For humans, projection areas are widely separated from one another, meaning anything we perceive from sight, sound and impulses must travel along fibre tracts with a great loss of time and information. The cetacean's paralimbic lobe brings this all together in one, processing information rapidly with a richness that we cannot understand. The unique evolution of the paralimbic system suggests that the animals are doing something very sophisticated or complex while they're processing together, emotions and sounds, and their brains may have adapted for a type of social connectivity unprecedented in the animals kingdom, taking the concept of social to a different level. Dolphins have a very strong cohesiveness in term of grouping: in fact, when one or two animals are sick and stranded, all the rest of the herd follows (Image 2). A lot of this comes down to the "emotional attachment", with a possible strong sense in these animals that if something happen to an individual, it happens to the entire group. Some scientist identify this type of cohesion among dolphins as a "collective soul".

So do we need dolphins to be "like us" to be considered intelligent? Cetaceans have the biggest of the brain among animals, including humans, but this does not make them

Image 2　When one or two animals are sick and stranded, all the rest of the herd follows

more intelligent than us. Defining intelligence is a tricky issue, and till now we did not yet completely understand the functions of human brain and found out the structure that defines intelligence. We, usually, define intelligence in other animals with the construction of our reality: we talk, we write, we do amazing things…and we classify animal species as less intelligent because they are not able to do things we do. But in a dolphin world we would be pretty stupid beings: we are not able to hear sounds underwater, to produce sonar with our heads, and to make the sounds as dolphins do. Are we less intelligent because of that? No. We are just different. So, do we need dolphins to be "like humans" to be treated as equal? Do we need other animals to be "like us" to have them treated as equal?

The problem lies in the fact that humans are mostly unable to treat as equal any being different from them.

(Yang Yunzhou contributed to this article)

About the Author

Sara Platto, associate professor, College of Life Sciences, Jianghan University; Secretary-general of Biology and Science Ethic, China Biodiversity Conservation and Green Development Foundation. Dr. Platto has worked as a veterinarian in different animal species in rescue centres in Spain, the United States and Canada, working with different species of wildlife, marine mammals, reptiles and birds. As an academic, one of Dr. Platto's major pursuits is to bring the knowledge of animal protection and behavioural study to young Chinese students by offering courses on these subjects at universities. Dr. Platto has made significant research contributions in the areas of animal welfare, animal behaviour, wildlife pathology and coronavirus pandemics.

第二章 工程世界

Engineering

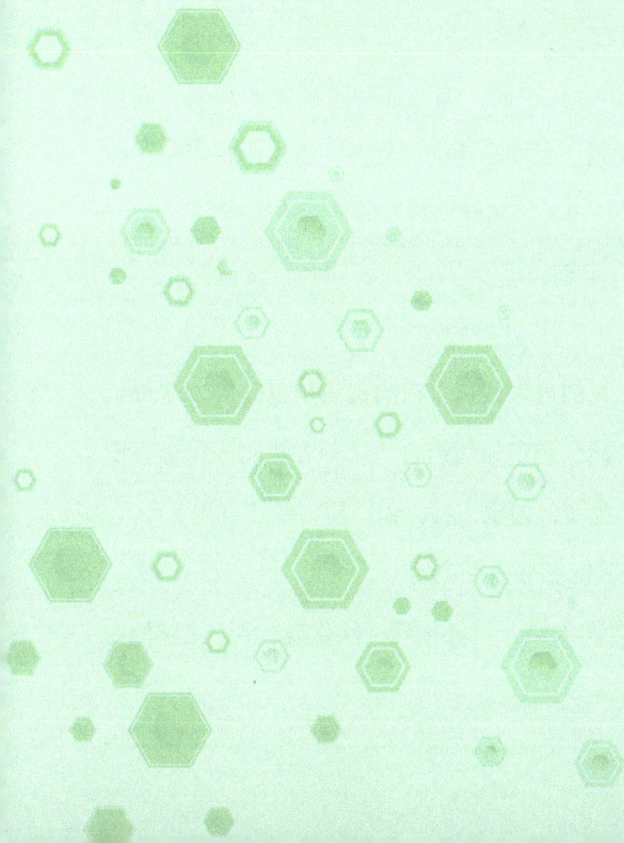

建筑材料的选择标准

文 / 加尼·瑞泽普（加拿大）　译 / 王一帆

　　爱因斯坦说过，物质与能量可以互相转化。世界上所有事物都是由物质与能量构成的。我们触摸不到能量，但是我们能感受到它们，我们能看到光，听到声音，感到热量。物质则是可以碰触的，它就存在于我们周围，无时无刻，无处不在，但我们却很少会去思考它。

　　假如我们能够用某种物质制作一样东西，那么那种物质就叫材料。利用各种各样的材料，我们可以修筑建筑、大坝、运河、铁路，也能生产手机、电脑、汽车等。材料与我们的生活息息相关，离开材料我们将举步维艰。

材料的分类

　　世界上有着数之不尽的材料，我们可以根据自己的需求用不同的方法将它们分类。其中一种是观察材料在自然状态下如何组合，这种方法叫作化学分类法。据此，我们将部分材料分类为金属，如金、银、铜、铁、锌等（图1），它们通常是有光泽和坚硬的物质，并且能够导热导电。

　　还有一类材料是陶瓷，包含了氧化铝、二氧化硅、碳化硅、瓷、混凝土、

图1 金属齿轮

玻璃等材料。它们都有很强的抗压能力，但是在受拉和弯折时十分易碎。例如，混凝土在抗压方面性能十分突出，但是，如果我们要用它制作柱子或横梁，则必须在混凝土里加入钢筋来增强它的抗拉力和抗扭力（图2）。

图2 钢筋混凝土

聚合物这一类中包含了塑料、橡胶、聚乙烯（PE）、聚苯乙烯（PS）、聚氯乙烯（PVC）、聚碳酸酯（PC）等。这类材料应用十分广泛，塑料制品在我们身边随处可见，如在笔、电脑屏幕、汽车、飞机等的生产中都需要塑料。聚合物的应用已经涵盖了我们生活的方方面面。

最后一类是复合材料，这类材料都是由至少两种上述材料组合而成的。现如今应用最广泛的两种复合材料是玻璃复合材料和碳复合材料。例如，复兴号动车组、C90飞机、C919飞机、部分火箭等都使用了碳纤维复合材料（图3），因为碳纤维既轻巧又有很高的强度。

图3　大型客机

我们还有其他的分类方法。根据材料是天然的还是人造的，可以将其分类为天然材料和人工材料。例如，钢就是一种人工材料，因为自然界中没有钢。天然材料包含了如木头、泥、石头等材料。在古代，人们通常使用天然材料，因为天然材料可以随取随用。中国的长城就是由石头修筑的。用泥土很轻松地就可以造出砖块，改变木头和石头的形状也不需要很复杂的技术，这就是古人对材料的运用。如今我们创造了更多的新材料，它们也取代天然材料成为主流。

如今，我们在工程建设中使用了大量的人工材料。利用它们，我们建设了桥梁、道路、铁路、机场、隧道等交通工程，房屋、办公楼、公寓楼、工厂、发电站等建筑工程，还建设了水坝、港口、运河、堰等水利工程。

无数的材料被运用于工程建设中，其中最重要的几种天然材料为泥土、木材和石材，而最重要的几种人工材料为钢材、混凝土和沥青。在面对两种材料时我们该如何选择？为什么我们选择混凝土而不是钢材来建筑房屋？问题的答案是，我们遵循了重要的材料选择标准。

首要的选择标准是性能。例如，一块跳板应该具备什么性能？当一个跳水者站在上面时，它应该向下弯，当跳水者跳起时，跳板应该为其提供弹力，并且，它还应该具有足够的强度而不会折断（图4）。这就是对跳板的性能需求。其余的选择标准包括材料是否方便获得，使用该材料需要怎样的技术，还有材料的环保性能及造价——我们应该选用最经济的材料来达成目标。

对材料的选择取决于我们对材料的需求。没有最好的材料，也没有最差的材料。材料的好坏取决于它是否既安全又经济，还能满足特

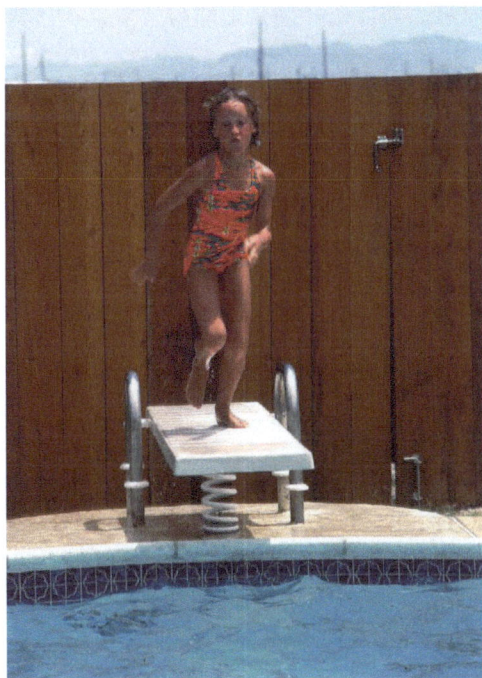

图4　跳板上的孩子（Linda Bartlett 摄）

定的需求。

钢有许多特征，它的光泽、导电性和导热性属于物理学特性；它的硬度和弹性属于力学特性；它的元素构成、易腐蚀性属于化学特性。任意材料的全部特性都可以根据物理学、力学和化学来分类。材料的性能往往由它的一种或多种特性决定。特性不分好坏，只在于它能否满足使用者的需求。拥有万金油特性的材料是不存在的。工程师会选择一种材料，一定是因为这种材料的性能比其他材料更能满足需求，如造价、环保等。

我们怎么确定材料的特性呢？每制造出一种新材料，工程师们就会取一些样品，使用特殊的技术和设备针对它的特性进行测试。在测试了大量的材料之后，工程师们会把这种材料的特性及相关数据记录在专门的手册中，方便他们以后为项目选择最合适的材料。生产材料的公司一般都会自行测试并提供自家材料的性能数据。

混凝土

现在我们介绍一些材料运用的实例。沥青混凝土常用于道路建设。它由沥青与石粒混合，可以冷铺或热铺，最后再用压路机压实（图5）。当工程师选用某种沥青时，他会考虑它的以下特性：它的黏性如何？它在不同温度下的稠度如何？它的相对密度如何？它的耐久性如何？

图5 道路工程中的沥青施工

它的固化速率有多快？它的延展性如何？老化、硬化以后它的性能如何？它的耐水性如何？它的温度敏感性如何？

同样，每当我们选择一种材料，我们都必须审视它的种种特性，看它是否符合我们的需求。

另一种材料是随处可见的混凝土，它主要由碎石、水泥和水构成。其实，混凝土是世界上除了水以外使用最多的材料。2018 年，全世界共使用了 370 亿吨混凝土。中国的混凝土产量和使用量均占全世界的 1/3。由于制造混凝土需要水泥，因此生产了大约 40 亿吨水泥。每生产 1 吨水泥都会产生超过 1 吨的二氧化碳——这是一种会导致气候变化的温室效应气体。

由于混凝土可以在任意地点制作成任意形状，所以在建设中我们不必一次就把整个建筑物建成。我们用混凝土建造出了很多伟大的桥梁，如世界上最长的桥梁——港珠澳大桥，世界上最高的桥梁——米洛高架桥（图6）。我们还用混凝土建造了很多伟大的建筑，如世界上最美丽的建筑之一多伦多市政厅

图 6 米洛高架桥

（图7）、世界上最高的大楼迪拜塔（图8）。我们还建造出了中国的三峡大坝、美国的胡佛大坝（图9）、瑞士的韦尔扎斯大坝，还有无数的公路与运河。

图7 多伦多市政厅

图8 迪拜塔

图9 胡佛大坝

和其他材料一样，混凝土有自己的优缺点。除了水泥，它的原料碎石、水都是天然易得的，它具有很强的抗压力，几乎能做成任意形状，并且造价低廉，生产和使用混凝土都不需要很高超的技能与技术，通常还有不错的耐久性。这些都是它的优点。

但是，混凝土需要时间来凝固，所以，使用混凝土的建造时间比钢材和木材都长；它容易开裂，特别是在干燥的气候环境里；它的抗拉力很弱，仅仅很小的拉力就可以让它断裂；它的能量吸收能力和延展性都很差。生产水泥能耗较高，同时产生大量二氧化碳。

如前所述，混凝土的抗拉性能很弱，所以不能单独应用于建造建筑或桥梁。而钢有着优秀的抗拉性能，因此，经过钢筋增强的混凝土可以同时拥有抗压性与抗拉性，这就是钢筋混凝土。它是一种非常优秀的复合材料，能在崩塌前吸收大量的能量，且强度高、造价低。

钢

钢在某种意义上也算是复合材料，但其实它是一种主要由铁和碳构成的合金。钢是现代社会中应用范围最广的工业材料之一。它的原材料是铁矿石。生产钢材的过程能耗很高，因此，同样会排出很多温室气体。

钢的生产过程很复杂，以下是比较重要的几步：把铁矿石分成小块，放入一种特殊的坩埚中，用火炉加热到 $1600\sim1700\ ℃$。熔化后的铁沉于坩埚底部，炉渣上浮。把分离出来的铁送入另一个炉中与碳和氧混合，最终的成品就是钢。把钢送到不同的工厂，就可以加工成各种零件与产品了。

钢具有很优秀的抗拉和抗压性，它有很强的韧性，在某些环境中十分耐久。钢在初次使用后是可以完全回收再利用的。钢结构的建筑工事的建造时间比混凝土框架要快得多，而且在建造时也不需要模板和临时主支撑。

但想要生产高质量的钢材、制作钢构件和构筑物都需要更高的技能与技术水平。在如海水、酸和高湿度这样的特定环境中，它会被锈蚀并失去耐久性。钢材造价相比混凝土和木头要更昂贵。生产钢材是高能耗的。钢结构建筑十分需要消防保护。

我们也用钢材建造过很多伟大的桥梁，如悉尼海港大桥（图 10）、旧金山的金门大桥。我们建造过很多伟大的建筑，如位于芝加哥的约翰·汉考克中心、位于曼哈顿的世界贸易中心一号楼、位于伦敦的"小黄瓜"瑞士再保险公司大楼（图 11）。

图 10　悉尼海港大桥

图 11 瑞士再保险公司大楼

木材

最后是木材。木材是一种天然环保的材料。它能吸收二氧化碳，减少温室气体的排放。在不直接暴露在潮湿环境的情况下，木材可以持续使用很长时间，它还有合理的强度与硬度。天然木材无法用于建造大跨度构筑物，但经过人工改良的木材可以增加跨度。如今，木材已经不再用于建造行车用的桥梁了。

木材重量很轻，易于砍伐、搬运及组装。它是环保材料并且造价低廉。生产木材只需要消耗很少的能量，同时，还能吸收温室气体二氧化碳，减缓气候变化。

当然，木材也有缺点，当它暴露在过度干燥或潮湿的环境时容易腐朽；它的强度弱于钢材、混凝土和一部分聚合材料；它的防火性能不强，并且不能随处取用。

如今，木材主要用于修建房屋与一些特别的建筑物，如位于温哥华的里士满冬奥会椭圆运动场馆的木质屋顶，其设计遵从了"保暖屋顶"的设计理念。

如上所述，木材的防火性能不强。近期，举世闻名的、美丽的、极具历史意义的巴黎圣母院几乎毁于一场大火（图12）。虽然它主要是由不可燃的砖石砌筑，但它是由木质的屋顶所覆盖，木材燃烧，整个屋顶都崩塌落下。可见防火性是我们在为建筑挑选材料时需要慎重考虑的重要特性。

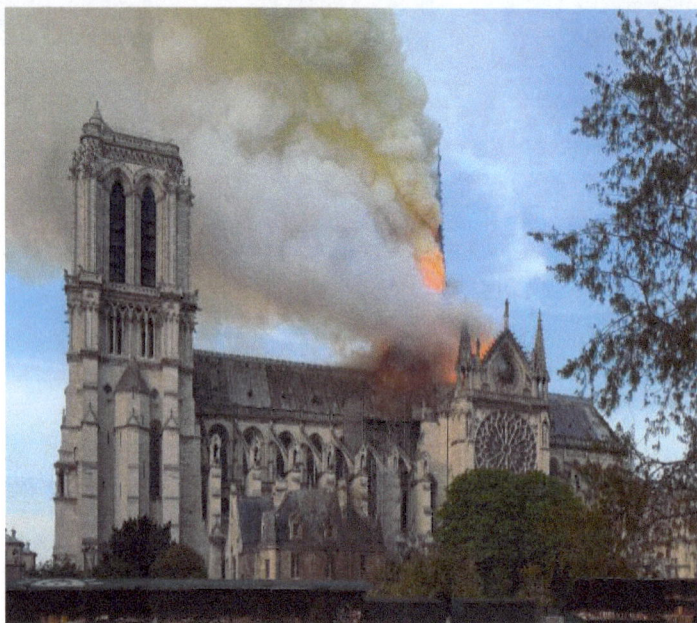

图 12　起火的巴黎圣母院

最后我要说，没有最好的材料，也没有最差的材料。性能符合要求的材料就是好材料。黄金具有很高的价值且价格昂贵，但我们不能用黄金造桥，也不能用黄金生产汽车和飞机，因为它的强度和硬度都不够。有一些材料之所以昂贵，是因为它不易获得，或者生产它消耗巨大。造价是在工程建造中一个重要的材料选择标准，我们都不想付出超过必要的成本。目前的研究主要专注于利用纳米技术和生物技术使材料更智能、更坚固、更便宜、更耐用。研究同时还致力于使材料可循环使用，并且更环保。

　　当我们将世界交接到你们年轻人的手中时，请让它变得更好。世界是一个封闭的系统，从外太空获取资源是不切实际的。被消耗的物质不会再次凭空出现。我们所拥有的都来自地球，如水和空气，这些都是无法被替代的资源。因此，你们应当学会像大自然一样进行循环利用与回收。大自然从不抛弃任何事物，一切都会被回收再利用。这是一个完整的循环，不停回到原点并再次向前。我们应当学习自然，努力地模仿它，回收利用所有的材料，让地球成为一个更好的地方。

作者简介

　　加尼·瑞泽普（Ghani Razaqpur）加拿大工程院院士、南开大学环境科学与工程学院讲席教授。他主持编写了世界首个纤维复合材料的设计国际标准，该标准成为 ISO 纤维复合材料标准的基础。Razaqpur 教授在再生混凝土的研究方面，也居于世界领导地位，他的研究解决了再生混凝土耐久性和强度等关键问题，研究内容为世界再生混凝土标准的制定提供了科学支撑。

扫描收看
本文视频课程

Selection Criteria for Construction Materials

By Ghani Razaqpur (Canada)

Einstein said: you can change energy to matter or matter to energy. In this world, everything we know is made from matter or energy. We can't touch energy, but we can feel it. For example, we can see light, we can hear sound, we can feel heat, etc., However, we can touch matter as it's around us everywhere and every day. We don' think about it too much!

If we can make something from some matter, we call the matter "Material". From materials we build buildings, dams, canals, railways and produce phones, computers, cars, etc. Materials are very important, and we can't live without them.

Materials Can Be Classified in Different Ways

There are millions of materials in this world that can be classified in different ways, depending on what you want and what the purpose of each is. One way to look at materials is to see how they are put together by nature. We call this the chemical structure of materials. In this way, we have materials that are metals like iron, steel, copper, zinc, gold, silver (Image 1) – generally shiny and hard, through which electricity and heat can travel.

There are also ceramics. These materials are inclusive to aluminum oxide, silicon dioxide, silicon carbide, porcelain, concrete, as well as glass. They are very strong when

Image 1　Gears made from metal

pushed upon but easy to break if pulled or twisted. For example, from concrete we build a lot of buildings. Concrete is very strong in compression, but we have to reinforce it by steel bars to give it resistance to tension (Image 2).

Image 2　Reinforced concrete

Then we have polymers, like plastic, rubber, polyethylene (PE), polystyrene (PS), polyvinyl chloride (PVC), polycarbonate (PC). They are very important because almost everything we see around us is made from plastic. For example, it takes plastic to produce pens, computer screens, cars, airplanes, etc. Polymer is used in practically everything now.

Finally, composites. This means they are materials that are made from combinations of the above materials. The most important composites today are glass composites and carbon composites. Fuxing trains, C90, C919 airplane, many rockets and many other things are creations of carbon fiber composites as carbon fiber is light and strong (Image 3).

Image 3　Airplane made from carbon fiber composite

We also classify materials in other ways. One of which is based on whether they are found naturally or under artificial conditions. We call them, under this guideline, non-engineered and engineered materials. For example, steel is an engineered material because we can't get steel naturally. Non-engineered materials would be like wood, soil, stone, etc. In the old days, people preferred to use non-engineered materials because they are naturally available. The Great Wall of China is made from stone. People made bricks from soil easily, and shaped wood and stone without complicated technology. That was what people did before. Today, we create many more new materials, and we use more engineered materials than non-engineered ones.

Nowadays, we use a large amount of engineered materials in construction. We build transportation structures like bridges, roads, railways, airports, tunnels. We build building structures like houses, office buildings, apartment buildings, factories and power plants. We build hydraulic structures like dams, harbours, canals and dykes.

There are many materials used in construction, but the most important materials are soil, wood and stone as non-engineered materials, and steel, concrete, asphalt as engineered materials. How do we choose one material versus another? Why do we choose concrete to build some buildings but not steel? There are important material selection criteria as follows.

Performance is the number one criterion. For example, what is the performance we want from a diving board? It should go down when a diver stands on it, then a bounce should be given to him/her when he/she jumps from it. It should be strong enough to do this repeatedly without breaking (Image 4). These are its performance requirements. The second criterion is material availability. The third criterion is the ability to properly use the material. The fourth criterion is not being harmful to the environment. The final criterion is the cost, as one should use the most economical material that can do the job.

So, choosing materials depends on what we want the material for. There is no such things as "the best material", just like there is no such thing as "the worst material". It just depends on whether it can safely and economically meet the specified need.

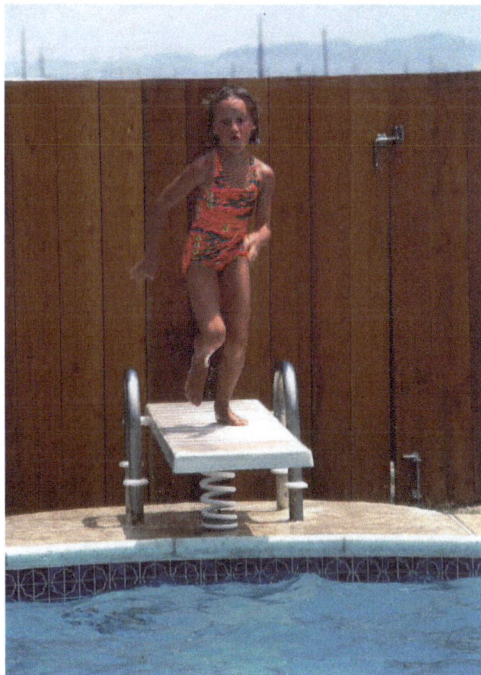

Image 4　Child on diving board(by Linda Bartlett)

When we talk about steel, we often say that it's shiny, it conducts heat and electricity. These are physical properties of steel. We also say that steel is strong and elastic. These are mechanical properties of steel. We say that steel is made from iron and carbon, steel rusts easily. These are chemical properties of steel. Properties of any material can be classified based on their physical, mechanical or chemical properties. Performance depends on one or more properties of a material. There is no good or bad property, this depends on what is required by the user. No single material can meet all performance requirements in every situation. Engineers choose a material because when compared to other materials, it may better satisfy the criteria.

How does one determine these properties? Every time a new material is produced, engineers take samples of it to the laboratory and test them for the property they are interested in, using special techniques and equipment. By testing many materials, engineers determine their properties and collect the data in special handbooks that they can later use to select the best material for a given job. Usually, companies that produce a material will test them and will provide information about the relevant properties of that material.

Concrete

Here are some examples of materials used in real construction. Asphalt concrete is used in road construction. It is made of asphalt mixed with stone particles, laid cold or hot, and compacted by a roller (Image 5). When a certain asphalt type is selected by engineers, they consider the following properties:

How well does it stick to the stone particles? (adhesion) What is its degree of liquidness or fluidity at any temperature? (consistency)What is its density?

Image 5   Road construction asphalt work

(specific gravity) Can it last a long time? (durability) How fast does it become hard? (rate of curing) Can it stretch without cracking or rupturing? (ductility) How well does it perform as it gets older? (aging and hardening) Does coming in contact with water change the asphalt properties negatively? (resistance to reaction with water) Do its properties change adversely with changes in temperature? (temperature susceptibility)

In a similar way, every time we engineers choose a material, we have to look at many properties of it to see if it will perform as we expect.

The other material is concrete, which is everywhere around us. Concrete is mainly made from stone, cement and water. In fact, no other material is used more than concrete in the world except water. In 2018, 37 billion metric tons of concrete was used globally. China produces and consumes one-third of all the concrete produced in the world. Since concrete is made from cement, approximately 4 billion tons of cement is needed to make that much concrete. Each ton of cement produces more than one ton of CO_2, a greenhouse gas, contributing to the climate change.

Concrete can be cast in any shape and anywhere, so we don't have to build the whole structure at once. From concrete we have built great bridges, like The Hong Kong-Zhuhai-

Image 6   The Millau Viaduct

Macao Bridge, the longest bridge in the world, and the Millau Viaduct (Image 6), the tallest bridge. We build great buildings like the Toronto City Hall (Image 7), one of the most beautiful buildings, and the Burj Khalifa in Dubai (Image 8), the tallest tower in the world. And we build dams like the Three Gorges Dam in China, The Hoover Dam in USA (Image 9), The Verzasca Dam. We build highways and canals.

Image 7   The Toronto City Hall

Image 8   The Burj Khalifa

Like all other materials, concrete has advantages and disadvantages. Raw materials of it, except cement, are natural and readily available. Concrete has high compressive strength. It can be made into practically any shape. The cost of concrete is competitive. It can be produced and placed with a relatively low level of skill and technology, and it's usually durable. These are its advantages.

But it needs time to gain strength. It requires a longer construction time than steel or wood. It shrinks and cracks, especially in dry climates. It has low tensile strength, and cracks under low load. Cement production produces a lot of carbon dioxide, which is a greenhouse gas and contributes to climate change.

As is mentioned above, concrete is too weak when subjected to pulling (tension), so

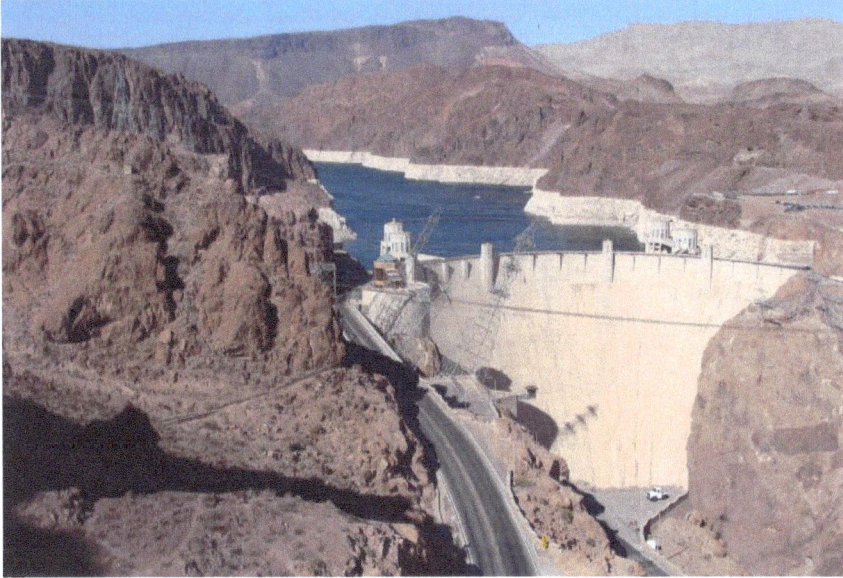

Image 9   The Hoover Dam

it cannot be used by itself to make buildings or bridges. But steel is very strong in resisting tension. So, concrete can be reinforced with steel bars or rods, then it can resist both push (compression) and pull (tension) forces. This type of concrete is called reinforced concrete. It is an excellent composite material and it can absorb a lot of energy before failure. It is also very strong and cost effective.

Steel

Steel is also in some sense a composite material, but it is actually an alloy of mainly iron and carbon. Steel is one of the most widely used industrial materials in the modern world. It is made from iron ore, which is extracted from the ground. A lot of energy is needed to make steel. Therefore, it is contributing in a significant way to greenhouse gas emissions.

Producing steel is a very time-consuming process, but here are some steps. First, we take iron ore from the mine, break it into small pieces, then put it in a furnace. Next, we heat it to around 1600-1700 degrees Celsius to melt it in a special crucible, with iron settling near its bottom and slag sitting on top of the iron. The two are separated and the iron is sent to another furnace where it is mixed with carbon and oxygen, and the final product is steel. Steel is then sent to mills to produce different steel shapes and products.

Steel has high tensile and compressive strength. It is very ductile, and very durable when not exposed to severe environments. Steel is completely recyclable after its initial use. Construction of steel frames requires much less time than similar concrete frames, and no forms or major temporary supports are needed during construction.

But it needs a higher level of skill and technology to produce good quality steel and fabricate steel components and structures. It corrodes and lacks durability when exposed to certain environments like seawater, acids and high humidity environments. It is generally more expensive than concrete and wood. Steel production is highly energy intensive and steel buildings need fire protection.

From steel we have built a lot of great bridges like the Sydney Harbour Bridge (Image 10), and the Golden Gate Bridge in San Francisco. We have also built great buildings like the John Hancock Center in Chicago, The No.1 World Trade Center in Manhattan, and the Swiss Re Building (the Gherkin) in London (Image 11).

Image 10　The Sydney Harbour Bridge

Image 11　The Swiss Re Building

Wood

And there is wood. Wood is a natural and environmental- friendly material. It stores carbon dioxide, so it reduces greenhouse gas emissions. When protected from humid conditions, it can last a very long time, and it has reasonable strength and stiffness. Natural wood cannot be used for very long span, but for longer spans engineered wood can be used. Wood is not currently used to build bridges for vehicular usage.

Wood is light, easy to handle and assemble, and easy to cut. It is environmentally friendly, and the cost is competitive. It requires low energy to produce, and as it stores the greenhouse gas CO_2, it mitigates the climate change.

Wood has disadvantages too. It rots when exposed to excessive wetting and drying and high humidity. It is not as strong as steel, concrete and some polymeric materials, it is not very fire-resistant, and it is not readily available everywhere.

Wood is currently used to mainly build houses and some special buildings, like the roof of The Richmond Olympic Oval in Vancouver that is designed on the "warm roof" principle.

As is mentioned above, wood can't resist fire. Recently, the famous, beautiful, and historic Notre Dame Cathedral in Paris was almost destroyed by fire (Image 12). Although it was mainly made from bricks and stones, which did not get hurt by fire, it was covered by a wood structure. Once the wood burned, the whole roof fell apart and was destroyed. So, fire resistance is an important property that we should consider in selecting materials for buildings.

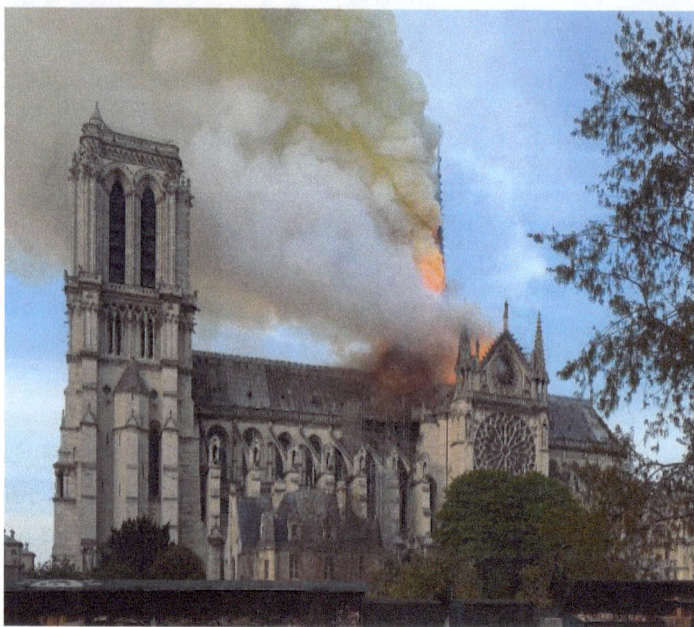

Image 12　The Notre Dame Cathedral in Paris

To finish, I can say that there is nothing as the best or worst material. Any material that can perform as required is good. You may know that gold is very valuable and expensive, but you cannot build a house with gold, you cannot make a car with gold, or make an airplane with gold, because gold is not strong and stiff enough. Some materials are expensive because they are not readily available or cost a lot to produce. Costs constitute a very important criterion for selection of materials in construction, as we don't want to pay more than we have to. Research currently focuses on making materials smart, stronger, cheaper, and more durable by using nanotechnology and biotechnology. Research is also going on to make materials reusable and environment friendly.

After we leave this world to you, please keep it in a good shape. We have not kept it in as good of a shape as you should. You should reuse and recycle materials because the world is a close-circuit system. You cannot bring materials from space into earth. Once you use something, it cannot be replenished. Practically, there is nothing you can replace on the earth by something from another planet. Everything is just from this planet. You cannot bring water or air from another planet. So, you need to reuse and recycle as nature does. You will never see nature throwing something away, and everything gets recycled. It's a full cycle, always goes back and forth. We should learn from nature and that's what we should strive to imitate, make all materials recyclable and make this world a good place for everyone to live in.

(Wang Yifan contributed to this article)

About the Author

Ghani Razaqpur is Member of Canadian Academy of Engineering and Chair Professor of College of Environmental Science and Engineering of Nankai University. He presided over the compilation of the world's first International Standard for Fiber Composite Material Design, which became the basis of the ISO fiber composite material standard. Professor Razaqpur is also a world leader in the research of recycled concrete. His research has resolved key issues such as the durability and strength of recycled concrete, which provides scientific support for the formulation of the world's recycled concrete standards.

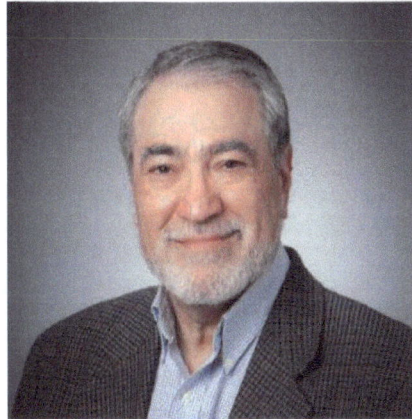

多姿多彩的桥梁

文 / 布鲁诺·布里斯杰拉（意大利）　译 / 孙梦格

　　我来自威尼斯，它位于意大利东北部，是威尼托大区的首府。这是全意大利最负盛名的旅行目的地之一，也是意大利的经济中心之一。威尼斯不仅拥有非凡的历史，还被称为"桥梁之城"。它坐落在亚德里亚海的一群小岛上，居住在那里的人们建造了 400 多座桥梁将整座城市联通起来，展现着这座令人着迷的魅力之都的历史和优美（图 1）。

图 1　威尼斯

在成长过程中，我一直被威尼斯宏伟的建筑、美丽的桥梁和独特的生活方式所吸引，因此我下定决心，在长大成为一名工程师后，将自己的时间和精力投入这些方面。图2展示了我作为工程师的一些工作成果。

图2　布鲁诺·布里斯杰拉作为工程师一些成果

作为土木工程师，我们可以建造世界上包括桥梁在内的各种各样的建筑，如位于纽约的曼哈顿中心大厦这样的摩天大楼，位于约翰内斯堡的国家银行体育场（2010年FIFA世界杯的主球场）这样的大型体育场，位于巴拿马和威尼斯的新型移动关口，以及位于乌克兰用于隔绝切尔诺贝利核电站的新型石棺。

中国也有许多令人印象深刻的建筑物。例如，上海的上海塔（632米）、深圳的平安金融中心（599米）和天津的高银金融117大厦（597米），它们都是世界排名前 10 位的最高建筑物。

今天，我们将从桥梁开始，学习一些基本的工程学知识。

桥梁概论

在全世界最长的 10 座钢拱桥中，有 6 座位于中国。位于广西的平南三桥是目前最大跨径的钢管混凝土拱桥（跨径 575 米）。紧随其后的朝天门大桥（跨径 552 米）是中国重庆市的一座横跨长江的公路铁路桥梁，于 2009 年通车。

我们要讨论的第一个问题是：为什么需要桥梁？

桥梁是为使某物越过或通过某种障碍而建造的结构。在日常生活中，我们经常注意到，人、汽车通过桥梁跨越铁轨、道路、河流或其他自然的或人为的障碍物。例如，位于英格兰梅德韦的罗切斯特大桥就横贯了梅德韦河。正因为桥梁要支撑人群和车辆从一侧穿过到另一侧，所以它们必须足够坚固，才能安全地支撑起自身的重量及经过其上的人员和车辆的重量。

动手实验！ 结构的影响力

我们只用非常基本的材料——一张打印纸和两堆书，就可以自己搭建一个基本的桥梁：将书堆放在桌子上，彼此之间保持一定距离，然后想象一下书堆之间的空隙就是你希望通过的障碍。现在，如果把纸片放在书堆上形成一个通道，我们就拥有了一座桥！

但是，我们会发现，这座桥极其脆弱，一旦在上面放上一支铅笔或一块橡皮，桥梁就倒塌了，同时我们假想的人和车也都会掉到深渊里。我们当然不能允许这种事情发生！我们需要改善这座桥梁的结构。

我们接着想到，纸桥的结构可以做出修改。因此，如果我们将刚才的纸卷成一个圆柱体，再将其放在书堆之间，它就变得稳固多了。现在，我们不仅可以在上面放一块橡皮，甚至可以放一个更大的物体，如铅笔盒。

为什么会这样？纸张不同承载力的秘诀在于它的形状。因此，我们要找到一个使纸桥变得坚固的结构。观察一下用作桥梁材料的这张纸，它很容易被弯曲或折叠，但是，一旦被卷成一根圆柱，它就不太容易向中心弯曲或对折了。这就是形状的改变所导致的强度改变。

我们还可以试验并观察纸张的另一个特点。如果我们两手抓住纸张的两边并向外拉，纸张将处于张紧状态，但是在大多数情况下，它不会被撕裂。然而，如果我们两手改变力的方向，将纸由两侧朝中心方向推，纸张就很容易变形并被弄皱。这就是纸材料本身的特性——推压时会塌陷，而拉伸时则保持形状。因此，在建造桥梁时要考虑的另一个重要问题就是如何选择和设计结构以增强材料本身的抗力，从而提供更好的支撑。

通常，工程师的任务就是寻找最佳的材料和最佳的形状。

桥梁的历史

最基本的桥称为梁桥（图3）。它由以下部分组成：主梁、桥面板、护栏、桥墩、桥跨和桥台。

为了进一步说明每个部分的工作原理，让我们先来讲个故事，回顾一下桥梁的历史，了解一下人类智慧如何与工程技术和建筑材料制造的进步相结合，逐步发展并稳固下来，形成了当今桥梁的外观和功能。

很久以前，一个原始人遇到了一条溪流，他很想跨过去，于是他就把一条木头架在河面上。此时，一座非常原始而古老的桥梁就诞生了。最初，桥梁的结构非常简单，并且是用很容易获得的自然资源（原木或石头）建造而成的。

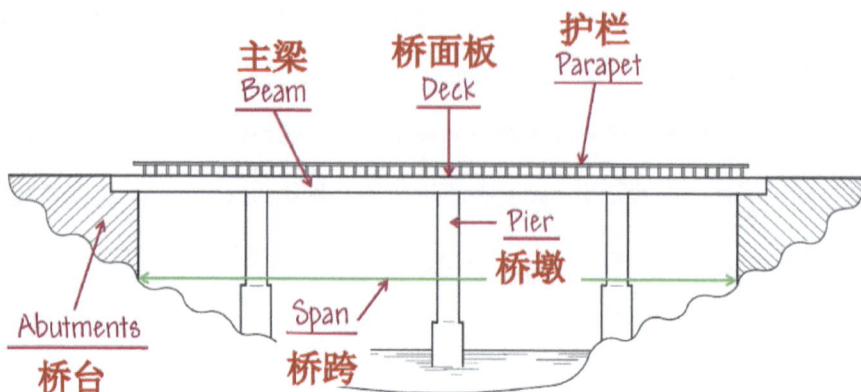

图 3　梁桥是最基本的桥

因此，它们只能跨越非常短的距离，并且结构也不是很稳定。桥梁建好后，原始人发现它摇摇晃晃的，很不安全，人走在上面很容易掉到水里。于是原始人灵机一动，把木头改造成了一个"主梁"，以此来使得它变得更稳定。但是，新的问题又出现了。下雨后，横梁的两端会陷入淤泥里面，桥又坍塌了。于是，他在横梁两端的下面堆砌了一些石头，形成了"桥台"解决问题。现在桥高多了，但是桥变高了后也空荡荡的，人走上去稍不注意就可能跌下来，令人害怕。原始人又想出了新的办法，他用木棍和绳索做了一个简单的栏杆和扶手，这样，有了"护栏"的桥梁看起来就安全多了。夏天的时候，降雨变多，河水变得宽阔，现在原始人想要跨越这条更宽的河流该怎么办呢？他搬来了很多石头，把这些石头堆砌在河流的中央，就制造好了一个"桥墩"，桥墩可以很好地为桥梁的中部提供支撑，而建造更多的桥墩也可以帮助原始人跨越更宽的河流。有了桥墩的帮助，再加上适当的护栏，一座在今天我们的生活中仍然很常见的桥梁就建造好了。

回顾建造桥梁的历史，我们发现，人类制造的历史其实也是一个试错的历史。从原始的工匠到今天的我们，进行创新都会犯很多错误。因此，不要害怕犯错误，有时这是学习和改进的唯一途径！

塔科马海峡大桥的灾难

　　塔科马海峡大桥是美国华盛顿州的一座悬索桥。它于 1940 年 7 月建成并通车，是当时世界上第三长的悬索桥，看上去像一条钢铁缎带一样纤细和优美。然而，仅仅过了 4 个月，这座大桥短暂的生命就在一场灾难中告终。

　　当年 11 月的某天，风速达到每小时 40 英里，大桥桥面板以交替的扭曲不断振荡，振幅逐渐增大直到板破裂。大桥之所以倒塌，是因为在强风下，那个位置产生了气体扰动力，而它的影响却在建造和施工时被设计人员和工程师忽略了。当时的桥梁建造通常不会考虑这些因素。

　　然而，我们工程师总是会从过去的错误中吸取教训，因此，这次桥梁坍塌事故极大地推动了相关领域对空气动力学和气动弹性力学的研究，从而影响了以后所有大跨度桥梁的设计。

动手尝试：纸桥挑战

　　现在让我们自己来动手尝试一下吧。跟随下面的步骤，我们亲自动手来建造一座纸桥。在这个活动中我们需要准备至少 4 张纸。

　　① 制作横梁，请先将两张纸彼此叠放，使角重叠。

　　② 将重叠好的纸片从一边开始向上慢慢卷起，确保卷起的纸管长度为 55 厘米。

　　③ 将两个卷起的纸管两端各弯起 5 厘米左右。

　　④ 将一根横梁的末端拼接到另一根横梁的末端。用胶带将它们粘在一起。

　　⑤ 最终做成一个四边形的主梁。

⑥ 取出剩余的 2 张纸，沿长边方向对折，并剪开。

⑦ 制作 3 个次梁。将剪下的 3 张纸也卷成管状作为次梁，并用胶带粘好。

⑧ 保持两个纸管笔直，将另一个纸管对折，将笔直的两个次梁连接到主梁上，并用胶带固定。

⑨ 将对折的次梁连接到主梁上，并用胶带固定。

⑩ 将前面步骤⑥中剩下的一张纸沿长边对折剪开，用来作为桥面板。

⑪用胶带将桥面板粘在做好的桥梁上。现在是时候测试您的桥梁了！

多彩的桥梁

世界上有许多种类型的桥梁。例如，一种常见的类型是拱桥。拱桥通常由石头或铁制成，两端各有一个弧形的桥台。在中国，现存最古老的拱桥是公元 605 年的赵州桥。世界上最长的拱桥是之前提到的中国重庆的朝天门大桥，跨度为 552 米。

另一种类型的桥称为悬索桥。悬索桥的样貌和拱桥很不一样，它的两端有垂直的塔架，塔架间的悬索拉住桥的桥面。这种桥的第一个现代实例建于 19 世纪初期。世界上很多著名的桥梁都是悬索桥，如洛杉矶的金门大桥（1280 米）、纽约的布鲁克林大桥（486 米）和日本的明石海峡大桥（1991 米）。

土木工程：值得奉献的职业

我是一名土木工程师，我一直认为这是世界上最古老，也是最好的工作。希望通过这篇简短的介绍，我能向大家说明工程的魅力，与大家分享我对工程的热情。

土木工程师负责道路、桥梁、建筑、大坝等建筑结构的建造、维护和保养，我们一直在努力寻找解决非常复杂的问题的简单方法。土木工程师的工作和职责将会影响全人类工作、休闲、学习和生活的环境，我们也将通过改造结构来应对不断发展的新技术、人口增长和气候变化所带来的挑战，从而帮助社会进步。这确实是一个值得奉献的职业。

作者简介

　　布鲁诺·布里斯杰拉（Bruno Briseghella）博士是福州大学土木工程学院的杰出教授兼院长，也是"可持续与创新工程研究中心"的创始主任。他毕业于意大利帕多瓦大学，获得学士和硕士学位，并在意大利特伦托大学获得博士学位。

　　他的主要研究集中于桥梁和结构设计、地震工程、地震隔离、整体桥台、耐久性、桥梁的监测和翻新，以及钢结构和钢混凝土结构方面，他不仅从事理论研究，也投身实践。他在国内和国际期刊和会议上发表了200多篇科学论文，并曾担任重要机构授予的多项研究计划的负责人或共同负责人。他当选为2019—2022年"国际拱桥大会永久性学术委员会"主席。

　　2013年，他获得福建省友谊奖和中国政府友谊奖；2018年，他获得2017年中国国际教育家奖。2014年，他被授予福州市名誉公民；2019年，他被授予福建省名誉公民。

Colorful Bridges

By Bruno Briseghella (Italy)

I am from Venice, a city located in northeastern Italy and the capital of the Veneto region. It's the most visited area in all Italy and one of the centers of the Italian economy. Venice is an amazing city with an extraordinary history. It is also known as the "city of bridges". Since it is situated on a cluster of small islands, people living there build over 400 bridges, many of which embody the beauty and history of this fascinating photographic city

Image 1　Venice

(Image 1).

Growing up, I've always been fascinated and inspired by the magnificent architecture, the beautiful bridges, and the unique lifestyle in Venice, so when I grow up to be an engineer, I decided to devote my time and energy to such aspects. Pictures below (Image 2) show some of my work as an engineer.

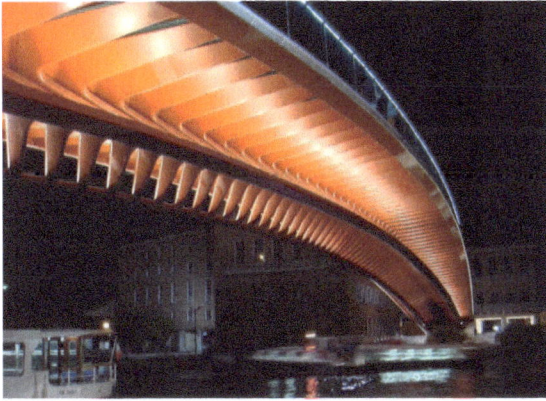

Image 2   Bruno Brisegbella's work as an engineer

And as a civil engineer, we can build all sorts of architecture in the world besides bridges, for example, skyscrapers like the Manhattan Center, big stadiums like the First National Bank Stadium Johannesburg, new mobile gates in Panama and Venice, and new confinement shelter in Chernobyl in Ukraine.

How about China? There are many impressive architectures here as well. For example, the Shanghai Tower (632 m) in Shanghai, the Pingan Finance Center (599 m) in Shenzhen, and the Goldin Finance 117 (597 m) in Tianjin are among the world's tallest buildings. Today, we are going to learn some basic engineering knowledge starting from the bridges.

An Introduction to Bridges

Among the top ten longest steel arch bridges in the world, six are located in China. The 3rd Pingnan Bridge in Guangxi is the longest steel arch bridge in the world (L=575 m), followed by Chaotianmen Bridge(L=552 m), a road-rail bridge over the Yangtze River in the city of Chongqing, China, which opened in 2009.

So, the first question is: why do we need bridges?

Bridges are structures built to get something over or under something else. We often notice, in our daily life, that bridges carry people, cars or traffic over railroad tracks, roads, rivers or some other obstacles, natural or artificial. The Rochester Bridge in Rochester, Medway in England, for example, is crossing the River Medway. Since they allow people or vehicles to cross from one side to another, they must be built strong enough to safely support their own weight as well as the weight of the people and vehicles that pass over it.

Experiment! How Structure Influences Everything

We can make a basic bridge by ourselves using only very basic materials: a piece of printing paper and two piles of books. Pile the books on your table with some distance in between, and imagine the space is the obstacle you wish to get pass through. Now if we place the piece of paper on top of the book piles to make a passageway, we have a bridge!

However, our bridge now is so fragile that even if we just put a pencil or eraser on, it will collapse. And our imaginary people and traffic will fall. Certainly, it cannot be that way! We need to do something to improve our bridge.

Then it comes to us, we can actually change the structure of the paper bridge. So, if we roll up our paper to make a cylinder and then put it between the book piles, it will do a much better job. Now we can not only put on one eraser, but even a bigger object like a pencil box.

Why? The secret lies with the shape. We want to make sure the materials we use to build bridges are shaped in a way to make them the strongest. Observe our piece of paper, if we try to bend or flex it, it will bend very easily, however, when rolled into a cylinder, it will not bend that easily. The changing of shape leads to the changing of strength.

We can also experiment and observe another particular feature of our chosen bridge material, the piece of paper. If we grip the sides of the paper and stretch it in opposite directions, the paper will be in tension, but it, in most cases, won't tear. However, if we change the direction of force and push two sides towards the centre, the paper will easily lose its shape and crumpled up. It collapses when being pushed while maintains shape when being stretched. So, another important issue to think about when building bridges is how to design the structure to give resistance to the bridge so that it provides better support.

Often, the job of an engineer is to find the best material and the best shape.

History of the Bridge

The most basic bridge is called a beam bridge (Image 3). It consists of the following parts: beam, deck, parapet, pier, span and abutments.

To further explain how each part works, let's go back to story telling the history of the bridge. See how combined human wisdom, together with the development of engineering and manufacture of building materials, gradually evolved and enabled steady adoption into today's bridges' look and function.

So, long time ago, a caveman encountered a stream that he wished to pass, so he put a log over it. Hence, we had a very primitive and ancient bridge. In the beginning, bridges were very simple structures that were built from easily accessible natural resources, namely wooden logs or stones. Because of that, they can only span very close distances, and their structure is not very stable. When the bridge was built, the caveman found it was very wobbly and precarious. So, he tried to change it a bit by cutting it into a beam. It became more stable. However, when it rained, the beam sunk into the mud and collapsed again. So, the caveman piled up stones under the ends of his beam to make abutments to fix this problem. Now the bridge was much higher up. But new problem emerged: the height

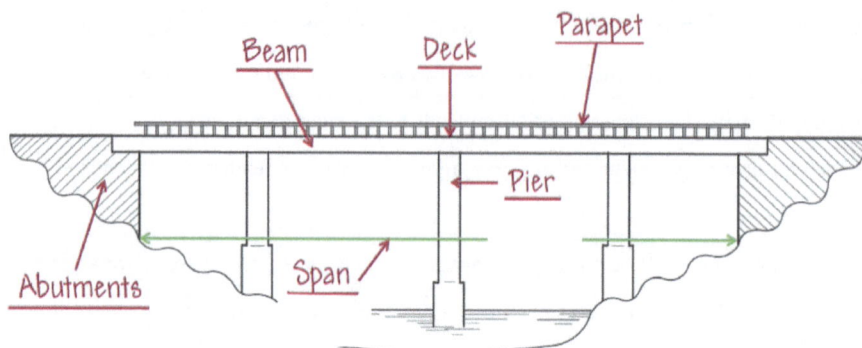

Image 3　The beam bridge is the most basic bridge

increased risks and now the caveman was scared walking on the bridge in the wind! So he came up with the ideas of making simple parapet rails out of sticks and string. With the guardrail, he felt much safer. Later, the caveman wanted to cross a much wider river, and he recalled what he had done before, so he piled up stones in the middle of the river to make a pier. Now he had a wider bridge, and it almost looked like the common bridge we see everywhere nowadays.

Looking back through the history of building bridges, we find that it takes a lot of mistakes to make any actual innovations, so do not be afraid to make mistakes. Sometimes, it's the only way to learn and improve!

The Disaster of the Tacoma Narrows Bridge

The Tacoma Narrows Bridge was a suspension bridge in the U.S. state of Washington. It was built in and opened to traffic in July, 1940. It was the third longest suspension span in the world at that time, and it looked slender, elegant and graceful like a steel ribbon. However, only four months later, the great span's short life ended in disaster.

One day in November when the wind speed reached up to 40 miles per hour, the bridge deck oscillated in an alternating twisting motion that gradually increased in amplitude until the deck tore apart. The reason for its collapse is that designers and engineers had not properly considered the aerodynamic forces that were in play at the location during a period of strong winds. At the time of construction, such forces were not commonly taken into consideration.

However, as engineers, we always learn from past mistakes, so the collapse boosted researches into bridge aerodynamics and aero-elastics, which has influenced the designs of all later long-span bridges.

Try Yourself: the Paper Bridge Challenge

Now let's try for yourself. Here I will provide you with a step-by-step solution to build your own paper bridge. You need to prepare four pieces of paper.

① To make two beams, place two sheets of paper over each other so the corners overlap.

② Roll the sheets into each other, ensuring that the total length of the tube is 55 centimeters.

③ Bend each beam approximately 5 centimeters from each other.

④ Tuck the ends of one beam into the ends of the other beam. Tape them together.

⑤ The result is a rectangle made of your beams.

⑥ Take the remaining 2 sheets of paper and cut in half lengthwise.

⑦ Make 3 secondary beams. Roll up each strip to make a tube. Tape to secure each beam.

⑧ Keep two beams straight and fold the third in half. Attach the secondary beams to the main beam and secure with tape.

⑨ Attach the secondary beams to the main beam and secure them with tape.

⑩ Find the strip that you set aside in ⑥ and cut it lengthwise. It's going to be the deck!

⑪ Tape your deck to your bridge. And now it's time to test your bridge!

Colorful Bridges

There are many types of bridges in the world. For example, the arch bridge. It is a bridge with abutments at each end shaped as a curved arch. An arch bridge is normally made of stone or iron. In China, the oldest existing arch bridge is the Zhaozhou Bridge of 605 AD. And the world's longest arch bridge is the previously mentioned Chaotianmen Bridge in Chongqing, China, with a span length of 552 m.

Another type of bridge is called suspension bridges. It is a type of bridge in which the deck is hung below suspension cables on vertical suspenders. And it looks very different from an arch bridge. The first modern examples of this type of bridges were built in the early 1800s. Some of the world's famous bridges are suspension bridges, such as the Golden Gate Bridge (1280 m), the Brooklyn Bridge (486 m), and the Akashi Kaikyo Bridge (1991 m) in Japan.

Civil Engineering: a Career Worthy of Devotion

I am a civil engineer, and I always regards it as the oldest and best job in the world. Hopefully, I can share with you my passion for engineering and show you the brilliance of it from this brief introduction class.

Civil engineers ensure safe construction, operation and maintenance of structures, such as roads, bridges, buildings and dams. We are always trying to find the beautiful simple solution to a very complicated problem. As a civil engineer, your work will influence where people work, relax, learn and live. You will pitch in helping society to become more advanced by adapting the infrastructure to meet challenges brought on by new technologies, population growth and climate change. It is truly a career worth devotion to.

(Sun Mengge contributed to this article)

About the Author

Dr. Bruno Briseghella is Distinguished professor and Dean of the College of Civil Engineering of Fuzhou University and Founding Director of the "Sustainable and Innovative Engineering Research Center". He graduated with a Bachelor's and Master's Degree from Padova University (Padova, Italy) and a PhD from Trento University (Trento, Italy).

His main research activities have been focused on bridge and structural design, earthquake engineering, seismic isolation, integral abutment bridges, durability, monitoring and retrofitting of bridges, and steel and steel-concrete structures, both from the theoretical and experimental point of view. He has published more than 200 scientific papers in national and international journals and conferences and has served as PI or CO-PI of several research programs granted by important Institutions. Dr. Briseghella has been elected as Chair of the International Conference on Arch Bridges-Permanent Scientific Committee from 2019 to 2022.

In 2013, he was awarded the Fujian Province Friendship Award and the China National Friendship Award, in 2018 the 2017 International Educator in China Award. In 2014, he was awarded Honorary Citizen of Fuzhou. In 2019, he was awarded Honorary Citizen of Fujian Province.

飞机与航空

文 / 韦恩·曼斯菲尔德（美）　　译 / 傅涵

历史

人们总是对飞行很着迷，但是过去他们不知道如何制造一个机器使他们离开地球。人们曾多次尝试制造飞行器，直到我们对飞行的基本物理学有了明确的了解，这一雄心壮志才得以实现。

我很幸运，因为我来自一个飞行家庭。我祖父大约在一个世纪前的 1929 年就开始飞行，我的父母也都成为飞行员，而且都是专业的飞行员（图 1）。他们是航空媒体行业的先驱，会在空中牵引横幅，用飞机拉烟在空中写字。我的父母教给了我所有关于航空的知识——如何驾驶飞机，以及如何使飞机保持良好的状态。

有许多女性已经成为世界著名的飞行员。阿米莉亚·埃尔哈特是女飞行员中的先驱，在我们还未乘飞机出国旅行之前，她就因飞越海洋而闻名世界。她的开创性的飞行探险使我们有可能旅行到遥远的大陆，探索新的地区。不幸的是，就在世界反法西斯战争前夕，她在太平洋上空消失了。她的命运至今仍是个谜。

图 1　1957 年准备起飞去做宣传的母亲

帕蒂·瓦格斯塔夫无疑是现代航空界最有名的女性。在近代航空史上，她赢得了很多特技飞行冠军，获得了很多的荣誉。她多次击败男女选手，赢得全国联赛特技飞行的冠军。

李霞卿（1912—1998 年），艺名李旦旦，是一名中国女电影演员，同时也是一名开创性的飞行员和慈善家。1936 年，她成为中国第一个获得民用航空执照的女性，并与人共同创办了中国第一所民用飞行学校。作为一个著名的女演员，她主演了《西厢记》。在中国女性还不能开车的时候，李旦旦比其他任何人——无论男人或女人——都更热衷于飞行。在第二次世界大战之前的 10 年里，如果你请任何一个中国人说出一个飞行员的名字，他们的答案很可能就是李霞卿。

在过去的几年里，我曾在中国的航展上飞行，用飞机悬挂横幅在空中飞行，用飞机拉起烟雾在空中书写（图2）。这都是小型飞机的一种用途——当然，用途还不止这些。

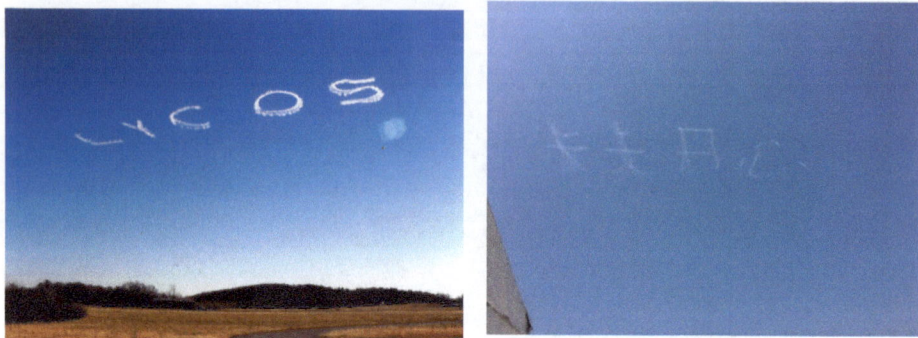

图2　我用飞机在空中书写

航空的重要性

飞机和直升机在许多方面为我们提供了服务：运输、保护我们的食物供应不受虫害、救火、空中巡逻、在发生自然灾害或疾病暴发时运送物资，还有航空旅游和航空体育。

图3是一张航空应用飞机的照片。这些飞机被用来喷洒杀虫剂，防止害虫侵害我们的食物，还可以给农作物施肥，让它们长得更快，种植更多的食物来养活我们。当人们难以进入被水淹没的田地时，飞机可以从空中播种水稻。如果没有飞机，粮食产量将大大减少。

飞机还被用于从火灾中拯救生命和财产。火灾可能发生在山区或茂密的森林中，此时消防员很难从地面到达火灾现场。这时，飞机会向火堆上洒水和化学混合物，以阻止火势蔓延，拯救生命和保护我们的财产。对于小型火灾，可以使用直升机或小型固定翼飞机；对于大型火灾，就要用与最大客机一样大的飞机，携带大量的水和化学混合物，投在森林大火上，以拯救附近的家庭和企

图 3　飞机的应用——杀虫

业，并保护人们的生命财产安全。

　　飞机的另一个用途是帮助警察和安全部门保护我们的安全。直升机可以用来追捕罪犯，防止他们逃跑。无人机和普通飞机也可以用来巡逻我们的城镇，以确保我们的公民免受非法行为或恐怖主义的伤害（图 4）。

图 4　飞机的应用——救援

在发生自然灾害或疾病时，飞机经常被用来运送物资。地震发生后，飞机可能是进入受灾地区运送医疗用品、急救人员和食物的唯一途径。这有助于拯救和保护人们的生命。小型飞机可能用于飞往较小的城市和乡镇，而大型运输机可以将大量物资运送到受地震、火灾或医疗紧急情况影响的大城市。这种方式在全世界范围内挽救了许多生命，特别是在那些不太发达的国家，他们的道路或应急服务可能无法达到在灾难来临时做出快速反应的水平。

此外，航空最重要的用途之一是让我们和朋友及家人在假期里见面，或者去探索世界上的新地方。乘坐民用航空公司的飞机出行在过去并不常见，但近年来，航空技术的进步降低了飞行成本，使更多的人可以到国外旅行，也使更多的人可以在假期乘坐长途飞行去看望朋友和家人。

随着越来越多的人学习飞行，空中运动越来越受欢迎。飞行的选择有很多，包括旋翼机、轻型运动飞机、小型直升机和常规固定翼飞机。最近，我们的公司晴空航空一直在为中国提供生产运动飞机和轻型飞机的合作机会，包括生态飞行者、猛虎、美洲豹双发飞机和海狼两栖飞机等机种。这些飞机将给中国更大的发展飞机制造基地的机会，并将使越来越多的人实现飞行的梦想。

让我们看看飞机是如何飞行的

首先，我们必须知道飞机的主要部件是什么。一架飞机由机身、机翼、尾翼、发动机、螺旋桨和起落架组成。

机身是飞机的主要部分，人们坐在里面，飞行员坐在前面。机翼附着在机身的两侧，机尾在后面。在小型飞机中，发动机和螺旋桨通常在前面；在大型喷气式飞机中，发动机通常安装在机翼下方，有时也安装在靠近机尾的机身侧面。

机翼从机身两侧伸出，是飞机产生升力的一部分，使飞机保持在空中。机翼由被称为襟翼的可移动部分、前缘板和副翼组成。襟翼和前缘板可改变机翼的形状，使飞机在起飞和着陆时飞行速度变慢，在水平飞行时，襟翼和前缘板缩回，使飞机能以更快的速度飞行。副翼用来倾斜机翼，帮助飞机转弯。

机尾部分包括稳定器、方向舵和升降舵。方向舵用来帮助飞机转弯。升降舵用来使飞机上升或下降。小型飞机会有一个类似于汽车引擎的发动机和一个用来拉动飞机在空中前进的螺旋桨。一架大型喷气式飞机有我们所说的喷气式或涡轮发动机，它把废气从尾部推出，然后推动飞机在空气中向前飞行。这些发动机能产生巨大的动力。一些较大的飞机在起飞时可以重达 400 万千克。

飞机还需要一个带轮子的起落架，这样它们才能在跑道上降落和起飞。许多小型飞机的轮子固定在一个位置，而大型飞机和喷气式飞机的轮子可以收回到飞机的腹部，从而使飞机以更快的速度飞行。要知道飞机是如何飞行的，我们需要知道 4 个重要的词：重力、升力、推力和阻力。重力是一种无形的力，它把物体拉向地心。如果你捡起一个球，然后抛它，它就会掉到地上。这是重力。升力是飞机机翼上流动的空气产生的力，它将飞机向上拉。推力是飞机的螺旋桨或推动飞机前进的喷气式发动机所产生的力。阻力是阻止飞机前进的力，也叫作空气动力阻力。

当推力大于阻力时，飞机就会前进。当飞机向前移动时，它会产生升力，当升力大于重力时，飞机就会飞行。

飞行员是如何控制飞机的呢？

一旦飞机升空，飞行员就可以通过调整机头向上或向下的角度和发动机的功率来控制高度和速度。飞行员用升降舵控制机头的角度，用油门控制发动机的功率。飞行员通过增加机头向上的角度以增加引擎的动力。对飞行员来说，保持飞机足够快地飞行以保持升力是很重要的；否则，如果没有足够的气流，翅膀失去升力，可能会停止飞行，这叫作空气动力失速。

为了让飞机着陆，飞行员会减少动力，降低速度，让飞机慢慢地向地面降落。如果飞行员想让飞机转向，他可以同时使用副翼和方向舵来将飞机转向他想要的方向。飞行员还有其他的考虑。例如，飞机的载重必须合理规划，以使它达到适当的平衡。如果所有的重量都在飞机的前部或后部，飞机就不能很好地飞行或可能无法起飞。每次飞行前，飞行员都要考虑很多事情并仔细计划。飞行员必须确保自己身体健康。此外，飞行员应该在飞行前仔细查看天气情况，以确保天气条件适合飞行。当飞行员到达机场时，他们要检查飞机以确保一切正常运行，飞机处于良好状态是非常重要的，而且飞机还需要有足够的燃料进行计划中的飞行。飞行员、机械师、航空工程师或空乘都是很好的职业。如果你喜欢飞行，那么你可以考虑上述职业。

有很多学习飞行的新机会。在学校里有各种实践项目和在线课程可以学习。现在，还有一些优秀的高中专门从事航空事业。你也可以从航展中学到很多东西。航空和飞行都是航空航天工业的一部分。航空航天包括许多更先进的知识和技术领域，如化学、冶金、气象学、生物科学、高科技电子、GPS导航和地球空间系统等。材料和航空航天设计方面的先进工程技术需要继续进步，以制造出更安全、更快的飞机，同时运营和航空系统也要环保。从职业规划上来说，你可以立志设计一个新的导航系统来减少飞机飞行所需的燃料量。或者可以发明一种新材料，让飞机更轻，使用更少的燃料，飞得更快更高。或者，为什么不大胆梦想自己成为第一个飞到火星的人呢？

最后，让我们记住我们的基本航空词汇：重力、升力、推力和阻力。而一架飞机的基本部件是机身、机翼、尾翼、发动机、螺旋桨和起落架。

作者简介

　　韦恩·曼斯菲尔德出生于一个航空世家，航空历史可追溯到 1929 年他的祖父。他的父母都是专业飞行员，他们开创了早期的航空事业。曼斯菲尔德将空中广告业务发展成为一家全球性营销公司。他曾在众多的中国航空展上亮相，并在 2018 年的郑州航展上首次在天空中用飞机书写汉字。最近，曼斯菲尔德发展了他的飞机制造业务，旨在将新技术、培训和就业带给中国。

扫描收看
本文视频课程

Aircraft and Aviation

By Wayne Mansfield (America)

History

People have always been fascinated about flying, but in old times they didn't know how to build a machine to lift themselves off the earth. Many attempts were made to build flying machines but until a clear understanding of the basic physics of flight was made it was nearly impossible.

I've been very lucky because I come from a flying family. My grandfather started flying nearly a century ago in 1929, and both of my parents became pilots (Image 1). Both my father and mother were expert pilots, and pioneers in the aerial media business. They could tow aerial banners and write messages in the sky with vapor. My parents taught me all about aviation - how to fly airplanes and how to maintain them in good condition.

Many women have become world-famous pilots. Amelia Earhart was a pioneer aviator who became famous for flying across oceans before air travel to foreign countries was possible. Her pioneering flights helped make it possible for us to travel to far off lands and visit new places. Sadly, she disappeared over the pacific Ocean just before the war on Fascism and her fate remains a mystery to this day. Patty Wagstaff is no doubt the most famous woman in modern aviation. She has won more aerobatic championships and received more honors than any other person in recent history in aviation. Not only did she

Image 1　Mom getting ready to take off on a publicity mission in 1957

win the national aerobatic championship multiple times, but she beat both women and men to become the top champion.

Li Xiaqing (1912–1998), also known by her stage name Li Dandan, was a Chinese film actress, a pioneering aviator, as well as a philanthropist. She was the first Chinese woman to be granted a civil aviation license in China in 1936, and also co-founded the first civilian flying school. As a famous actress, she starred in Romance of the Western Chamber.

More than any other figure—man or woman—Li demonstrated her passion for flight throughout China at a time when her countrywomen weren't even allowed to drive cars. In the decade before World War II, if you had asked anyone in China to name just one pilot, the answer you probably would have gotten was Li Xiaqing.

For the past several years we have been flying at air shows in China, flying aerial banners and writing messages in the sky with vapor，as shown in Image 2. This is one use for small airplanes and there are many more.

Image 2   Writing messages in the sky with vapor

Aviation Is Important for Many Reasons

Airplanes and helicopters serve us in many ways: transportation, protecting our food supply from pests, fighting fires, carrying police aloft to protect us, moving supplies when there is a natural disaster or outbreak of disease. Air tourism and air sports are popular and common uses of aircraft.

Here's a photo of an aerial application airplane (Image 3). These airplanes are used to spray pesticides to keep insects from eating our food and to fertilize crops to make them

Image 3   Aerial application airplane

grow more quickly and to produce a larger amount of food to feed us. Aircraft are also used to plant rice from the air when it is difficult to enter fields flooded with water. Without airplanes, the mount of food produced would be much less.

Airplanes are also used for saving lives and property from fires. Sometimes it's very difficult for firefighters to reach a fire from the ground because it might be in the mountains or heavily forested areas. That's when aircraft are used to drop a water-chemical mixture on top of these fires to stop the flames, saving lives and protecting our property. For small fires they may use a helicopter or a small fixed-wing airplane; for big fires they use airplanes as large as the biggest airliners and they carry thousands of gallons of water-chemical mixture to drop on huge fires in forests, to save nearby homes and businesses and to protect peoples' lives.

Another use for aviation is for the police and security services to keep us safe，as shown in Image 4. Helicopters can be used to chase criminals and keep them from escaping. Also drones and regular aircraft can be used to patrol our cities and towns to make certain that our citizens are kept safe from illegal behavior or terrorism.

Airplanes are often used to fly with supplies during natural disasters or disease. After

Image 4　Rescue aircraft

an earthquake an airplane might be the only way to reach an area affected to bring in medical supplies, emergency personnel and food. This helps save and protect people's lives. Small planes maybe used to fly into smaller cities and towns whereas large transport aircraft can move huge volumes of supplies to largest cities affected by an earthquake or fire or in the case of a medical emergency. Many lives have been saved this way throughout the entire world, especially in countries that are less developed and may not have roads or emergency services able to respond quickly to a disaster.

One of the most important uses of aviation is to fly us and our friends and family to meet one another during the holidays, or to travel to explore new places in the world. Flying in an airline are used to be unusual, but more recently advances in aviation have reduced the cost of flying allowing many more people to visit foreign lands and for more people to fly long distances to visit their friends and family during holiday or vacation times.

Air Sports are becoming increasingly popular as more and more people are learning how to fly. There are many ways to enter sport flying including gyrocopters, light sport aircraft, small helicopters and regular fixed-wing airplanes. Most recently our company Clear Sky has been offering sport aircraft and light aircraft manufacturing opportunities for China including planes such as the EcoSport flyer, the Tiger, the Cougar and the Sea Wolf Amphibian. Planes like these will give China an opportunity to develop a much larger aircraft manufacturing base and will make flying available to more and more people.

Let's Look at How Planes Fly

First of all, we have to know what the main parts of an airplane are. They consist of the fuselage, the wings, the tail, the engine, the propeller, and the landing gear.

The fuselage is the main part of the airplane where people are seated inside, with the pilot sitting in front. The wings are attached to the side of the fuselage, and the tail is on the back. And in small airplanes the engine and propeller are usually on the front. In large jet planes the engines are usually attached underneath the wings or sometimes on the side of the fuselage near the tail.

The wings extend out from each side of the fuselage and are the part of the airplane that creates the lift that keeps the airplane in the air. The wings have movable sections called flaps, leading edge slats and ailerons. The flaps and leading-edge slats change the shape of the wings to allow the plane to fly more slowly for takeoff and landing, and in level flight they are retracted to allow the airplane to fly at higher speeds. The ailerons are used to tilt the wings to help the airplane to turn.

The tail section includes the stabilizers, the rudder and the elevators. The rudder is used to help the airplane to make turns. The elevators are used to make the airplane climb or dive.

Small planes will have an engine similar to the engine in a car, and a propeller which is used to pull the airplane forward through the air. A big jet plane has what we call a jet, or turbine engine which pushes exhaust gas out the rear that then pushes the airplane forward through the air. These engines can create tremendous power. Some of the biggest airplanes can weigh 0.4 million kilos when they take off.

Planes also need a landing gear with wheels so that they can land and take off on a runway. Many small planes have the wheels fixed in one position, whereas the larger planes and jet airliners have wheels which can be retracted up into the belly of the airplane thereby allowing the airplane to fly at a higher speed.

To know how an airplane flies we need to know about four important words: gravity, lift, thrust, and drag.

Gravity is an invisible force the pulls objects down towards the center of the earth. If you pick up a ball and let it go, it falls to the floor. That is Gravity!

Lift is the force created by air flowing over the airplanes wings to pull it upwards.

Thrust is the force created by the airplane's propeller or the jet engines which move the airplane forward.

Drag is the resistance that tries to stop an airplane from moving forward. In an airplane this is called aerodynamic drag.

When thrust is greater than drag, the airplane will move forward. When the airplane moves forward it creates lift, and when lift is greater than gravity the airplane will fly.

Now Let's Look at How the Pilot Controls the Airplane

Once the airplane is in the air the pilot controls the height and speed by adjusting the angle of the nose up or down and adjusting the power from the engine. The pilot controls the angle of the nose with the elevators, and the engine power with the throttle. When he or she wants to claim they have to both increase the angle of the nose upwards and increase the power from the engine. It is important for the pilot to keep the airplane flying fast enough to maintain lift; otherwise the wings may stop flying without sufficient airflow. This is called an aerodynamic stall.

In order to land the airplane, the pilot reduces power, reduces the speed and lets the plane settle gently toward the ground.

If the pilot wants to turn the plane, he uses both the ailerons and the rudder to steer the plane in the direction he desires.

There are other considerations for a pilot as well because the airplane has to be loaded carefully so that it is properly balanced. If all of the weight is in the front of the plane or in the back of the plane, the airplane won't fly well or may not be able to take off.

Before every flight, a pilot has to consider many things and plan carefully. The pilot must make sure that he or she is feeling well and in good health. Also, the pilot should carefully check the weather before the flight to make certain that the conditions are good for flying. When the pilot arrives at the airport, it is very important that they check the airplane to make certain that everything is functioning properly, and the aircraft is in good condition; and that it has enough fuel for the proposed flight.

Being a pilot or a mechanic, an aerospace engineer or a flight attendant can be a wonderful career. If you love the idea of flying, then you should consider it for yourself.

There are many new opportunities to learn about flying. There are children's programs, online lessons, and learning in the school. There are now excellent high schools that specialize in aviation career including learning for mechanics, pilots, flight attendants, flight dispatchers and all the people involved in the logistics of operating and in managing an airline. You can also learn a lot by going to an airshow. Aviation and flying are all part of the aerospace industry. Aerospace includes many more areas of advanced learning and technology, such as chemistry metallurgy meteorology, biosciences, high technology electronics, the Global Positioning Satellites (GPS) navigation and geospace systems.

Advanced engineering in materials and aerospace design are required to continue to advance to make safer and faster aircraft, and also the operation system and the aviation system should be environmentally friendly. You could be the person that designs a new navigation system that reduces the amount of fuel required for an aircraft to fly. You might be the person that invents a new material allowing aircraft to be lighter, use less fuel and to fly faster and higher. Why not be the first person who flies to Mars?

For now, let's remember our basic words: gravity, lift, thrust, and drag. The basic parts of the airplane are the fuselage, the wings, the tail, the engine, the propeller and landing gear.

(Fu Han contributed to this article)

About the Author

Wayne Mansfield comes from an aviation family going back to his grandfather in 1929. Both his father and mother were competent professional pilots who started an early aviation business. Mansfield developed this aerial advertising business into a worldwide marketing firm. He has participated in numerous Chinese air shows, and wrote Chinese characters in the sky in Zhengzhou Air Show in 2018. More recently Mansfield has developed his aircraft manufacturing business with the intention of bringing new technologies, training, and employment to China.

建筑空间与技术中的仿生学

文 / 罗杰威（意大利）　　译 / 唐庆超

　　大自然造就了人类，人类又与自然息息相关。了解大自然对现如今深陷环境污染困扰的我们来说有着极为迫切的重要性。今天，我们就要从一个新颖的角度讲解一下大自然与人类之间的关系。在仿生学科学家看来，大自然永远有着解决所有问题的最好办法。因此，我们才需要学习自然，遵循自然界的种种规律。希望通过本文，大家能更深入地了解自然的高效与美丽，也更积极地投入尊重大自然、保护大自然的行动中来！

　　生命是如此奇妙，我们唯有了解自然的运作方式，才能更好地保护自然；况且，自然的法则坚不可摧，如果我们不遵循自然规律，自然就将给予我们惩罚。仿生学正是一门致力于了解自然、模仿自然运作方式的学科。

何为仿生学？

　　仿生学的概念是由英国人达西·汤普森提出的，其含义源自古希腊词语"βίον"，意为"重要的元素"。汤普森先生对物体的形状和物理规则之间的关系进行了研究，并将这些从生命系统中学习到的规则运用到了人工系统当中。从这个层面上来说，仿生学是一门非常严谨的科学，但同时，仿生学也是一门艺术。

哲学家圣多马斯·阿奎那曾言："艺术是对自然运作方式的模仿。"在他看来，艺术并不单指绘画，生活中的建筑、科技也可以称为艺术。既然艺术是对自然运作方式的模仿，那么，致力于寻找大自然的运作方式，并将其运用到我们的日常生活当中的仿生学自然也是一门艺术。

所以，仿生学可不是一门枯燥繁难的科学。我们不如将其称为一种"自由又科学、严谨"的研究方式吧！

了解了仿生学的概念之后，我们应该如何学习仿生学呢？首先，我们需要将仿生学的研究对象拆分成两部分来认识：一部分是受到重力作用的陆地生物和非生物对象；另一部分则是受到压力作用的海洋生物。重力和压力的差异在很大程度上会影响生物的形状。例如，生活在水里的鱼和陆地上的马就长得不一样，因为它们所受到的力不同。

汤普森先生发现，人类的头骨和猴子的头骨十分相似。只要将人类的头骨施加压力稍微变形的话，我们就能得到猴子的头骨了。生活在深水区和浅水区的鱼类也存在这种相似性，由于水压不同，深水鱼和浅水鱼的形状也不同。重力和压力决定了生物运动的形式和动态，这一规律渗透于大自然的方方面面。

那么，这一规律对于我们而言有什么意义呢？我们又该如何去运用这一规律？事实上，在重力和压力的作用下，大自然中诞生了形形色色的物体结构，而这些物体结构又遵循着一定的物理和数学规则。只要找到这些奇妙的规则并运用它们，我们就能将自然的奇迹转变为人类技术的奇迹。

我们可以做一个有趣的实验。将一滴牛奶滴进牛奶或浓稠的液体中，你会发现牛奶滴溅起形成了一个皇冠的形状（图1）。这个皇冠的形状实际上是一个对称的图案，并蕴含着一个复杂的数学模型。实际上，许许多多简单的形式背

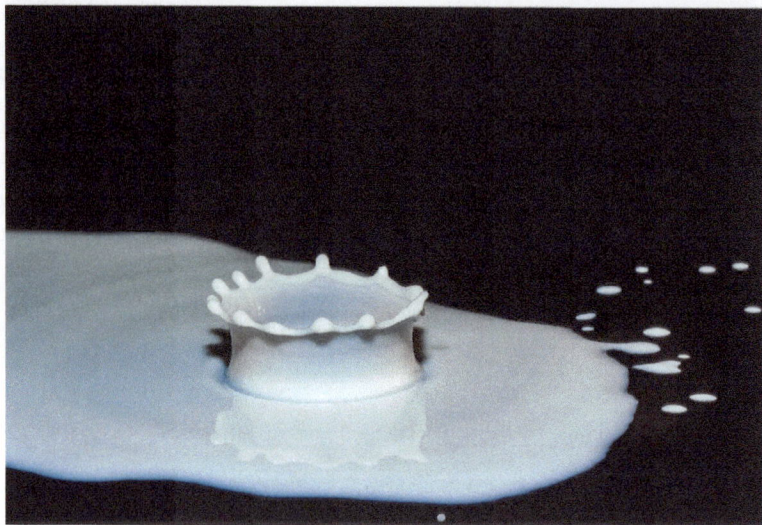

图 1　牛奶滴形成了皇冠

后都隐藏着复杂的数学规则，大自然也是如此。寻找并发现这些规则，找到大自然的运作方式并运用它们，这就是仿生学的意义所在。

斐波那契序列

　　我们首先来看看植物。它们身上存在着一些奇特的对数螺旋规则——植物的叶片、花和芽都隐含着螺旋线形状。螺旋线是由一个"序列"不断重复所形成的形状，其整体形状和部分形状彼此相同，可以说，整体是部分的重复。而它们所重复形成的序列实际上就是数学中的斐波那契序列（1，1，2，3，5，8，13，…）。

　　为什么植物身上会存在着这样奇特的序列呢？这是出于它们的生存需要。只有遵循斐波那契序列的模型，它们的每一片叶片才可以均匀地受到阳光和雨水的滋润，才能更好地生长，这是大自然的黄金法则。斐波那契从兔子繁殖中发现了这一规律，但大自然早已在其造物的过程中将这个规律运用得炉火纯青了，如在植物、贝壳和人类的耳朵、头发等地方，你都能发现这一规律的身影。事实上，不仅地球如此，宇宙也同样遵循这一规则，著名科学家哈勃就曾对不同星系进行了研究，最终发现某些星系的模样同样遵循着斐波那契序列的规律。

除了螺旋线形状外，双螺旋形状也同样时常在大自然中出现（图2）。双螺旋是由一个斐波那契序列和一个镜像的斐波那契序列重叠而成。向日葵和宇宙中的重力波都遵循了这一规则。如果你将衣服扭转一下，你同样也会发现螺旋形状。

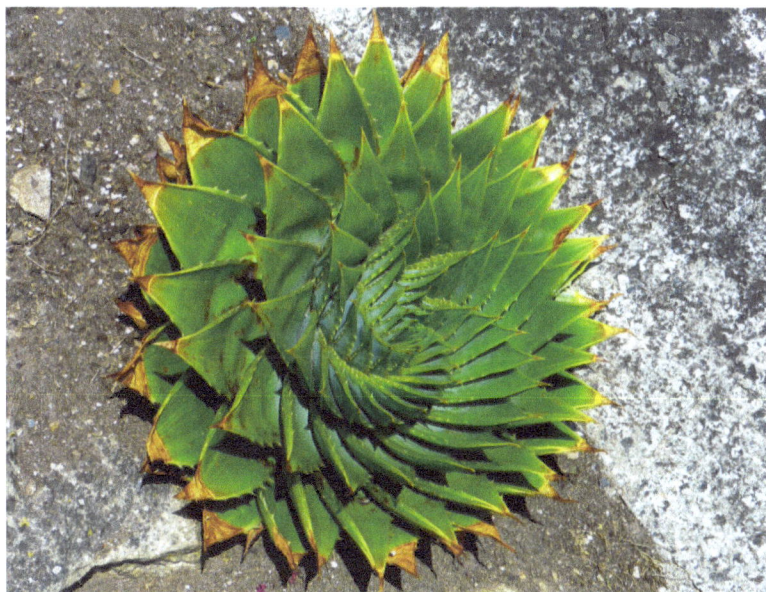

图2　叶片呈双螺旋形状的多叶芦荟

自然中存在的斐波那契序列给予了人们创造的灵感，德国音乐家约翰·塞巴斯蒂安·巴赫就曾根据斐波那契序列作曲。遵循自然规律的音乐听起来美妙悦耳。斐波那契序列同样被运用于建筑当中，如哥特式大教堂中的某些结构便是如此。

紧密的 3D 结构蜂巢与球形结构

领略了斐波那契序列的奇妙，我们接下来要了解的是更为复杂的三维空间。三维空间同样存在着奇妙的自然结构。有一个非常有趣的实验：如果将一些小铅球放进一个容器里，然后挤压它们，它们之间的缝隙就会变得越来越小，直至消失。最后，就连球体也都变形了。

这些小球最终形成的几何体并不是随机的，而是 20 面体或 12 面体。12 面体在晶体学中是极为稳定且节省空间的结构。当人们挤压小球时，它们就自动形成了这种非常坚硬稳定的形态。一些建筑师从中得到灵感，仿造这种几何体形状来建造房子，北京的水立方便是如此。

这样的规律同样发生在二维空间当中。当我们把很多圆形放在一起并不停挤压时，这些圆形最终将形成蜂窝结构，这种蜂窝结构的基础就是六边形。六边形也是非常稳固的形状（图 3）。

图 3 蜂窝结构

如果我们想要得到一个结构非常紧密的几何体，我们需要的基础图形并不是圆形、正方形、三角形或者其他的形状，而是六边形。蜜蜂没有靠学数学而只是遵循自然的准则便自己找到了这个规律。

生活在海里的海绵需要面对来自四面八方的海水的压力，它们不像鱼那样能够只朝一个方向前进，而是会在海水中不停旋转。因此，海绵身体的各个部分都要具有很强的抵抗力，这样看来，海绵的骨架是球形并且几乎是完全对称的也就不难理解了。

仔细观察，我们可以发现海绵的球形骨架之所以如此坚硬，是因为它是由众多的小六边形组成的。但一个封闭的结构全是一种图形也不行，这就像一个房间必须要有一个门一样，如果我们想让这个球体闭合，就必须要有至少一种其他的图形才行。因此我们可以发现，在海绵的球形骨架上存在着一些小的五边形结构。没有这些五边形或者其他形状的图形，球体就无法闭合（图4）。

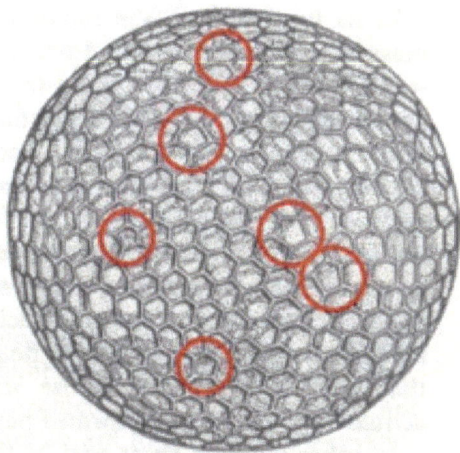

图4 海绵球型骨架上的五边形[①]

————————

① 达西·汤姆森.生长和形态 [M].都灵：博拉蒂·博林希里出版社，1992；175.罗杰威对该图书进行了注解。

看到这里，大家可能会疑惑，我们了解这么多自然中的结构有什么用处呢？我们又该如何利用它们？事实上，这些规律和结构已经被运用到建筑当中了。了解自然中的结构有助于我们设计和建造建筑。有时候，建筑结构和自然中的结构是不谋而合的。

肥皂泡与最小面

建筑师曾在动物的骨骼上寻求到了灵感。蜻蜓的体型很小，翅膀振动频率却很快。因此，蜻蜓的翅膀必然需要足够坚硬才能在高速的振动下保持安好。当我们仔细观察蜻蜓的翅膀就会发现，它们的翅膀上布满了网格样的形状。这些形状就是肥皂泡堆积在一起的形状，这其中蕴含着一个奇妙的数学规则——最小面积原理。

我们可以借助肥皂泡来解释这个最小面积原理。取一个圆环浸入肥皂水中，然后取出，此时，圆环表面覆盖着一层肥皂水。弯曲圆环，我们会发现，此时圆环表面的肥皂水用量最少，肥皂泡的面积最小，肥皂泡各处的受力也都相等。这同样是一个十分重要的数学原理。

最小面积原理不仅可以运用在数学中，同样也可以运用于建筑当中。在意大利有一座由伟大的工程师塞尔吉奥·穆斯梅奇设计建造的桥梁。这座桥的工程与其他普通的设计过程有很大不同。塞尔吉奥并没有通过数学计算的方式去设计桥梁，而是运用了肥皂泡原理。他借鉴了肥皂泡的结构和形状，并将其建造成桥梁。事实证明，这种遵循自然的建造方式非常有效，他成功地建造出了一座迄今屹立已有 50 余载的桥梁。

自然中的结构无一不遵循着牢固、节约、优美等原则。将自然结构运用于建筑当中，我们可以得到更为牢固而更为节约空间的建筑。如何设计建筑？或许，大自然早已告诉了我们答案。

不仅在建筑领域，自然在许多其他领域都永远掌握着解决问题的最好办法。在如何寻找问题的最优解这一方面，自然永远是我们的老师。因此，让我们一起向自然学习，共同成为我们美丽家园的保护者吧！

作者简介

罗杰威教授是一名建筑师，建筑与环境技术博士，毕业于米兰理工大学。自 2004 年起，他担任天津大学建筑学院教授、硕士和博士生导师，以及建筑学院国际交流办公室副主任、仿生建筑与规划研究中心实验室主任。他曾出版专著 8 部，合作著作 10 部，发表论文 600 余篇和 1 部小说，指导 70 多名国内外学生完成硕士论文和博士论文，其中多名学生的论文或设计竞赛获奖。他是中国银川大学干旱地区中阿资源与环境治理特色国际合作实验室的顾问。主要研究方向涵盖建筑设计、建筑规划中的仿生方法、城市规划、传统建筑和村落的修复、现代建筑史、古代建筑的形而上学、可持续建筑、生态村、数据驱动分析和数据驱动设计。

扫描收看
本文视频课程

Bionic Approach for the Architectual Space and Technology

By Paolo Vincenzo Genovese (Italy)

Nature generated human beings, and human beings are a part of Nature to which it is closely related. Therefore, understanding Nature is an extremely urgent issue for us who are deeply troubled by pollution and technological life. Today, I will explain the relationship between Nature and human beings from a novel perspective: Bionics. Nature always follows the most performative way to solve problems. Therefore, we need to learn from Nature and follow the laws of Nature.

Hoping that through this article, everyone can have a deeper understanding of the wonderful beauty and efficiency of Nature and be more active in respecting Nature and protecting Her!

What is Bionics?

Life is so wonderful, we can only protect Nature better if we understand how Nature works. In another perspective, if we do not follow the rule of Nature, Nature will get rid of us because her laws are unbreakable. Bionics is a discipline dedicated to understanding and imitating the process of Nature.

The concept of Bionics was founded by the Englishman D'arcy W. Thompson, and its meaning is derived from the ancient Greek word "βíόν", which means "vital element". Mr. Thompson studied the relationship between the shape of objects and physical rules, and applied these rules learned from living systems to some artificial systems. At this level, Bionics is a very rigorous science, but at the same time, Bionics is also an art.

The Scholastic philosopher St. Thomas Aquinas once said: "Art is the imitation of the Nature in its way to operate." In his view, art does not only refer to painting. Architecture and technology in life can also be called art. Art is an imitation of the natural processes in their way of working. Thus, Bionics dedicated to finding out how nature works and applying it to our daily lives is also an art.

Therefore, instead of calling Bionics a boring and difficult science, we might as well call it a free and scientifically rigorous research method at the same time.

After understanding the concept of Bionics, how should we learn Bionics? First of all, we need to divide the research object of Bionics into two parts to understand: one is terrestrial living and non-living objects subjected to gravity, and the other is the marine one generated under pressure. The difference in gravity and pressure affects the shape of living things to a large extent. For example, fish living in water and horses on land look different because the forces are different.

Mr. Thompson discovered that human skulls are very similar to monkey skulls, and by applying pressure to deform the human skull a little, we can get the monkey skull. This similarity also exists in fish living in superficial or deep waters. Fish in deep and shallow waters have different shapes due to different water pressures. Gravity and pressure determine the shape and dynamic of motion of living things, and this rule permeates all aspects of Nature.

So what is the meaning of this rule for us, and how do we apply this rule in the human artifacts? In fact, under the action of gravity and pressure, Nature has formed a variety of different object structures, and these object structures follow certain physical and mathematical rules and processes. Finding these wonderful rules and applying them, we can turn the miracle of Nature into technology.

Everyone can do an interesting experiment. You can drop a drop of milk into milk or other dense liquid, and the milk drop splashed in the shape of a crown (Image 1). You can discover

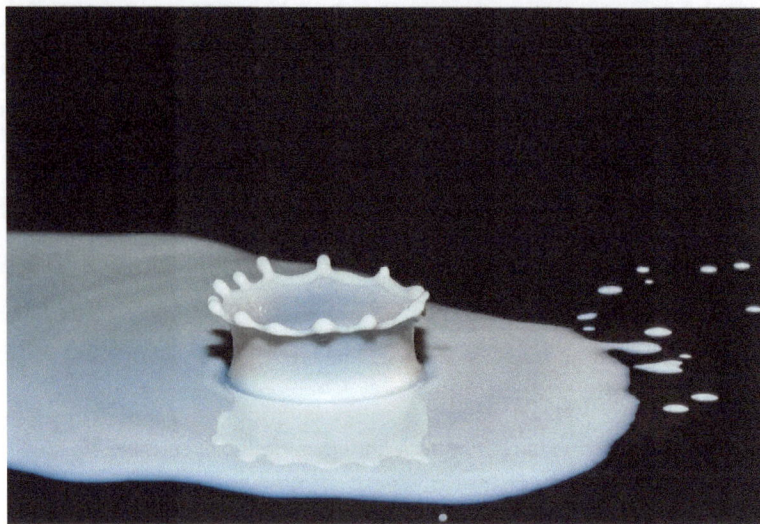

Image 1   The milk drips into the liquid to form a crown

that the shape of this crown is actually symmetrical and contains a complex mathematical model. In fact, many simple forms hide complicated mathematical rules, and so does Nature. Finding and discovering these rules, finding out how Nature works, and applying them is the meaning of Bionics.

The Fibonacci Sequence

We first put our eyes on the plants, and will find that there are some peculiar logarithmic spiral rules in them-leaves, flowers and buds of plants all have a spiral shape implicit. A spiral is a shape formed by a continuous repetition of a sort of "program". The overall shape and the partial shape are the same. It can be said that the whole is a partial repetition. The sequence they repeat is actually the Fibonacci sequence(1,1,2,3,5,8,13,...).

Why are there such peculiar sequences in plants? This is because of their survival needs. Only by following the Fibonacci sequence, can each of their leaves be evenly moistened by sunlight and rain, and grow better. This is the Golden Ratio of Nature. Fibonacci discovered this law in the reproduction of rabbits, but actually the Nature used this law in every aspect of his manifestation in order to optimize the performance of its creation. For example, you can find this in plants, shells, human ears and hair, etc. In fact, not only the earth, but the universe also follows this rule. The famous scientist Hubble has studied different galaxies and finally found that some of these galaxies also follow the Fibonacci sequence.

In addition to the spiral shape, the double spiral shape also often appears in Nature (Image 2). The double helix is formed by the overlapping of a Fibonacci sequence and a mirrored Fibonacci sequence. Sunflowers, gravitational waves in the universe follow this rule. If you twist your clothes, you will also find a single helix shape.

Image 2　Aloe polyphylla with double helix-shaped leaves

The Fibonacci sequence in Nature gives people the inspiration for creation. The German musician Johann Sebastian Bach once composed music according to the Fibonacci sequence. Music that follows the laws of Nature sounds beautiful and pleasant. The Fibonacci sequence is also used in architecture, for example in some structural system in the Gothic cathedrals.

Compact 3D Structure:honeycomb and Spherical structure

After understanding the wonders of the Fibonacci sequence, what we need to understand next is a more complex three-dimensional space, which also has a wonderful natural structure. There was a very interesting experiment. If you put some small lead balls into a container and press them with heavy weight, what happen is that the space between them will become smaller and smaller, and finally, disappear. At the same time the sphere will deform.

The final geometry formed by these small balls is not random, but will form a 20-hedron or a 12-hedron. Dodecahedron is an extremely stable and space-saving structure in crystallography. When people squeeze the balls, they automatically form this very hard and stable form. Some architects have taken inspiration from this, and imitated this geometric shape to build houses. The Water Cube in Beijing is a convenient example of this structure.

This rule also occurs in two-dimensional space. When we put a lot of circles together and kept squeezing them, in the end, these circles will form a honeycomb structure. The basis of this honeycomb structure is a hexagon, and the hexagon is also a very stable shape and space-optimized. If we want to get a very tightly structured geometry, the basic figure we need is not a circle, square, triangle or other shapes, but a hexagon. This law, the bee found it not rely on learning mathematics, but by following "the nature of the Nature" (Image 3).

Sponges living in the sea need to face the pressure of sea water from all directions. They are not like fish which only need to move in one direction, but will keep spinning in the sea. Therefore, all parts of the sponge body must be very resistant, so it is not difficult to understand that the skeleton of the sponge is spherical and almost symmetrical.

Observing carefully, we can find that the reason why the spherical skeleton of the sponge is so robust. Because it is composed of many small hexagons. But a closed structure is not all a kind of figure, liking a room must have a door, if we want to close the sphere, there must be at least one other figure. Therefore, we can find that there are some small pentagons on the spherical skeleton of the sponge. Without these pentagons or other anomalous figures the sphere can not be closed (Image 4).

Image 3   Honeycomb structure

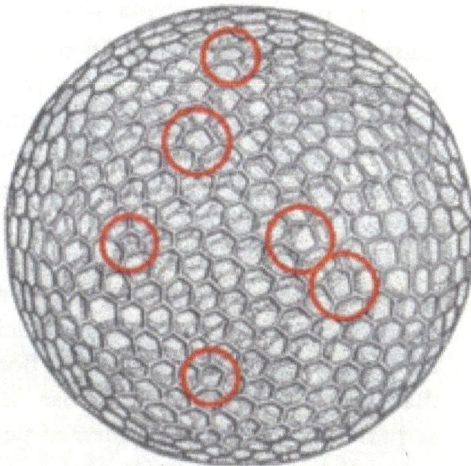

Image 4   Small pentagons on the spherical skeleton of the sponge[①]

---

① THOMPSON D W. Crescita e forma[M]. Torino: Bollati Boringhieri, 1992: 174. Graphic elaboration by Paolo Vincenzo Genovese.

Seeing this, you may be wondering, what use is there for us to understand so many structures in Nature, and how should we use them? In fact, these laws and structures have been applied to architecture. Understanding the structure in Nature helps us design and construct buildings. Sometimes, the structure of a building coincides with the structure in Nature.

Soap and Minimum Surfaces

Architects have found inspiration in animal bones. Another case are dragonflies; they are small in size, but their wings vibrate very quickly. Therefore, dragonflies' wings need to be stiff enough to stay safe under high-speed vibrations. When we look closely at the wings of a dragonfly, we will find that the wings of a dragonfly are covered with grid shapes. These shapes are the shapes of soap bubbles stacked together, which contains a wonderful mathematical rule — the principle of minimum surfaces.

We can use soap bubbles to explain this minimum surfaces principle. Take a ring and immerse it in soapy water, and then take it out. At this time, the surface of the ring is covered with a layer of soapy water. Bending the ring, we will find that at this time the amount of soapy water on the surface of the ring is the least, the surfaces of the soap bubble is the smallest, and the force on the soap bubble is equal. This is a very important mathematical principle.

The principle of minimum surfaces can be used not only in mathematics, but also in architecture. There is a bridge in Italy made by the great engineer Sergio Musmeci. The engineering of this bridge is very different from ordinary process of design. He did not design the bridge through mathematical calculations, but used the soap bubble principle. He borrowed the structure and shape of soap bubbles and built it into a bridge. The facts proved that this natural construction method was effective. He successfully built the bridge. Today, the bridge has stood for 50 years.

Structures in Nature follow the principles of firmness, economy, and beauty. By applying natural structures to buildings, we can get stronger and more space-saving architectural structures. How to design a building, perhaps Nature has already told us the answer long, long ago.

Not only in the field of architecture, but in many fields, Nature will always follow the best way to solve the problem. In terms of how to find the optimal solution to the problem, Nature will always be our teacher. Therefore, let us learn from Nature and become the protectors of our beautiful home together! I have designed a skyscraper with this principle. In the future, you can do the same!

(Tang Qingchao contributed to this article)

About the Author

Professor Paolo Vincenzo Genovese is an architect and Ph.D. in "Architectural and Environmental Technology", graduates from Polytechnic of Milan. Since 2004 he is a full-time professor and also Master and Ph.D. tutor in the School of Architecture of Tianjin University in China, the Deputy Director of International Exchange Office as well, and the Director of Lab of Bionic Architecture & Planning Research Center in this university. He has published eight monographs, ten books in cooperation, more than six hundred papers and a novel. He is tutor of over 70 Ph.D. and Master Dissertations in China and abroad, some of which gained prizes in designing competitions. He is advisory consultant of China-Arab International Joint Laboratory on Featured Resources and Environmental Governance in Arid Regions in Yinchuan University, China. His study, research and expertise concern designs of architecture, Bionic approaches in the architecture planning, urban planning, restoration of traditional buildings and villages, history of modern architecture, metaphysics of ancient architecture, sustainable architecture, eco-villages, data-driven analysis and data-driven design.

第三章　科技魅力

Amazing Science

机器人的神奇功能

文 / 新井健生（日本）　译 / 唐庆超

近年来，世界范围内人口老龄化问题愈发严重，日本也不例外。面对青壮年劳动力人口减少、新生儿数量下降、老龄化人口不断增加的现状，人们该何去何从？

开发机器人的神奇功能是解决问题的一个思路。如何制作机器人，如何利用机器人，将成为未来的重要课题。我将从介绍机器人的种类开始，一步步带领大家进入一个机器人的新天地。

机器人种类繁多，用途多样，想一个个介绍清楚它们可不容易。

图 1 中这个蹦蹦跳跳能轻松翻越各种障碍，看起来和孙悟空一样灵敏的机器人阿特拉斯，它就有着极为出色的运动能力，可是个优秀的运动员呢！

如果没有见过埃里卡，小朋友们大概不会想到现在已经有和真人如此相似的机器人了吧！埃里卡外表上看起来就像一个有着棕色头发、可爱面容的亚洲女郎。我现在还没有想好埃里卡的用途，但或许某一天，埃里卡会像真人一样和你聊天，在你无聊的时候陪伴你！

制作像埃里卡这样高仿真机器人的专家可不少，石黑教授就制作了一款以

图1　机器人阿特拉斯

他自己为原型的机器人。教授和机器人面容高度相似,他们站在一起的画面可真是太不可思议了!

当然,为了追求一些特殊功用,机器人的外表也会随之发生变化。阿斯塔里斯克的设计灵感和外表就来自蜘蛛,它有着6条腿,不仅可以爬行,还能像手一样抓取物体,6条腿赋予它出色的爬行能力,使它可以轻轻松松到达人类很难触及的地方(图2)。这是多么让人羡慕的机器人的神奇功能呀!

图2　外表近似蜘蛛、拥有出色爬行能力的机器人

此外，还有一类可以用来攀爬的机器人，它们爬起墙来可是一把好手，清洁各种高层建筑或桥梁支柱等不在话下。用于负重的机器人也不能少，机器人大狗的名字很可爱，事实上它可以在复杂地形条件下搬运重物，是非常实用的机器人。野猫顾名思义，有着快速移动的能力，奔跑速度可达 40 km/h。

有一类机器人大家可能常常忽视，或感到困惑，那就是自动驾驶汽车。事实上，这也是一种机器人。工厂领域也存在很多机器人的身影，如可以用来抓取、组装、焊接等的工业手臂和机床。

制造和使用机器人已经成为全世界的共识。2013 年，多用途工业机器人的使用量显示，日本以 23% 的份额占据世界第一的位置，其次是占据 14% 份额的美国。然而，两年后的 2015 年，日本份额下降至 18%，紧随其后的是占据 16% 份额的中国，一举跃居世界第二。而到 2018 年，中国已跃居世界第一。中国的工业机器人正在高速增长当中。

在全球机器人数量高速增长的背后，实际上是多数国家普遍面临的一个问题——人口老龄化。日本的人口老龄化问题尤其突出。老龄化社会导致劳动人口迅速减少，将会给工业和经济带来严峻的挑战。

中国也存在类似的人口老龄化情况，随着时间的推移，中国的老年人口也将不断增加，劳动力进一步减少。未来谁来工作成为老龄化社会亟须解决的难题。

于是，机器人应运而生。

未来，人们不仅需要更多的工业机器人，也需要更多的服务型机器人。这些机器人可用于家务、护理、医疗、安全保卫等人们生活的方方面面，本用于工业的机器人也将逐渐走进人们的生活。

大家在家里常用的扫地机器人其实就是一个典型的服务机器人。此外，服务型机器人还有校园、机场、小区等常用来巡逻的保安机器人，长得像小海豹的安抚型机器人。对于行动不便的患者而言，还有专用来日常护理的机器人，可满足患者日常饮食起居的需要（图3）。

服务型机器人还包含娱乐机器人，可以像真人一般唱歌跳舞、吹奏音乐；也可用于教育，或许未来的某一天，机器人也可以成为老师站上讲台呢！

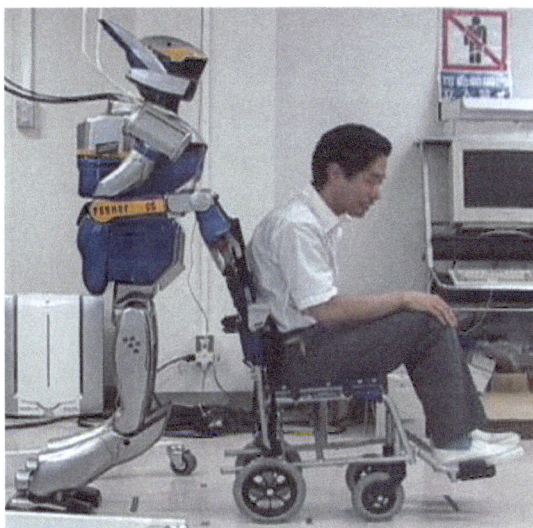

图3 可用于日常护理的机器人

还有一些医疗服务机器人，可用来做微创手术，相对于人类而言，医疗机器人更为精确、冷静，更少会有体力和心理负担。我的实验室里就开发了不少这样的医疗机器人。

事实上，建筑机器人在机器人领域也占据着重要的地位，日本从20世纪70年代便开始研发建筑机器人，这些机器人可用来搅拌混凝土、焊接钢架、喷涂防火材料等。然而，建筑机器人投入使用的过程却一直不太顺利，毕竟那时，青壮年劳动力充足，雇用建筑工人的成本可比使用机器人低多了。但对于如今步入老龄化社会的日本来说，建筑机器人可就能起大作用了。

农业领域同样存在机器人的身影，如用来自动播种收割的机器人、可遥控割草的机器人等。

在中国，我们也可以看见许多机器人的身影，并且许多已进入市场及人们的日常生活了，如酒店和餐厅常常使用的送餐机器人、展馆和校园内使用的保安机器人、用来启智的机器人玩具等。

介绍了这么多种机器人，大家想必也非常好奇机器人是如何制作出来的吧。以下是机器人的设计理念。

我们需要通过对形态、功能和生命智能进行建模来设计自动化的机器和系统。机器人的形态一般参考各种生命形态，如蜘蛛、海豹等，也可以参考人类的形态。而机器人的功能包括攀爬、运输、医疗等，其形态需要根据功能来进行调整。最后，我们需要赋予机器人生命智能，以实现其自动化运作。

虽然没有像哆啦A梦这样神奇的机器人，机器人的智能水平也达不到人类的水平，但机器人给人类带来的便利已经渗透到人们生活的方方面面。从大的方面来说，它们足以支持一个国家的经济发展，填补劳动力空缺；从小的方面来说，它们可以陪伴你、照顾你、治愈你。可以说，总有一天我们需要的东西会被机器人实现。机器人在大小和功能上的优势是人类无法企及的，而且它们还有最温暖人心的使命——让人类生活得更幸福。

我在实验室里就设计了一款微型机器人，它可以抓取1毫米的物体，甚至可以抓取细胞，如此精确的能力让它在医疗生物领域可以发挥巨大的作用，如通过抓取细胞来查探人体细胞的状态，甚至可以用来克隆（图4）。

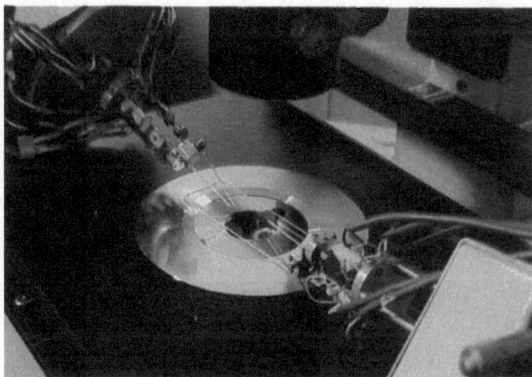

图4 可抓取1毫米大小物体的机器人

了解了这么多神奇的机器人，想必小朋友们也对机器人世界产生了不小的兴趣，希望未来会有更多人在机器人领域取得成就，战胜人口老龄化！

作者简介

新井健生（Tatsuo Arai），1952 年出生于日本，2017 年加入北京理工大学，目前为北京理工大学教授，也是日本大阪大学名誉教授。主要研究方向为微型机器人在生物学中的应用。

The Magical Function of the Robot

By Tatsuo Arai (Japan)

In recent years, the worldwide problem of aging has become more serious, and Japan is of no exception. Faced with a shrinking workforce of young adults, a decline in the number of newborns and an increasing number of aging population, what should people do?

Developing the magical function of the robot is an idea to solve the problem. How to make robots and how to use them will become imcreasingly important topics in the future. I will start by introducing the types of robots to lead you into a new world of robots step by step.

There are many types of robots with various uses. It is not easy to introduce them one by one.

The robot Atlas (Image 1) which looks as agile as the Monkey King, can easily surpass various obstacles by jumping. It has excellent athletic ability to make itself an excellent athlete!

If you haven't seen Erica before, you probably wouldn't have thought that there are now robots so similar to real people. Erica looks like an Asian girl with brown hair and a cute face. I haven't thought about what purpose should Erica serve yet, but maybe one day, Erica will chat with you like a real person, and accompany you when you are bored!

There are many experts who specialized in making high-simulation robots like Erica.

Image 1   Atlas robot

Professor Ishiguro has made a robot based on his own image. The faces of the professor and the robot are highly similar which makes the picture of them standing together really amazing!

Of course, in order to pursue some special functions, the appearance of the robot will also change accordingly. The design inspiration and appearance of Astarisk comes from a spider. It has 6 legs, which can not only crawl, but also grab objects like a hand. The 6 legs give it excellent crawling ability, making it easy to reach the place where humans are difficult to get to (Image 2). What an enviable magical function of the robot!

Image 2   These robots look like spiders and have excellent crawling ability

In addition, there is a class of robots that can be used for climbing. They are good at climbing up walls and can clean up various high-rise buildings or bridge pillars, which greatly reduces the danger of humans working at heights. The robots designed to carry heavy loads are also indispensable. The robot Big Dog has a very cute name. In fact, it is a very practical robot which can carry heavy objects on complex terrains. It looks like a big steel dog. Wild Cat, as the name suggests, has a fast-moving ability. It's running speed can reach 40 km/h.

There is a type of robot that people may often overlook or be confused upon. That is the self-driving cars. In fact, this is a type of robot, too. In addition, there are also many robots in the factories, such as industrial arms and machine tools that can be used to grasp, assemble, and weld.

Manufacturing and using robots has become the consensus of the world. In 2013, the estimated operational stock of multipurpose industrial robots showed that Japan ranked first in the world with a 23% share, followed by the United States with a 14% share. However, in 2015, two years later, Japan's share fell to 18%, followed by China with 16% of the share, ranking second in the world in one fell swoop. By 2018, China has leapt to number one in the world. China's industrial robots are growing rapidly.

Behind the rapid global increase in the number of robots is actually a problem commonly faced by most countries' aging populations. Japan's aging problem is particularly prominent. An aging society has led to a rapid decrease in the labor force, which will cause serious damage to industry and economy.

China also has a similar situation. Over time, China's elderly population will continue to increase and the labor force will further shrink. This will become an urgent problem for an aging society in the years to come.

In this case, robots came into being.

Robots can take on most of the work: they can act as construction workers to build homes, as nurses to take care of children, as doctors to perform operations on people, and they can become teachers and so on. In an aging society, there is a shortage of labor which robots can fill up.

The function of the robot is not only as is mentioned above. In the future, people will not only need more industrial robots，we also need more service robots. These robots can be used in all aspects of people's lives, such as housework, nursing, medical care, security and so on. Robots originally used in industry will gradually enter people's lives.

The sweeping robot commonly used in your home is actually a typical service robot. In addition, service robots include security robots commonly used for patrols on campuses, and healing robot which looks like a small seal. For patients with limited mobility, there are also robots dedicated to daily care, which can meet the daily needs of patients in diet (Image 3).

Service robots also include entertainment robots, which can sing, dance, and play music like real people; they can also be used for education. Perhaps one day in the future, robots can also become teachers on the podium!

There are also some medical service robots that can be used to perform minimally invasive surgery. Compared with humans, medical robots are more precise, calmer, and have less physical and psychological burden. Many such medical robots have been developed in my laboratory.

In fact, construction robots also occupy an important position in the field of robotics. Japan has been developing construction robots since the 1970s. These robots can be used to mix concrete, weld steel frames, spray fireproof materials, and so on. However, the process of putting construction robots into use has not been smooth all the way. After all, at that time, they had sufficient young and middle-aged people to work, and the cost of hiring construction workers could be much lower. But for Japan, which is now entering an aging society, construction robots can play a bigger role.

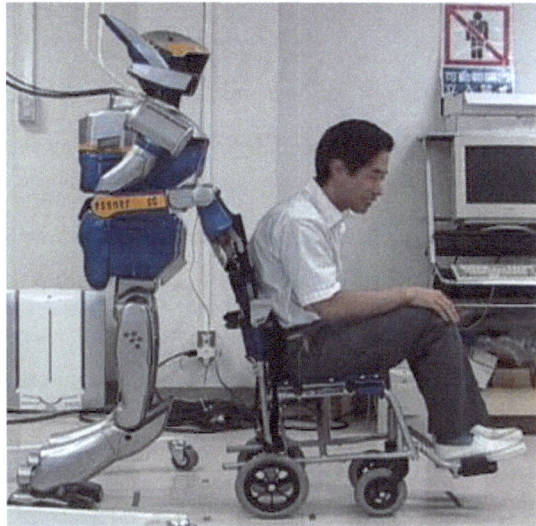

Image 3　A robot that can be used for daily care

There are also robots in the agricultural field, such as robots for automatic sowing and harvesting, robots that can remotely mowing grass, and so on.The application of agricultural robots has greatly improved the efficiency of agricultural work. By controlling the robots, more things can be accomplished with less human interference, and the number of labor requirements will be reduced.

In China, we can also see many robots, and many have already entered the market and people's daily lives. For example, food delivery robots often used in hotels and restaurants, security robots used in exhibition halls and campuses, robot toys used to inspire intelligence and so on.

After introducing so many kinds of robots, everyone must be very curious about how robots are made. The following is the design concept of the robot.

We need to design automated machines and systems through modeling morphology, functions, and intelligence of life. The shape of the robot generally refers to various life forms, such as the spiders and seals that appeared in nature. It can also refer to human forms and so on. The functions of the robot include climbing, transportation, medical treatment, etc. The shape needs to be adjusted according to the function. Finally, we need to give the robot life intelligence to realize its automated operation.

Although there is no magical robot like Doraemon, and the level of intelligence of robots cannot reach the level of human beings, the convenience brought by robots to humans has penetrated into all aspects of people's lives. Their roles can be large enough to support a country's economy and fill labor vacancies, yet also small enough to accompany you, take care of you, and heal you. It can be said that what you need will be realized by robots one day. They have advantages in size and function that humans cannot reach, and they have the most heartwarming mission-to make human life happier.

I designed a miniature robot in my laboratory. It can grasp objects as small as one millimeter, and even grasp cells. Such precise capabilities allow it to play a huge role in the field of medical biology. For example, by grabbing cells to investigate the state of human cells, it can even be used for cloning (Image 4).

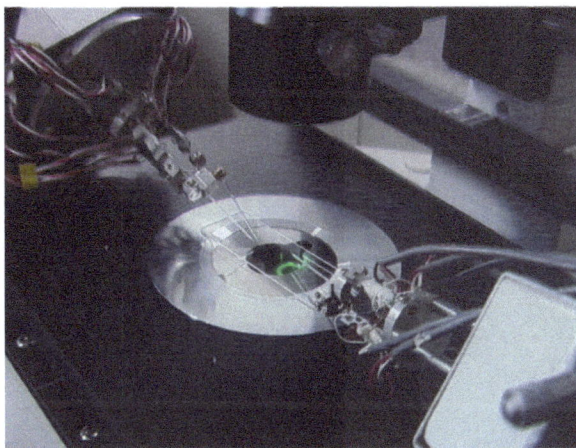

Image 4   A robot which can grab objects as small as
one millimeter

Knowing so many magical robots, presumably children have also developed a lot of interest in the world of robots. I hope that more and more people will make achievements in the field of robots in the future and overcome the problem of aging population!

(Tang Qingchao contributed to this article)

About the Author

Tatsuo Arai was born in Japan in 1952 and entered Beijing Institute of Technology in 2017. He is currently a professor at Beijing Institute of Technology and an Honorary Professor at Osaka University, Japan. The main research direction is the application of micro-robots in Biology.

纳米科技：从晶体管的发明到纳米技术的兴起

文 / 亨利·阿达姆松（瑞典） 译 / 黄稊茵

纳米技术是属于微小世界的科学。当今，纳米技术无处不在，已经充分融入了人们的日常生活之中，也将在未来扮演更加重要的角色。纳米材料的制作需要极高的成本与最先进的科技。在本文中，我将同你一起探索纳米技术的世界，包括它在现实生活中的重要运用、它的工作原理（主要是纳米晶体管）及它为我们带来的无限可能。

如图 1 所示，如果我们把 1 毫米的长度放大、再放大，我们会发现——头发的粗细不过是这 1 毫米的 1/10；细胞还要小，是 1 毫米的 1/50；细菌是 1/100；病毒甚至小到只有它的 1/1000~1/10 000；比一个病毒还小的就是分子和原子了。

图 1 中画阴影的部分就是我们纳米工程技术的研究范围。其中一个重要部件就是纳米晶体管。它的大小仅仅如同病毒一般，却是纳米技术里不可或缺的一分子。另一个重要的成员是碳素管，它在未来将对癌症的治疗起到重大作用。在接下来的文章中，我会带你们熟悉它们。

纳米技术已经在我们的生活中得到了广泛运用，如食品农业、生物医药、

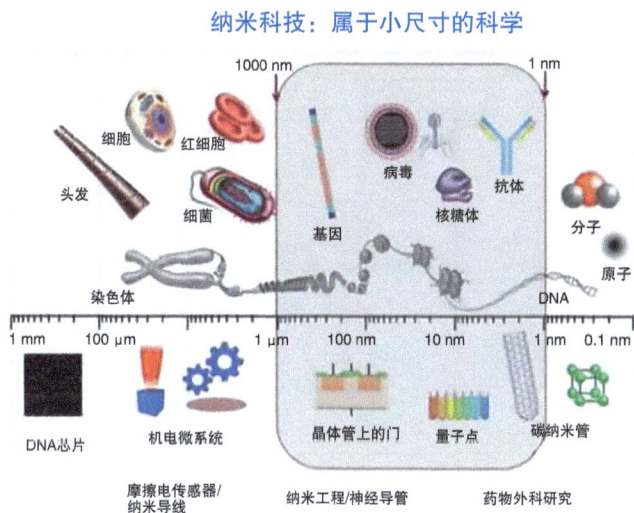

图 1　纳米在 1 毫米中所处的位置

能源储备及电子科技行业。纳米材料可以做成防水材料，如我们都熟悉的阿迪达斯运动鞋就运用了这一技术。除此之外，纳米材料还是抗衰老护肤霜的原料之一。纳米护肤品一经推出就得到了女士们的一致青睐。还有，许多电子设备的显示屏也用到了纳米材料。可是，纳米材料实在太小了，在加工过程中非常难处理，导致并不是所有人都能生产、运用纳米级的材料。也正是因为它的"小"，纳米实验室中必须保证没有任何其他微小颗粒的干扰。在这样的实验室要求下，研究人员必须用罩衣和帽子把他们的身体和头发都包起来，这也让工作的难度有所加大。图 2 就是我的团队在纳米实验室里工作的场景。

　　我们团队在纳米技术研究中最突出的领域是纳米光子学、纳米电子学和纳米医学。我们在研究这样一个概念，叫作"纳米医院"。我们希望将传统意义上治病救人的医院转移到人们的身体内部。科学家先在人体内搭起一个"纳米医院"，然后再把纳米材料放在碳素管中，又把碳素管放入"纳米医院"内。这

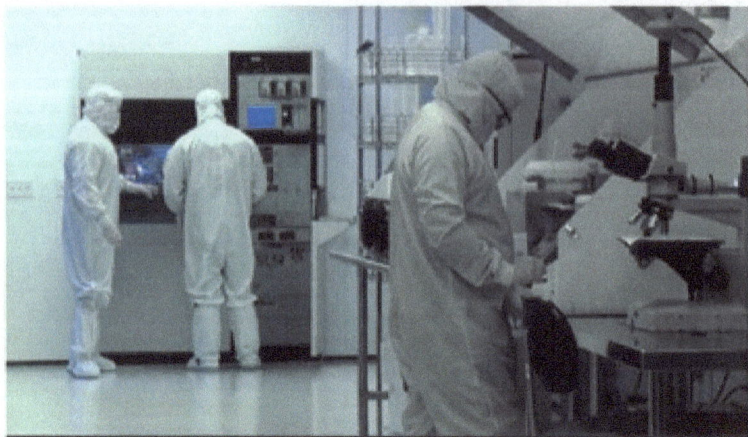

图2　纳米技术加工工艺实验室及亨利教授的团队

就可以将患者血液中的病毒隔离开，并精准地把它们消灭干净。我们还可以想象一下，如果我们身体内部有一个小机器人，可以通过编程对它进行操控，那么在这种纳米机器人的帮助下，我们不需要研发新的疫苗就可以消灭体内存在的冠状病毒。我们把这些能够帮助我们治病的小机器人称作"纳米机器人"（Nanorobot）。

此外，纳米光子学也是一个重要的研究方向（图3）。不可见光常被称作红外光。运用纳米技术，我们可以制造一种可以捕捉到红外光的摄像机，使我们能够在黑暗中或云层里仍然拥有清晰的视觉。更重要的是，这种摄像机运用的短波红外成像技术还能协助我们检测到人体内部的癌细胞。

当晶体管晶片与设计的纳米材料（如锗）连接使用时，它们就变成了一个短波红外成像设备。红外光被纳米材料吸收，然后由晶体管放大，最终产生出电信号。这种类型的摄像头现在被广泛安装在汽车的前部，以帮助司机在夜间驾驶时拥有更加清晰的道路视野。这样一来，夜间行车的安全性就得到了提高。

除此之外，纳米技术在其他方面也有许多应用，如癌症的治疗。在碳素管

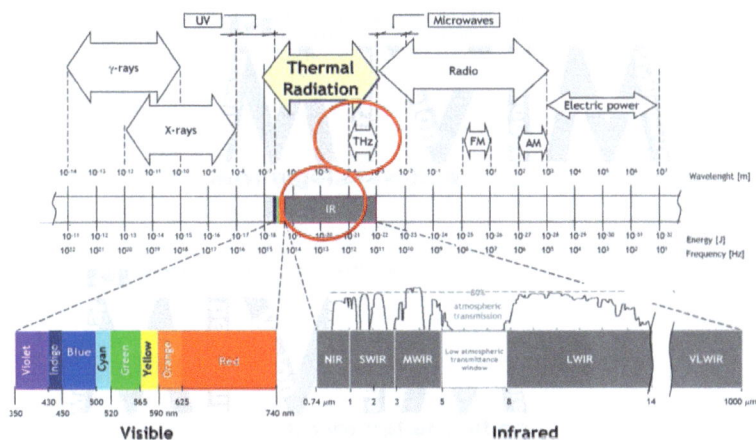

红外和太赫兹成像

图3　纳米光子学

的帮助下，药品可以被直接输送到病灶部位。我们的研究在未来的一个重要方向就是利用短波红外成像技术快速、方便地检测乳腺癌。

在许多情况下，肿瘤必须切除。但外科医生常常没办法一下子弄清楚肿瘤生长的数量。于是，许多癌症患者可能会遇到癌症复发的情况。一个原因是癌细胞不能被准确定位和追踪，导致其没能被完全清除，而残留的癌细胞就增加了患者再次患病的风险。就像人在黑暗中看不见路一样，我们也看不清人体内的癌细胞。这时纳米技术就非常有用。基于太赫兹技术，波长较长的光可以照射到身体的癌变部位并进行对比。摄像头可以获取癌变部位的图像并显示在iPad上。这样外科医生就可以清晰地观察癌变部位的具体情况，轻松切除所有的肿瘤。

除了医学，在未来，纳米技术还可以用于找出利用身体携带枪支炸药的恐怖分子。太赫兹源可以向被测物体发送波段，而波在遇到金属和爆炸材料时会发生反射。此时，带有纳米材料阵列的照相机可以接收到反射回来的波。纳米技术在安全监控和反恐战争中能够发挥出关键性的作用。

将来，纳米芯片可以与人脑相连接，帮助收集、整合我们的记忆，这样人类再也不需要花时间学习就可以直接记住许多知识。例如，一个纳米芯片可以储存学习一种语言所需要的所有信息，如果科学家将这个芯片与人脑连接，人不用坐在教室里学习就能轻松掌握这门语言。

说完了上面这些纳米技术的广泛运用后，让我们更加深入地探索一下纳米晶体管与纳米电子技术的世界吧。1947年，第一个移动电话诞生了。当时它还非常大，且只在军事活动中使用。商业用的移动电话出现于1983年，但是它当时的价格达到了惊人的4000美元，是富人才买得起的奢侈品。不过，移动电话现在正变得越来越小，几乎人手一个。这是为什么呢？

如果我们拆开一个移动电话，仔细观察它的内部结构，我们会发现里面有许多的集成电路。我们接着打开集成电路，会发现里面有数以百万计的晶体管（图4）。这就是现在为什么手机越变越小、越来越流行的秘密。晶体管由3个

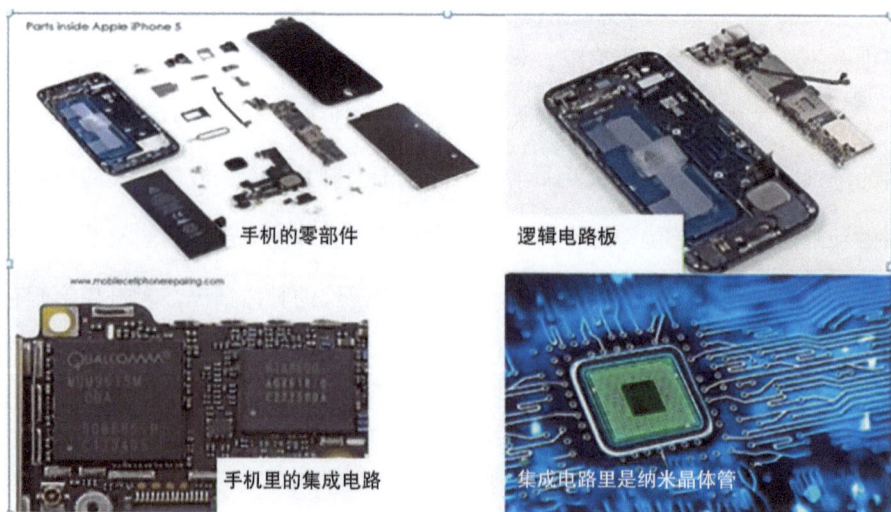

手机的零部件

逻辑电路板

手机里的集成电路

集成电路里是纳米晶体管

图4　手机里面是什么样子的？

部分组成：漏极、栅极、源极。电子们会从源极流向漏极。我们可以通过关上栅极来控制它们的流动。我们用水和阀门来举例说明：当水在管子里从上到下流动时，如果我们关上位于中间的阀门，水就不会继续流下去了。

晶体管有许多类型，最常见的两种是场效应晶体管和双极型晶体管。晶体管可以作为开关来打开或关闭电子传输，也可以放大电信号。例如，计算机中的双极型晶体管就可以放大电子信号。又如，你在旅行时会需要 GPS 来导航，GPS 的信号来自地球周围的卫星，这种信号非常小，但晶体管就可以解决这个问题。它通过放大接收到的信号来指引你到达目的地。

双极型晶体管的另一个应用是安装在麦克风、手机等设备中的小天线。我本人用正常声音说话是很难让一整个大教室中的人都听清的。但是有了麦克风后，大家都可以听得一清二楚。这是因为麦克风中的晶体管将我的声音信号放大了。

对过去一个世纪中的历史事件和趋势的认识可以帮助我们更好地了解未来的一系列可能。第一支晶体管是由 3 位美国工程师在 1956 年发明的——他们是威廉·肖克利、约翰·巴丁和沃尔特·布拉顿。它是一个双极型晶体管，比今天的晶体管要大得多。

晶体管的发现后来获得了诺贝尔奖。可不幸的是，当时还没有人完全认识到它的潜力，以及它会给我们未来的生活带来多么巨大的影响。在报纸上，晶体管的发现只占了一个小专栏，没有激起多大的水花。的确，在那个时期，没有人意识到晶体管的无限可能。

两年后的 1958 年，杰克·基尔比发明了第一个集成电路，简单地说，就是把晶体管集合起来形成电路。而后，两名工程师——罗伯特·诺夫斯和果根·摩尔——联手创办了一家名为英特尔的新公司。这两位创始人的经营理念是制造各式各样的集成电路，并逐年提高业绩。为了获得更多的利润，他们制定了目标：定期增加晶体管的数量，或减小芯片中晶体管的尺寸。这个就是后来半导体技术中著名的"摩尔定律"。根据摩尔定律，每过 18~24 个月，集成电路中的晶体管数量就要翻一番。

这个定律对手机的功耗有直接的影响。过去的手机需要 1.5 个供电电压，而现在只需 0.7 个左右。因此，当晶体管的体积变小、能耗更低时，手机电池就变得越来越薄了。这么多年来，晶体管的设计一直是二维的，但今天我们已经有了三维的晶体管，性能也变得非常高效。手机的功能大大增加，智能手机也越发方便。摩尔定律已经即将达到其自身的极限，而新的定律也将很快被制定出来，从而进一步优化晶体管。

在未来，我们还将尝试和测试新材料的运用，并利用它们继续生产未来的晶体管。你听说过石墨烯吗？这是一种实用的碳材料，非常适合制作晶体管。等到某一天，当你在纳米领域工作时，你就会明白纳米技术在改善人类生活方面具有巨大的潜力和能力。我真诚地欢迎你们从事纳米技术的工作，成为社会生产中的优秀一员。

作者简介

　　亨利·阿达姆松（Henry H. Radamson）是一名纳米科学领域的教授，以研究员的身份供职于中国科学院微电子研究所和瑞典皇家理工学院，同时也是斯德哥尔摩 Nocilis Materials 公司的联合创始人之一。目前，阿达姆松教授在国际期刊上发表 SCI 论文已有 230 余篇，其中包括 2 本科学专著，3 篇评论文章和 7 个书籍章节。

扫描收看
本文视频课程

Nanotechnology: from Discovery of Transistor to Emerging of Nanotechnology

By Henry H. Radamson (Sweden)

Nanotechnology is a science of small sizes. It is omnipresent in people's daily life now and will also be playing a more important role in the future. The cost of nano materials is high, and we have to apply advanced technology. In this article, we will explore the world of Nanotechnology together with its significance in the real-life application, its working principles, main transistors and the possibilities it will bring to us.

If we magnify the length of 1 millimeter, we will find that hair is 10 times as small as 1 mm. Cells in our body are 50 times smaller than 1 mm, bacteria 100 times, virus 1000 even 10000 times. The following are the molecular and atom. Atoms are the smallest unit that everything is made of.

Nanoengineering mainly focuses on the shadow area as is shown in Image 1. One of the elements in this shadowed area that is worth mentioning is the Gates of Transistors. A transistor, with its size as small as the virus, is an indispensable component in nanotechnology. The other important element is carbon nanotubes(CNT), which will be significant in curing cancers one day. I will explain more specifically in the later paragraph.

Nanotechnology has already been widely applied in our routine life such as agriculture

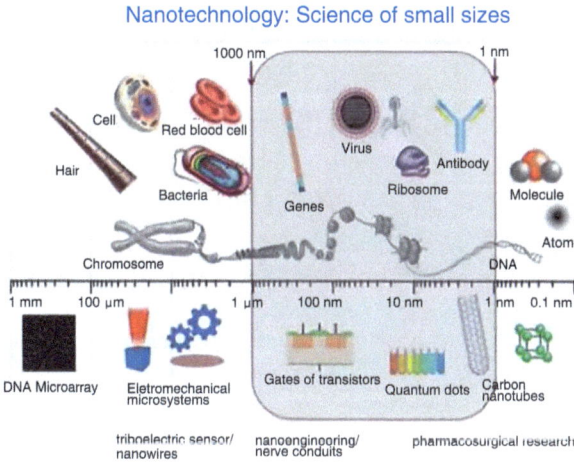

Image 1　Location of nm within 1 mm range

and food, bio-medical, energy storage and electronics. Nanomaterials can make water resistive material which can be used in shoes, like Adidas. Also, nanomaterials can help produce anti-wrinkle cream, which is very welcomed by women who are worried about the aging of their skins. Other than these, many mobile displays also use nanomaterials. You have nanomaterials almost everywhere. People, however, seldom put it on table because they are scared that it is too small to deal with. Its small size makes it a must that laboratory should have essentially no particles. To work in such a lab, researchers should cover their body and hair. Therefore, under these conditions, you will find it hard to move around at ease . This is exactly how my team works as shown in Image 2.

The most significant applications of our research are in nanophotonics, nanoelectronics and nanomedicine. One focus could be towards transplanting the concept of physical hospital to people's inner body. In such case, we create a nano-hospital where nanomaterials are put inside to isolate the virus from patients' blood and kill them accurately. Moreover, imagine if there is a small robot in our body that can be controlled through programming. They can even fight against coronavirus without inventing vaccine. We call these small robots which are able to fix innate health problems "nanorobots".

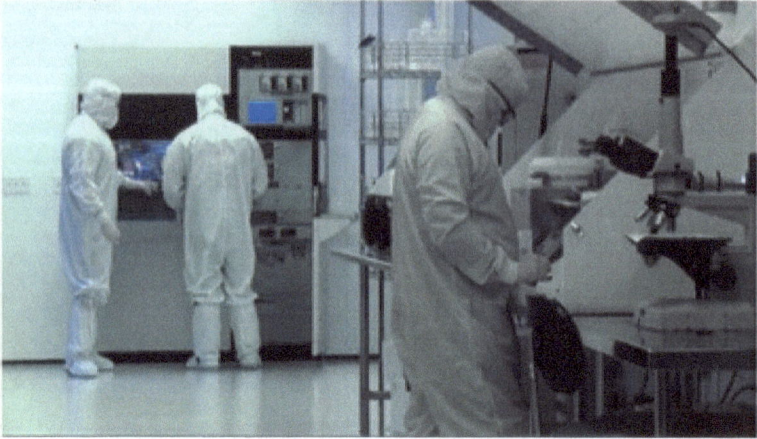

Image 2   Nanotechnology process laboratory

In addition, nanophotonics also matters (Image 3). Invisible light is often called infrared light. Nanotechnology can help to fabricate a camera which enables us to see clear in the darkness or through clouds and, more importantly, detect cancer cells by using short wavelength infrared (SWIR).

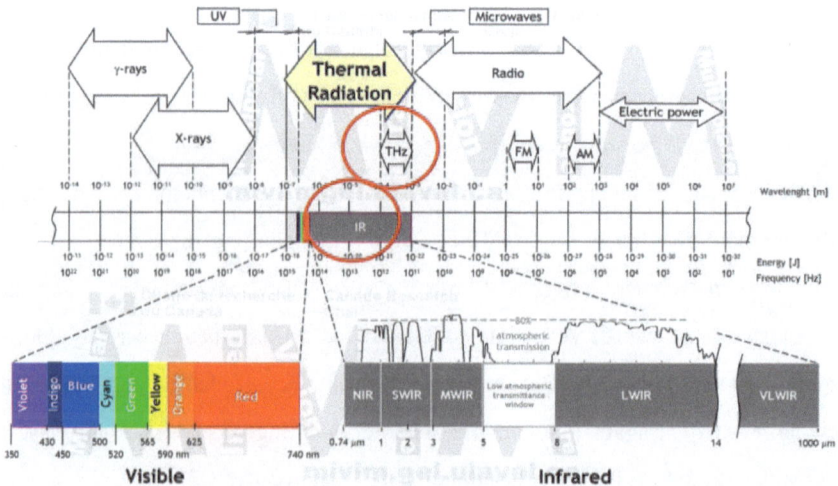

Image 3   Nanophotonics: Imaging of IR and Teraherz

SWIR imaging devices are manufactured when the transistor wafer is connected to the designed nanomaterials such as germanium. The electrical signals are created when infrared light is absorbed by the nanomaterials and later are amplified by the transistors. This type of camera is now inserted in the front of cars to help the driver to have better vision when driving in the night. In this way, the safety on the roads is increased.

There are also other applications of nanotechnology in medicine which could be applied to cure cancer. With the help of carbon tubes, the drug could be pin-pointedly delivered to the cancer tumors and make a better condition for the patients to fight against this disease. One important outcome from our research is SWIR imaging to scan for breast cancer easily in the future. In many cases, the cancer tumors have to be removed but the amount of the cancer growth is often not clear for surgeons. Then, many cancer patients may die when the cancer comes back after some time. This is due to the difficulty that cancer cells could not be accurately located and tracked, thus not being removed completely. Otherwise the remained cancer cells increase the risk for the patients to be ill again. However, just as people cannot see in the darkness, we cannot clearly see the cancer cells in people's body. Therefore, nanotechnology matters.

Based on terahertz technology, light with long wavelength may shine on the cancerous part of the body and make a contrast of the cancer cells which helps the surgeon to easily remove the tumor as shown in the picture. The image obtained by the camera will be displayed on the iPad, so that cancer cells can be easily observed.

In addition to nanomedicine, future nanotechnology can also contribute to discovering the terrorists who have guns or bombs in their bodies by using THz imaging. A THz source can send waves to the subjects and then the waves would be reflected in presence of metals and explosive materials where the camera with nanomaterials arrays can receive it. Therefore, nanotechnology plays an important role for surveillance and wars against terrorism.

In future, nanochips can be associated with human's brain helping to collect memories so that people can memorize knowledge without spending time learning. For instance, a chip can store all information of a language. If scientists may connect the chips to the brains, people then don't need to spend a lot of time any more in the classroom but still can learn and manage to speak a new language instantly, thanks to the chip.

After explaining the wide application of nanotechnology, we are going to dig deeper into the nano transistor world, talking about nanoelectronics in the following paragraphs.

The first mobile phone in 1947 was very big and was used only for military applications. The commercial one appeared in 1983 which was considered as a luxury, costing almost 4000 dollars. But as we know, mobile phones are getting smaller and smaller and nowadays are accessible almost to everyone. Why does it become smaller and cheaper?

If we dismantle a phone and look into its inner structure, we will see there are several integrated circuits (IC). Continually, we open the IC, there are millions of nano transistors inside (Image 4). These are the secrets to the popularity of mobile phones nowadays. Transistors consist of 3 parts—the drain, the gate and the source. Specifically, the electrons are going from the source to the drain, and we can close this transport with this gate. To better understand this electron transport, I use water and valve as a metaphor. Water is equal to the electrons and valve is the gate. When we close the valve, water is stopped from flowing down.

Parts of the mobile phone   Logic board

ICs inside the mobile phone   Inside ICS are nano transistors

Image 4   How does it look like inside a mobile phone?

There are many types of transistors, but two of them are most common ones: field effect transistors (FET) and bipolar transistors (BT). The transistors operate either as a switch to close and open the electron transport as the water valve or to amplify the electrical signals. For example, the transistors in computers are of the bipolar type and amplify the electron signals. For instance, if you want to go to a certain address, you will need the guidance of the Global Positioning Satellites (GPS). The signal of GPS comes from the satellites around earth. Transistors in GPS can resolve this issue by amplifying the signals and thus leading you to the destination. The other application of bipolar transistors is in microphone or mobile phone's antenna. As an example, my voice is not high enough to be heard clearly in a huge classroom. With the help of a microphone, however, this goal can be fulfilled. This is because of the transistors in the microphone that amplify my voice signals.

Understanding historical events and trends, especially over the past century, gives a better understanding and knowledge to even greater events about to take place in the future. Regarding the history of transistors, the first one was invented by three American engineers, William Shockley, John Bardeen, and Walter Brattain in 1956. The first transistor was bipolar type and was much bigger than today's transistors. The discovery of transistor won the Nobel Prize. Unfortunately, nobody understood and recognized its potential and huge impact it can bring to our life in the future. In the newspapers, the discovery of transistors received a little column and caught very little attention. Indeed, during that period, nobody realized the endless possibilities of transistors.

Two years later, in 1958, there is another person named Jack Kilby who made the first IC. Simply, the transistors were integrated in a circuit or integrated circuit, IC. Later, two engineers, Robert Novce and Gorgon Moore who worked at Fairchild Semiconductor Company resigned in order to obtain better working conditions. They started a new company called Intel. The business idea of the founders was to fabricate various ICs and increase their performance year by year. In order to make more profits, they aimed to increase regularly the number of transistors or decrease the size of the transistors in the chip. This roadmap was later named as the famous Moore's Law in the semiconductor technology.

The Moore's Law requires the doubling of the number of transistors every 18-24 months. This has a direct effect on the power consumption of the mobile phones. In the past, the mobile phones needed 1.5 supply voltage, but nowadays it is only around 0.7 voltage. As a result, batteries became much thinner when the mobile phones consume significantly lower energy due to the smaller size of transistors. for many years, the transistors had a 2-dimentional (2D) design but today's transistors are 3D whose performance has become remarkably better. At the same time, the range of functions has been increased in the mobile phones. That's why our smartphone is constantly more and more convenient. Moore's law is going to reach its limit soon in the future, and a new law will be created to further improve the transistors.

In the future, we will also try and test new materials, utilizing them to produce future transistors. Have you ever heard of graphene? This is one of the practical materials made of carbon, suitable for transistors. We will not go through more materials here, since they may be difficult for you to understand now. But someday, when you really work in the nano business, you will understand this. Nanotechnology has huge potential and capability to improve human's life. I sincerely welcome you to work in nanotechnology and become a productive member of the society.

(Huang Zixi contributed to this article)

About the Author

Henry H. Radamson is a professor in Nanotechnology. He is a researcher of the Integrated Circuit Advanced Process R&D Center of IMECAS (ICAC IMECAS), a researcher in semiconducting material of KTH Royal Institute of Technology, and co-founder of Nocilis Materials Company. Until now, Prof. Radamson has published more than 230 SCI papers in international journals, including 2 scientific monographs, 3 review articles and 7 chapters in some books.

天体物理学和黑洞

文 / 瑞尼 · 威尔海姆 · 思博森（德国） 译 / 孙梦格

我叫思博森，来自中国科学院国家天文台（National Astronomical Observatories）。现在，我和我的团队正在筹办一个名为"丝绸之路计划"的大项目。我们团队关注的主题包括行星系统、星团、星系和星系核、黑洞和引力波发射相关的演化计算问题。我们研究的领域主要有：静止和活跃的星系核中的双重超大质量黑洞和引力波、星系核和致密星团中恒星和气体的动力学演化、行星系统（在星团中）如何形成和演化，以及我们应该如何设计速度更快、能耗更低的超级计算机。

我们的两个主要项目节点分别位于中国北京（NAOC 和 KIAA）和德国海德堡（ZAH-ARI）；我们与基辅（乌克兰）、阿拉木图（哈萨克斯坦）及其他一些国家（如智利、意大利、英国、巴基斯坦、奥地利等）的机构和同事有着密切的合作。我们长期致力于中外新型超算设施的教学和推广应用。我们的项目在中、德两国间起到了桥梁的作用，同时还与亚、欧、美三大洲之间建立了众多的联系。通过这个桥梁，我们可以实现学生、知识和科学家的交换，共同为技术创新而努力，也为不同文化间的相互尊重和理解而努力。

国家天文台的总部设在北京。我们的机构在中国的很多地方都设有分站，如长春和乌鲁木齐。这些分站都配备有大型的天文仪器。有时候，我会在北京大学科维里天文与天体物理研究所办公。我在德国海德堡大学还有一个办公室。在我们的科学院团队里，大家都来自不同的国家和地区，在文化上可谓非常的多元。

我希望本文能给你一些启发：也许你会想成为一名天文学或物理学的科学家；也许在今后，你也会在一所顶尖大学的实验室里工作。希望在不久的将来，我们能有机会一起合作！

天文学和天体物理学

当在夜晚仰望天空的时候，我们会看到一颗颗小星星。小时候，我曾经对它们非常着迷。每当在夜晚凝视它们的时候，我都会想知道它们的秘密。长大后，我意识到，为了更好地观察和研究它们，我需要学习更多的数学和物理知识。而把这些知识结合起来的学科就是天文学。于是，我选择了天文学和天体物理学作为自己未来的努力方向。那么，天文学是什么？天体物理学家又是做什么的呢？让我们一起来了解一下吧。

天文观测——望远镜

在天文学中，科学家们会利用望远镜来更好地观测星空。你可能已经很熟悉望远镜了。望远镜是我们用来观测远方物体的仪器。然而，天文学家使用的望远镜要比普通的望远镜大得多、复杂得多。

现在，让我向大家介绍一些目前世界上最先进的天文望远镜吧。例如，哈勃太空望远镜（常被称为 HST 或哈勃）是为了纪念伟大的天文学家埃德温·哈勃而命名的。哈勃是一个大型的天基天文台，自1990年由"发现"号航天飞机发射和部署以来，它为天文学研究带来了革命性的变化。哈勃至今仍在太空中运行，是世界上最大、用途最广、最著名的望远镜之一。你可以在NASA的网站上找到更多关于哈勃的详细描述和图片（图1）。

图1　哈勃太空望远镜（图源：NASA）

我还想向大家介绍位于智利的欧洲南方天文台（ESO）。ESO在智利运营有3个非常独特的世界级观测点。图2就是位于2600米高的帕拉纳尔站点的

VLT（甚大望远镜阵列）。帕拉纳尔站点称得上是欧洲天文学的旗舰设施。它坐落于智利安托法加斯塔以南约130千米处、距离太平洋海岸12千米的内陆。这里是世界上最干燥的地区之一。(https://www.eso.org/public/about-eso/esoglance/)

VLT是一种很不寻常的

图2　位于帕拉纳尔站点的VLT

望远镜。它其实是一个由 4 台单元式望远镜组成的阵列，每台主镜的直径为 8.2 米。在一个小时的曝光时间内，一台单元望远镜就可以生成微弱到 30 级的天体图像。这相当于观测到了比肉眼所见的天体暗淡 40 亿倍的天体。（https://www. eso.org/public/about-eso/esoglance/）

图 3 中的望远镜大家一定非常熟悉。它就是 500 米口径球面望远镜（FAST），绰号"天眼"。FAST 是中国建设的世界上最大的单碟射电望远镜。它位于贵州"大窝凼"洼地天然盆地中，由一个直径 500 米的固定天线组成，与自然景观融为一体。FAST 于 2011 年 3 月开工建设，于 2016 年 9 月 25 日首次点亮，2020 年 1 月 11 日宣布全面投入使用。"天眼"的设计很新颖，采用了金属板制成的活动表面，可以通过计算机控制角度，帮助将焦点对焦到天

图 3　500 米口径球面望远镜（FAST）

空的不同区域。

天体物理学——太阳系

天体物理学是天文学的一个分支，它运用物理学、数学和化学的原理来研究恒星、太阳、星系和太阳系外行星等天体的性质。作为天体物理学家，我们非常想透彻地了解整个宇宙，以及我们在其中身处的位置。

天体物理学家对我们的太阳系很感兴趣。宇宙中有许多行星系统。我们的行星系统被命名为太阳系（Solar System），因为太阳在拉丁文中被命名为"Sol"。

我们的太阳系包括太阳和 4 颗类地行星——地球、水星、金星和火星。它们之所以被称为类地行星，是因为它们有一个紧凑的、像地球一样的岩石表面。除此之外，还有 4 颗气态巨行星，分别是木星、土星、天王星和海王星。与类地行星不同的是，气态巨行星的成分多为气体，如氢气和氦气。我们的太阳系还有冥王星等矮行星、几十颗卫星和数百万颗小行星、彗星和流星体。

直到现在，太阳系仍在不断带给我们惊喜。例如，加州理工学院的天文学家迈克·布朗领导的团队在 2003 年发现太阳系中的一颗矮行星"塞德娜"。在搜索过程中，布朗的团队利用了帕洛玛天文台的"塞缪尔·奥斯钦"望远镜。塞德娜是太阳系中发现的最遥远的天体之一，有人说，它处于"太阳系中最孤独的地方"。塞德娜有一个围绕太阳的高度椭圆形轨道，这意味着它离太阳的距离从近日点的 76 个天文单位（AU）到远日点的 936 个 AU 不等。而它绕着太阳运行一圈可能需要超过 1 万年的时间。AU 是天文学中的长度单位，大概等于从地球到太阳的距离。现在你知道它离我们有多远了吧，这也是为什么我们称它为最孤独的一个（图 4）。

天体物理学还关注恒星的"生死"。在历史上很长一段时间里，我们认为恒

图4　在矮行星塞德娜上看地球和内太阳系（艺术渲染）

星是恒定存在的，它们只是在那里，没有变化，也不会去任何地方。后来，在大望远镜的帮助下，我们发现事情并没有那么简单。

虽然星星没有生命，但我们仍然可以用"生死"来比喻它们的起源和终结。望远镜帮助我们发现了宇宙中美丽的星云，这可以为我们了解恒星的演变提供线索。

简而言之，星云是占据实际空间的巨大尘埃和气体云。有些星云来自垂死的恒星（如超新星）爆炸时抛出的气体和尘埃；另一些星云则是新恒星开始形成的区域。中国古代有关于超新星爆炸的记录。中国宋代的天文学家记载到，在1054年，他们观测到天球上有一颗明亮的恒星，它在日光下可见3个多星期。他们把它称为"客星"（图5）。直到1731年，

图5　蟹状星云 (1054年的超新星）

英国天文学家约翰·贝维斯才在中国天文学家首次观测到"新星"的同一地点发现了一片星云。

黑洞

当恒星们走到生命尽头时，会发生什么呢？这要看情况了。恒星的最终命运取决于它的质量。小恒星，如我们的太阳，会坍塌形成被称为白矮星的物体。中子星则是大恒星的进化最终产物——那些大到太阳 1.4~2 倍的恒星。如果一颗垂死恒星的体积是太阳的 2 倍以上，会发生什么呢？当完全坍塌时，它会发生变化，超越中子星阶段，变成一个更小、更密集的物体。有科学家计算出，这种物体表面的引力场会变得非常强大，连光都无法逃脱，所以我们称它为黑洞。

我们能看到黑洞吗？很遗憾，答案是不能。没有任何东西，连光都逃不出黑洞。所以，我们其实是无法"看到"它的。那么，科学家是如何知道或证明黑洞的存在的呢？虽然他们不能用望远镜直接观察黑洞，但可以通过探测黑洞对附近其他物质的影响来推断黑洞的存在，并对其进行研究。其实，在大约 20 年前，恒星围绕银河系中央黑洞的运动就已经被观测到了。

既然黑洞如此强大，那我们是否有担心它们的必要呢？目前，黑洞离我们太远，还无法从太阳系中吸取任何物质。但科学家已经观察到黑洞将恒星撕裂的现象，这个过程会释放出巨大的能量。至于个人，我们其实丝毫不用担心一不小心"掉到"黑洞里面去。

我目前的研究

宇宙中有数以百万计的黑洞。有时，它们可能会发生碰撞。而黑洞间的碰撞是一个灾难性的事件。这个过程会在短时间内释放出比宇宙中所有恒星都要高的能量！不过这股能量并不会释放出亮光。它会在太空中产生"地震"，类似于我们在池塘表面看到的波浪和涟漪。而我们想要探测的就是这种引力波。

我们如何探测引力波呢？可以用"处女座"干涉仪来探测。它是一个大型干涉仪，旨在探测宇宙中远处黑洞碰撞所产生的引力波。该仪器的两臂长达3

图6 位于意大利比萨附近的"处女座"干涉仪

千米，位于意大利比萨市附近的圣斯特凡诺－马切拉塔（图6）。

我正在参与"丝绸之路计划"和MPA下的"龙模拟项目"。这是迄今为止规模最大、最逼真的大规模球状星团的直接N体模拟项目。通过高效的算法，我们可以在现代超级计算机上对百万恒星运行进行模拟，包括恒星和双星演化的算法。这种模拟能够提供有关大型球状星团动态行为的前所未有的见解。

为了实现更好的模拟效果，我们需要超级计算机的帮助。"神威·太湖之光"是中国的一台超级计算机，截至2018年11月，它的运算能力在超级计算机的五百强榜单中排名第三。太湖之光由国家并行计算机工程与技术研究中心设计，位于中国江苏省无锡市的国家超级计算中心。

作者简介

瑞尼·威尔海姆·思博森是中国科学院国家天文台研究员。思博森博士的主要研究领域包括：恒星动力学、星团、黑洞、星系核、引力波、多核超级计算和平行程序设计。

Astrophysics and Black Holes

By Rainer Wilhelm Spurzem (Germany)

My name is Rainer Spurzem, I'm a scientist from National Astronomical Observatories (NAOC), Chinese Academy of Science. Currently, I'm working on a big project called The Silk Road Project. Our team is dedicated to computational studies of the evolution of planetary systems, star clusters, galaxies and galactic nuclei, black holes and gravitational wave emission. Some of our main research projects are: Binary Supermassive Black Holes and Gravitational Waves in Quiet and Active Galactic Nuclei, Dynamical Evolution of Stars and Gas in Galactic Nuclei and Dense Star Clusters, How are planetary systems forming and evolving (in star clusters)? How can we design supercomputers which are faster and consume less energy?

Our two main project nodes are Beijing, China (NAOC and KIAA) and Heidelberg, Germany (ZAH-ARI); we collaborate closely with institutions and colleagues from Kiev (Ukraine) and Almaty (Kazakhstan) and several other countries (e.g. Chile, Italy, UK, Pakistan, Austria, etc). We are dedicated to teaching and promoting the use of new supercomputing facilities both in China and abroad. Our project is a bridge between China and Germany, with links to Asia, Europe and America. Through this bridge, we exchange students, knowledge, scientists, work together for new technologies, and also for mutual cultural respect and understanding.

The NAOC Headquarter is sited in Beijing and our institution has many locations in China, such as Changchun, Urumqi. They have all equipped with big astronomical instruments. One of my office is the Kavli Institute for Astronomy and Astrophysics in Peking University. I also work in an office in Astronomisches Rechen-Institut(ARI) at the University of Heidelberg in Germany. I work in a multi-cultural scientists team with colleagues and students from all over the world as well.

I hope you will find some inspirations in this article. Maybe your passion to become an expertise in astronomy or physics one day will be boosted and maybe you also want to work in a big lab in a top university. I hope in the near future, we will have a chance to work together!

Astronomy and Astrophysics

When we look up in the sky at night, we see stars. When I was a kid, I used to be so fascinated about them, wondering about their secrets while staring into them at night. When I grow up, I realize that, in order to better observe and study them, I need to learn more about math and physics, and the subject that combines these is the astronomy. So, I chose astronomy and astrophysics. What is astronomy? And what do astrophysicists do? Let's find out.

Astronomy Observations – Telescopes

In astronomy, scientists use telescope to better observe stars. You may be familiar with the telescope as an instrument we use to see faraway objects. However, the telescopes that astronomers use are much bigger and more complicated.

I'll introduce to you some of the world's most advanced telescopes now. For example, the first is the Hubble Space Telescope. The Hubble Space Telescope (often referred to as HST or Hubble) is named in honor of the trailblazing astronomer Edwin Hubble. It is a large, space-based observatory, which has revolutionized astronomy since its launch and deployment by the space shuttle Discovery in 1990. It remains in operation today and is one of the largest and most versatile, well-known telescopes in the world. You can find more detailed descriptions and pictures of Hubble on the website of NASA (Image 1).

Another telescope I want to show you is in the European Southern Observatory (ESO) in Chile. ESO operates three unique world-class observing sites in Chile,

Image 1　Hubble Space Telescope (Photo credit: NASA)

and the Image 2 shows the VLT (very large telescope array) in the 2600 m high Paranal site. Paranal site is the flagship facility of European astronomy and is situated about 130 km south of Antofagasta in Chile, 12 km inland from the Pacific coast, in one of the driest areas

Image 2　VLT at Paranal

of the world. (https://www.eso.org/public/about-eso/esoglance/)

The VLT is a most unusual telescope which is based on the latest technology. It is not just one, but an array of 4 Unit Telescopes, each with a main mirror measuring 8.2 metres in diameter. With one Unit Telescope, images of celestial objects as faint as magnitude 30 have been obtained in a one-hour exposure. This corresponds to observing objects that are four billion times fainter than those seen with the naked eye. (https://www.eso.org/public/about-eso/esoglance/)

The next one will be much familiar to you and it is the Five-hundred-meter Aperture Spherical Telescope (FAST), nicknamed Tianyan ("Eye of the Sky")(Image 3). FAST is a Chinese megascience project to build the largest single dish radio telescope in the world. It is located in the Dawodang depression, a natural basin in Guizhou. And it consists of a fixed 500m diameter dish constructed in the landscape.

Image 3   Five–hundred–meter Aperture Spherical Telescope (FAST)

Construction commenced in March, 2011, and FAST had first light on 25 September, 2016.

Tianyan has a novel design, using an active surface made of metal panels that can be tilted by a computer to help change the focus to different areas of the sky. Construction on the FAST project began in 2011 and it was declared fully operational on 11 January, 2020.

Astrophysics – Our Solar System

Astrophysics is the branch of astronomy that employs the principles of physics, math and chemistry to ascertain the nature of the astronomical objects like stars, the sun, galaxies and extrasolar planets. As astrophysicists, we seek to understand the universe and our place in it.

The first thing that astrophysicist really interested in is our solar system. There are many planetary systems in the universe and ours is named the solar system because our sun is named "Sol" in Latin.

Our solar system consists of the Sun, four terrestrial planets including our planet, the Earth, Mercury, Venus, and Mars. They are called terrestrial because they have a compact, rocky surface like Earth's. There are also four gas giants namely Jupiter, Saturn, Uranus and Neptune. Unlike terrestrial planets, gas giants have a mostly gaseous composition, such as hydrogen and helium. Our solar system also has dwarf planets such as Pluto, dozens of moons and millions of asteroids, comets and meteoroids.

Until now, we are still making amazing discoveries about our solar system. For example, the dwarf planet Sedna was discovered in 2003 by a team led by Mike Brown, an astronomer at the California Institute of Technology. It is discovered using the Samuel Oschin Telescope at the Palomar Observatory. Sedna is one of the most distant bodies found in our solar system, someone says that it is in "the most lonely place in our solar system". Sedna has a highly elliptical orbit around the Sun, which means it ranges in distance from 76 astronomical units (AU) at perihelion to 936 AU at aphelion. And it could take more than 10,000 years for it to orbit the Sun. AU is the astronomical unit, it is a unit of length, roughly the distance from Earth to the Sun. Now you know how far it is and why we call it the loneliest one (Image 4).

Astrophysics also focuses on the life and death of the stars. For a long time in history, we thought stars were fixed, they were just there without developing or going to anywhere. Then, with the help of the big telescopes, we have discovered that things are not that simple.

Although stars are not alive, we can still use "life and death" as metaphors to their origins and ends. For example, telescopes help us discover beautiful nebulae in the universe,

Image 4   See Earth and Inner Solar System from Dwarf planet Sedna (artist render)

which could serve as clues for us to understand the development of stars.

In short, a nebula is an enormous cloud of dust and gas occupying the space. Some nebulae (more than one nebula) come from the gas and dust thrown out by the explosion of a dying star, such as a supernova. Other nebulae are regions where new stars are beginning to form. In ancient China, there was also record of supernova explosion. Chinese astronomers of the Song dynasty documented seeing a bright star on the celestial sphere in 1054, it was visible in daylight for more than three weeks, and they classified it to be a "guest star" (Image 5). It was not until 1731 that John Bevis, an English astronomer discovered at the same location, where the Chinese astronomers first saw the "new star", a nebula.

Image 5   The Crab Nebula (supernova in the year 1054)

Black Holes

What will happen when stars "live" towards their ends? Well, it depends. The final destiny of stars depends on its mass. Small stars, such as our Sun, will collapse to form objects called white dwarfs. Neutron stars are the evolutionary end products of larger stars — those 1.4 to 2 times as large as the Sun. What happens to a dying star that is more than twice as large as the Sun? When it collapses completely, it changes beyond the neutron-star stage, to an even smaller, denser object. Some scientists calculated that the gravitational field at the surface of such an object would become so strong that even light would be unable to escape, so we called it: black hole.

Can we see black holes? The answer, unfortunately, is no. Remember nothing, not even light can escape the black holes? So we cannot actually "see" it. So, how do scientists know or prove the existence of black holes? While we can't directly observe black holes with telescopes. We can, however, infer the presence of black holes and study them by detecting their effect on other matter nearby. Actually, motion of stars moving around the central black hole in our Galaxy has been observed for about 20 years.

If the black hole is so powerful, should we be worried about them? For now, black holes are too far away to pull in any matter from our solar system. But scientists have observed black holes ripping stars apart, a process that releases a tremendous amount of energy. As for individuals, you do not need to be worried about "falling" into a black hole.

My Current Research

There are millions of black holes in our universe. Sometimes they may collide. And when it happens, it is a catastrophic event, the process will emit energy (for a short time) higher than all stars in the universe! The energy does not release light, however, it creates an earth-quake in space, similar to waves and ripples we see on the pond surface. And it is this space waves that we are trying to detect.

How can we detect gravitational waves? For example, we have the Virgo interferometer, which is a large interferometer designed to detect gravitational waves of colliding black holes far out in the universe. The instrument's two arms are three kilometers long and located in Santo Stefano a Macerata, near the city of Pisa, Italy (Image 6).

Image 6 The Virgo interferometer near the city of Pisa, Ltaly (http://www.oca.eu/ images/Artemis/slideshow/Virgo_Vueaerienne.jpg)

I'm working on the Dragon Simulation Project of NAOC (Silk Road Project) and MPA. It is the biggest and most realistic direct N-Body simulation of massive Globular Cluster (GC) so far. Efficient algorithms allow the simulations to be run on modern supercomputers for millions of stars. Including algorithms for stellar and binary evolution, the simulations offers unprecedented insights into the dynamical behavior of large GCs.

To achieve better simulation, we need the help of the supercomputers. The Sunway Taihu Light is a Chinese supercomputer which, as of November 2018, is ranked third in the TOP500 list. It was designed by the National Research Center of Parallel Computer Engineering & Technology (NRCPC) and is located at the National Supercomputing Center in the city of Wuxi, in Jiangsu Province, China.

(Sun Mengge contributed to this article)

About the Author

Rainer Wilhelm Spurzem is a fellow researcher at the National Astronomical Observatory of the Chinese Academy of Sciences. Main research areas of Dr. Spurzem include: Stellar Dynamics, Star Clusters, Black Holes, Galactic Nuclei, Gravitational Waves, Many Core Supercomputing and Parallel Programming.

狭义相对论：奇妙的时间和空间

文 / 斯蒂芬·帕克（美）　译 / 孙梦格

导论

　　我们的生活中有许多高速运动的事物，如在赛道上冲刺的跑步者，在大街上疾驰的汽车，或者是上海的磁悬浮列车。但是，我们却从未遇到过经典物理学无法描述的奇异现象。这是因为，相对于爱因斯坦提出的"光速极限"（光速用"c"表示，c = 300 000 km/s），上述物体的运动速度依旧很慢。爱因斯坦预测，当物体运动速度极快时，会发生一些很奇怪的现象。现在，通过研究爱因斯坦的相对论，我们来带领大家一起探索这个引人入胜的世界。

相对速度

　　在讲狭义相对论之前，我们先来认识一个被称为"相对速度"的概念。请思考以下情景。

　　情景 1：一列火车以相对于地面 10 m/s 的速度运动，一个人以相对于火车 2 m/s 的速度在列车上运动。请问，人相对于地面的速度是多少？

根据日常经验，我们会得出答案是 12 m/s，方法是将上述速度加在一起（10 m/s＋2 m/s＝12 m/s）。因此，火车上的人对于地面的相对速度为 12 m/s。

情景 2：火车现在以相对于地面 0.1c 的速度移动（别忘了 c 是光速的缩写），火车上的人以 0.01c（相对于火车）的速度移动，现在人相对于地面的速度是多少？

按照之前的思路，答案是 0.11c，因为 0.1c＋0.01c＝0.11c。尽管爱因斯坦的理论会告诉我们这并不完全正确，但已经很接近了（图 1）。

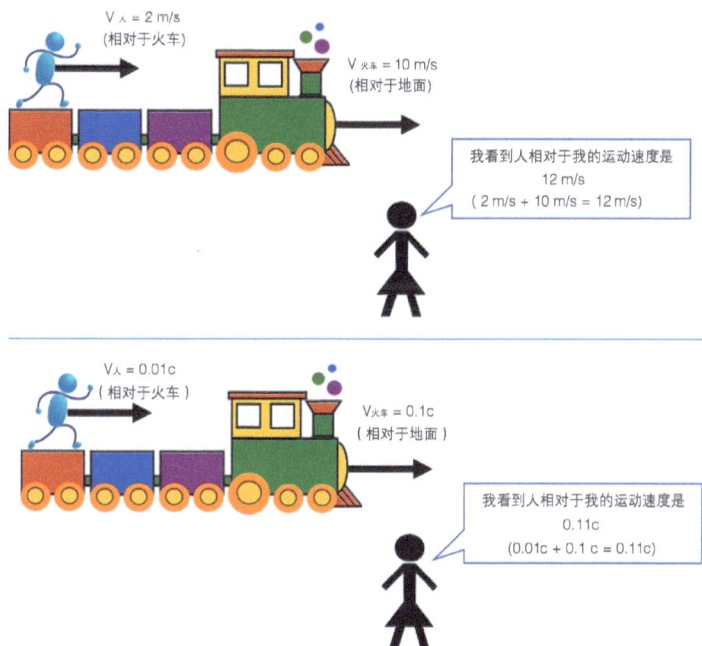

图 1 （上）速度很小时，相对速度很容易计算。如果火车以 10 m/s 相对于地面运动，火车上的人相对于车以 2 m/s 运动，则地面上的观察者会看到车上的人的相对速度是 12 m/s；（下）即便火车和人的速度分别达到 0.1c 和 0.01c，按照上述相对速度的计算法则得出的结果也没有太大偏差

即便速度已经很快，但我们的日常经验也没有发生太大变化。但当速度变得更快时，事情就不简单了。

情景 3：火车以 0.75c（相对于地面）的速度移动，而人以 0.75c（相对于火车）的速度移动。现在人相对于地面的速度是多少？

如果你认为答案是 1.5c（因为 0.75c + 0.75c = 1.5c），这就与爱因斯坦为狭义相对论所假设的基本原理相抵触了！爱因斯坦认为，没有什么能超过光速。所以，为了解决这个悖论，他需要创建一个新的规则来计算相对速度。运用这种新的计算规则，他要证明 0.75c + 0.75c = 0.96c！并且，在新的运算体系下，任何事物的运行速度都不可以超过任意参考系中的光速。

情景 4：现在火车上的人不想走路了，他打开一把手电筒，根据定义，手电筒的光（相对于火车）以光速 c 传播，火车仍以 0.75c（相对于地面）的速度

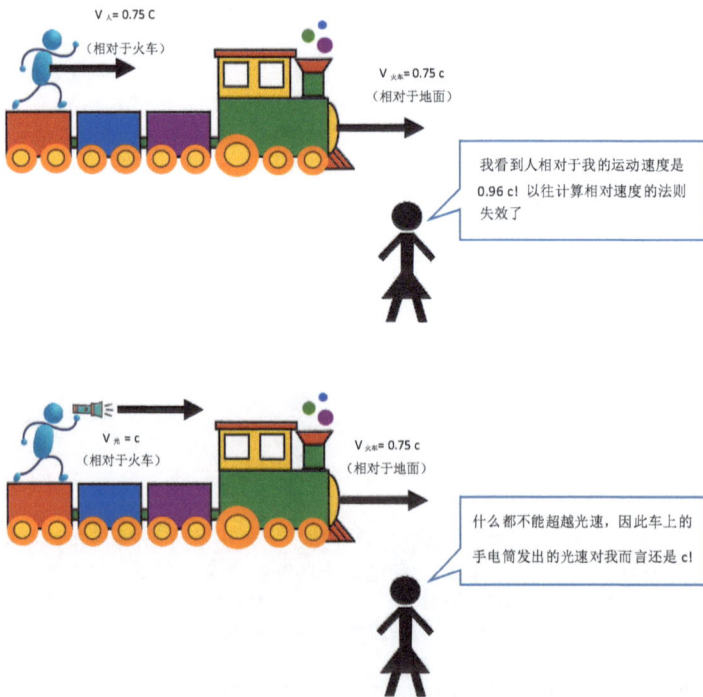

图 2 （上）当速度接近光速时，以往用简单光速计算相对速度的办法会失效；（下）如果车上的人拿着一把手电筒，它发出的光速对于车上的人和地面上观察的人而言是一致的，即无论参考系是什么，光速永远是 c

行驶。在这种情况下，光相对于地面的传播速度有多快？

因为爱因斯坦认为没有什么能超过光速，所以，如果我们用他的新法则推算出 0.75c + c = c，这就是正确答案！即使火车有速度，手电筒的光也必须相对于地面以 c 的速度移动（图 2）。因为光速就是光速！

也就是说，当以极快的速度运动时，物体会产生某种现象或发生某种变化，以此来维护此宇宙速度极限。值得注意的是，我们也经历过运动对日常生活的感官体验所产生的影响。例如，"多普勒效应"就是由于相对运动——即便速度不快——而使得声音频率发生了改变。当一辆救护车驶向观察者时，其警笛的音调会更高；而当它远离观察者时，警笛音调则会降低。

爱因斯坦告诉我们，在高速运动的世界中，时间和空间本身的结构都会发生扭曲。

时间膨胀

"时间膨胀"描述了时间在高速运动时会发生的变化。假设我在火车上随着火车移动，而你是一名地面上的观察者。火车的速度可以用来计算相对论中著名的系数 γ （希腊字母，读作" gamma"）。计算 γ 的方程我们不必太在意，但要记住 γ 必须始终等于或大于 1，并且速度越快，γ 的数值越大。作为参考，如果物体的速度是 0.75c，则 $\gamma = 1.5$。如果某物以 0.97c 的速度运动，则 $\gamma = 4$。

狭义相对论预测：

$$（静止时间） = \gamma * （运动时间）。 \tag{1}$$

因此，如果我所在的火车以 $\gamma = 2$ 的速度运动，那么我在火车上的 1 秒钟（运动时间）就相当于你在地面上的 2 秒钟（静止时间）。时间会随着运动而发生变化。我们的时钟不会保持同步。很奇怪吧！还有更奇怪的事情呢！

为了进一步探讨时间膨胀，我们来研究一下"双胞胎悖论"。所谓悖论，就是对一个问题得出的完全相反却都有道理的结论。但是，由于我们（至少在理论上）总是能用实验对结论进行验证，因此，问题应该只有一个解。

在"双胞胎悖论"中，我们假设，有一个名为 Pippi（读作"皮皮"）的小猫和一个名为 Riley（读作"莱利"）的小狗，它们在同一天出生（就像双胞胎）。Pippi 一直住在地球上，而 Riley 则坐上了宇宙飞船去旅行，Pippi 看着 Riley 乘着高速飞船向远离地球的方向运动了 8 年的时间（该时间由 Pippi 测量）。因为火箭速度很快，我们将系数 γ 设定为 4。

对于 Pippi 而言（它处于静止状态），它用爱因斯坦的方程（1）计算出运动中的 Riley 度过的时间是 2 年。如果此时 Riley 掉头返回地球，那么因为往返路程一样，Pippi 的时间又过了 8 年，而 Riley 的时间则又过了 2 年。因此，当它们再次在地球上相遇时，Pippi 已经 16 岁了，而 Riley 只有 4 岁。

但是，从 Riley 的角度来看，情况又会如何呢？对它来说，自己是静止的，而 Pippi（和地球）则相对于它在高速运动，使得 γ=4。因此，当 Riley 看着自己的表，发现在地球上的 Pippi 远离自己运动了 2 年时，按照爱因斯坦方程，Pippi 的时间应该度过了 1/2 年！此后 Pippi 和地球一起往回走，Riley 又过了 2 年，而 Pippi 又过了 1/2 年。这意味着，当它们再次相聚时，Riley 会是 4 岁，而 Pippi 只有 1 岁！（图 3）

悖论出现了！

对于 Pippi 而言，Riley 是运动的，所以当它们又在地球重逢时，Riley 是 4 岁，而 Pippi 是 16 岁（一只小狗和一只老猫）。

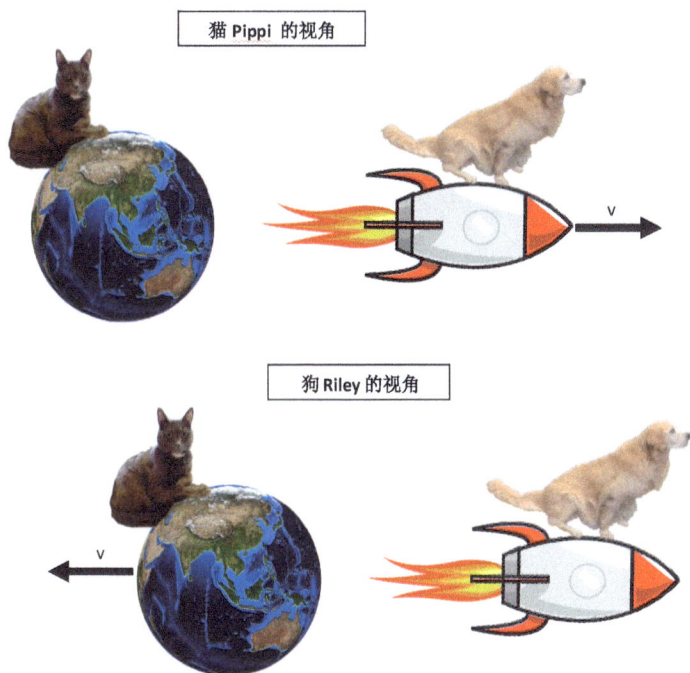

图3　（上）从猫 Pippi 的视角来看，狗 Riley 正在乘着飞船向右移动；（下）从狗 Riley 的视角来看，猫 Pippi 正在地球上向左移动

而 Riley 却说，自己认为 Pippi 是运动的，所以再次相遇时，Riley 是 4 岁，而 Pippi 只有 1 岁（一只老狗和一只小猫）。

实际情况究竟是什么样呢？

你可能会说，因为我们"知道"坐着飞船的 Riley 是运动的一方，所以应该是 Pippi 的年纪大而 Riley 的年纪小。虽然这个答案是对的，但我们还应该解答一个基本问题："我们如何知道自己是运动的，还是静止的？"

我们可以用搭乘电梯的体验来回答。当电梯向上移动时，你会觉得自己变重了（如果这时站在秤上，你的体重读数会比平时大）。在电梯运动的中段，你的体重又恢复了平常的读数。当电梯要停下时，你会感觉自己变轻了（秤的读数会比平时小）。我们现在知道怎么在人群中认出物理学家了，他们搭电梯总会带着体重计！（下次乘电梯时，你也可以试试！）

在你感受到（或测量到）体重变化时，电梯就在改变速度。在物理学中，我们称这种变化的速度为加速度。"感知"到（或测量到）加速度时，我们就处于运动状态。因此，加速度可以用来确定物体的运动状态。

回到刚才的悖论。狗狗 Riley 在返回地球的时刻会体会到加速度，因为它要让飞船向一个方向减速刹车，再向另一个方向加速，才能完成往返。感受到加速度的 Riley 就会知道自己的状态是运动的，而 Pippi 因为一直待在地球上，从未感到过加速，所以它一定是静止的。所以，Pippi 是正确的。当 Riley 走下太空船时，Pippi 已经变老了，而 Riley 还很年轻，它们不再是双胞胎了。

您可能会争辩说，这永远不会真正发生，因为我们不能造出那么快的太空飞船。但实际上，我们已经使用最精确的原子钟通过非常精确的实验看到了时间膨胀的效果。实验非常简单：我们先同步两个时钟。然后，让时钟 1 保持在地面上（使其处于静止状态），将时钟 2 放在飞机上环绕世界飞行（使其处于运动状态）。当飞机降落时，我们会发现时钟 1 和时钟 2 的时间不同步了！由于飞机的速度仍然较小（系数 γ 仅略大于 1），时钟读数的差距仅仅是数百纳秒（约 0.000 000 1 秒），但差异仍是真实存在的。由于运动，时间本身发生了变化。

我们还可以用生活中常见的导航设备——全球定位卫星（GPS）系统来观察时间膨胀的影响。导航卫星围绕地球运动，由于时间膨胀，它们的系统时钟必须不断调整，才能够正常工作。

尺度收缩

长度和距离也会因为运动状态发生改变。

狭义相对论预测：

$$(运动长度) = (静止长度) / \gamma \text{。} \tag{2}$$

如果物体以足够快的速度运动，使得 $\gamma = 2$，则静止时长度 2 m 的杆子实际上在运动时只有 1 m。物体在运动时比静止时短。为了说明这种有趣的现象，我们来看看"谷仓悖论"。

假设我有一根极易碎的玻璃杆，静止时测得的长度为 2 m。在地面上还有一个静止时测量长度为 1 m 的谷仓，两端有两扇门。

我们又叫来了狗狗 Riley 和猫猫 Pippi 一起做实验。Riley 控制谷仓左侧的门，Pippi 控制谷仓右侧的门。你和它们一起站在地面上观察这个了不起的实验。

我拿起杆子（水平于地面）快速跑向谷仓。为了好玩，假设我可以高速运动，使得 $\gamma = 2$。当杆子完全进入谷仓中，Riley 和 Pippi 会迅速关闭谷仓的门，然后立即重新打开。由于杆子的移动速度很快，通过方程（2），我们算出它相对于地面上的观察者的长度为 1 m，因此它能勉强装进 1 m 长的谷仓内。也就是说，等 Riley 和 Pippi 再把门打开，我能毫发无损地继续穿过谷仓，杆子不会折断（图 4）。

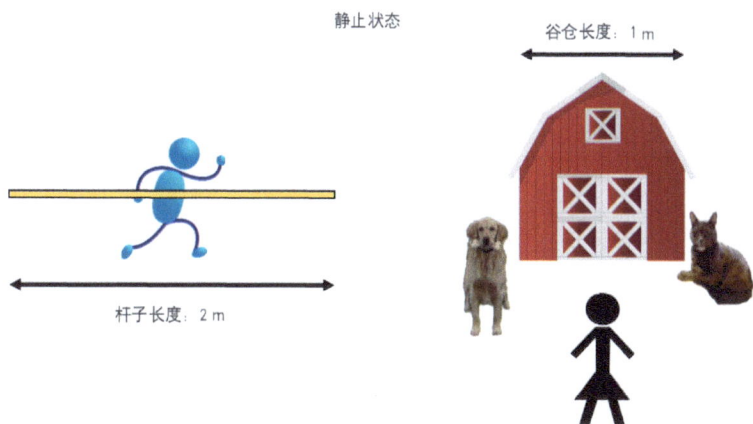

图 4　静止时，杆长 2 m，谷仓长 1 m

现在，我们换个思路，从我的视角看一看。杆子相对于我是静止的，因此长度为 2 m。谷仓、Riley、Pippi 和你则以很快的速度向我靠近，使得 $\gamma=2$。对我来说，所有物体都变得很窄！静止时长度为 1 m 的谷仓在高速运动时看起来只有 0.5 m 宽。我会很担心，因为 2 m 的长杆不可能装在仅 0.5 m 宽的谷仓内。也就是说，在 Riley 和 Pippi 同时关门时，我的杆子会被其中一扇门截断（图 5）。

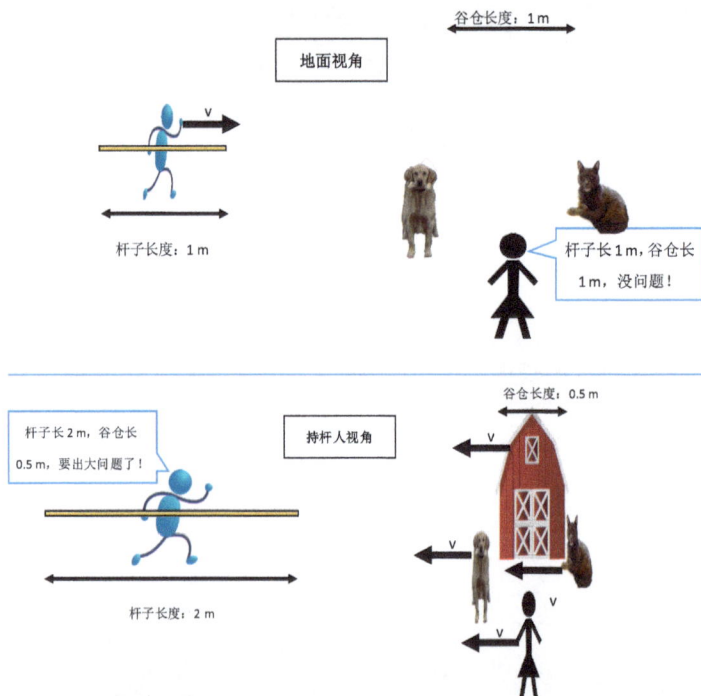

图 5　（上）对于地面上的观察者，运动的杆子看上去 1 m 长，Riley 和 Pippi 可以同时关闭和打开它们看守的门，因为谷仓可以"装下"杆子，所以杆子不会断；
（下）对于拿着杆子的人，运动的谷仓看上去长度是 0.5 m（杆子是 2 m）。如果 Riley 和 Pippi 同时关闭又打开它们看守的门，杆子不能完全被容纳进谷仓中，杆子会被折断

悖论出现了！

对你而言，静止时 1 m 长的谷仓可以容纳一个运动时 1 m 的杆子，Riley 和 Pippi 可以同时快速关闭和打开门，我可以拿着长杆毫发无损地跑过。

对我而言，静止时 2 m 的长杆无法放入运动中 0.5 m 宽的谷仓，如果 Riley 和 Pippi 快速同时关闭并打开门，我的杆子将被截断。

这怎么可能呢？杆子到底会不会被截断呢？

这个悖论的解答比第一个要难一些，它涉及"同时"这个概念在运动和静止时的变化。在你看来，Riley 和 Pippi 在同时开门关门，然而，在我看来，它们的开门关门则不是同时的。在我的参考系中，当杆的右端到达谷仓的右端时，Pippi 会先关门、开门。然后，我穿过谷仓，直到杆的左端位于谷仓的左端，Riley 再关门、开门。实际上，对我来说，Pippi 和 Riley 的开门、关门存在时间差，所以我能够用 2 m 长的杆子毫发无损地穿过 0.5 m 宽的谷仓（图 6）。

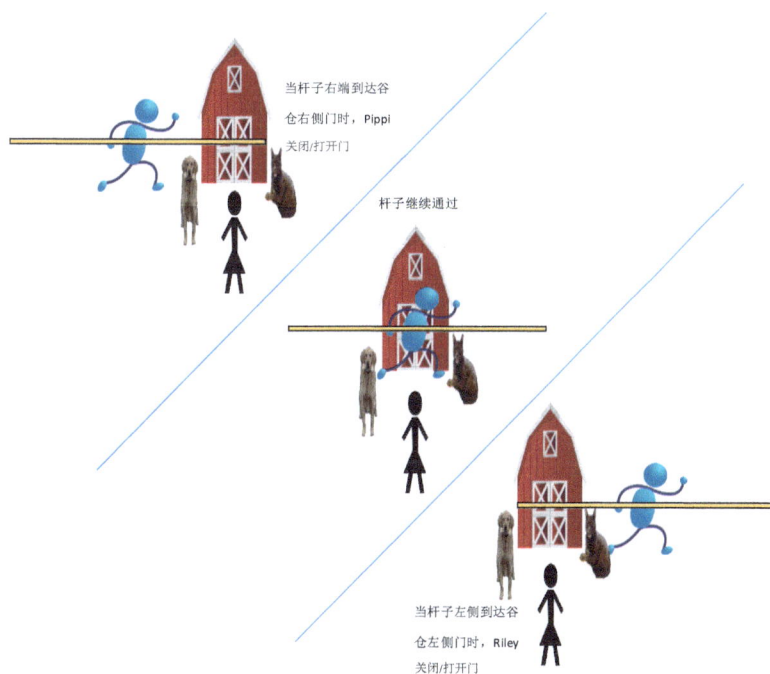

图 6　"谷仓悖论"的解释：杆子将完好无损，因为在持杆人看来，Riley 和 Pippi 是在不同的时刻关闭并打开各自所把守的门的（尽管在地面上的人看来，它们是同时开关门的）。在一个参考系中"同时"发生的事，在另一个参考系中却并非如此，这是相对论解释的最奇怪的事！但它却是真的！

狭义相对论将这种很酷的现象称为"同时性"。在一个参考系中同时发生的事情，对于另一个参考系的观察者而言则不是同时发生的。这是相对论中最复杂的概念之一，因为我们之前总是认为时间是绝对的。而实际上，时间也只是相对的！

多学一点！

爱因斯坦的狭义相对论能够说明物体的相对运动对时间和空间（通常被物理学家称为"时空"）的影响。他还发现重力也可能扭曲时空，并将此效应称为"广义相对论"。直到今天，科学家仍在探索这一问题。

例如，美国有一个叫作"激光干涉仪引力波天文台"（LIGO）的实验室。它的主要任务是检测来自宇宙源的引力波对设备产生的微小影响。LIGO 的隧道非常长（4 km），激光束在其内部的镜子上来回反射，科学家们由此测量到相当于 1/10 000 质子宽度的管道长度的变化，这种变化是由引力波导致的。这是一个非常复杂的实验，中国也在计划建造类似的实验室。

结论

相对论是我在学校里学习过的内容，它让我非常好奇宇宙运行的方式。因为我们日常体会不到时间膨胀和尺度收缩的现象，所以很难想象"时间不是绝对的"。但是，有许多物理实验表明，这的确是高速运动的世界的运行法则。像爱因斯坦这样的科学家从根本上改变了我们对事物的看法。我也确信，下一个重大科学突破将来自敢于大胆想象宇宙运行方式的年轻一代。科学实验的重要性不仅来源于它为社会带来的巨大进步（例如，如果我们不理解相对论，就无法使用 GPS），还在于它是一个充满着求知的快乐的过程！

作者简介

斯 蒂 芬 · 帕 克 (Stephen Parker) 博士于 2001 年 获得了华盛顿大学 (位于美国华盛顿州西雅图市) 的物理学博士学位。随后,他在丹麦技术大学(位于丹麦的孔恩斯灵比)进行了博士后研究。帕克博士在过去的 15 年中一直在大学教授物理学,他目前在圣马丁大学(美国华盛顿州莱西市)任教,曾获得 2012 年圣马丁杰出教授奖。在过去的两个夏天,他一直在华北航空航天工程学院(中国廊坊)开设物理入门课程。

扫描收看
本文视频课程

Exploring Special Relativity:
Fun with Space and Time

By Stephen Parker (America)

Introduction

All around us, we see things that we think are moving fast. It might be a runner sprinting around a track, a car speeding down the street, or maybe even the Shanghai Maglev train racing along its tracks. At these speeds, we never experience strange things that classical physics can't describe because they all are still moving very slow when compared what Einstein believed was the ultimate speed limit of the universe, the speed of light. We use the abbreviation "c" to represent the speed of light, where c = 300 000 km/s. Once Einstein made this assumption, he predicted that some very wacky things would happen as objects started moving faster and faster. In this article, we will explore this fascinating world by looking at Einstein's Theory of Special Relativity.

Relative Velocity

Before we can begin to understand special relativity, we first need to think about a concept called "relative velocity". Consider the following scenarios.

Scenario 1: A train is moving 10 m/sec (relative to the ground), and a person is moving on the train with the speed of 2 m/sec (relative to the train). How fast is the person walking relative to the ground?

From our everyday experiences, we know that the answer is 12 m/sec, because all we need to do is add these velocities together (10 m/sec + 2 m/sec = 12 m/sec). We say that the relative velocity of the person on the train to the ground is 12 m/sec.

Scenario 2: The train is now moving 0.1c (relative to the ground). Remember that "c" is just an abbreviation that means "the speed of light". The person on the train is moving with the speed of 0.01c (relative to the train). How fast is person walking relative to the ground now?

Using similar logic as before, the answer would be 0.11c, because 0.1c + 0.01c = 0.11c. Although Einstein's theory would tell us that this isn't exactly correct, it is close enough (Image 1).

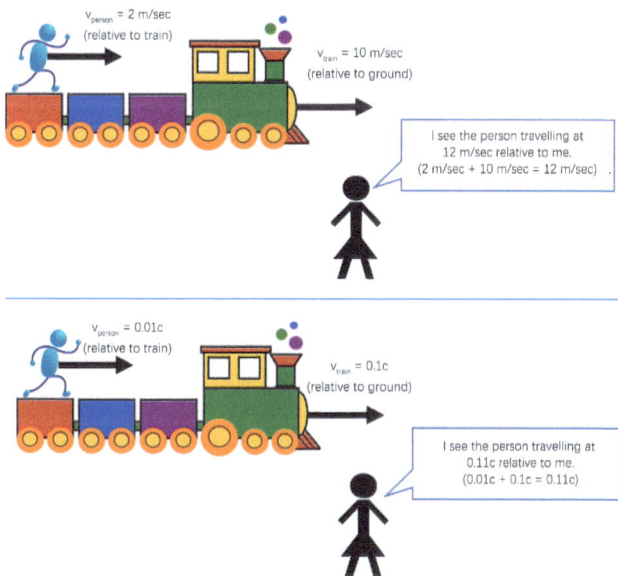

Image 1 Upper Panel: When speeds are small, relative velocities are easy to calculate using simple addition. If a train travels at 10 m/sec relative to the ground and a person walks at 2 m/sec relative to the train, an observer on the ground will see the person on the train travelling at 12 m/sec.
Lower Panel: Even when the speeds are 0.1c and 0.01c for the train and the person respectively, addition still basically gives the correct answer

Even at these extremely fast velocities, there isn't much that changes from our everyday experiences. Things start to change when objects start moving even faster, though.

Scenario 3: The train is moving 0.75c (relative to the ground), and the person is moving 0.75c (relative to the train). Now how fast is the person walking relative to the ground?

If you say 1.5c (because 0.75c + 0.75c = 1.5c), then you end up violating the fundamental principle that Einstein hypothesized for his theory of special relativity. Einstein thought that nothing can go faster than light. In order to answer this question, he needed to create a new rule for calculating relative velocities.

Using his new math, he was able to show that in this scenario, 0.75c + 0.75c = 0.96c! Furthermore, this new math will never allow anything to go faster than the speed of light in any reference frame.

Scenario 4: The person on the train gets tired of walking. He turns on a flashlight,

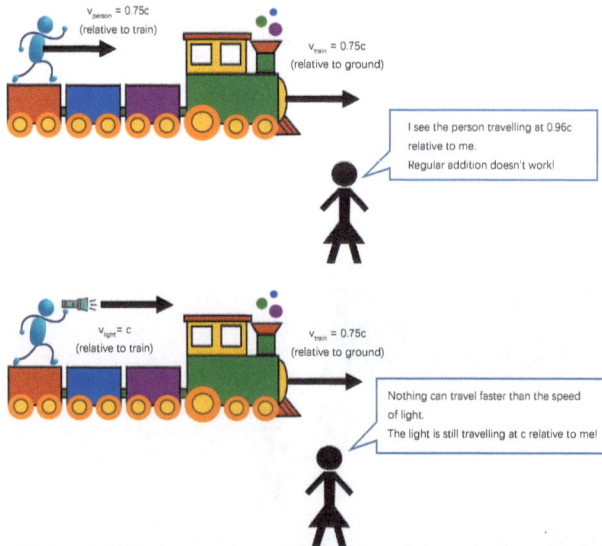

Image 2 Upper Panel: When speeds starting getting comparable to the speed of light, relative velocity calculations using simple addition will fail.
Lower Panel: If the person on the train has a flashlight, the speed of light will be the same for the person on the train as it is for the person on the ground. Light always travels at a speed of c, regardless of the reference frame

which by definition has to travel with a speed c (relative to train). The train still travels with a speed of 0.75c (relative to the ground). How fast will the light be travelling relative to the ground in this scenario?

Since Einstein said that nothing can travel faster than the speed of light, then if you said his new math would predict that 0.75c + c = c, then you would be correct! Even though the train is moving, the light must still be moving with a speed of c relative to the ground as well (Image 2). The speed of light is the speed of light!

This means that something must happen as objects start moving very fast in order to safeguard this cosmic speed limit. It is worth noting that it isn't completely counterintuitive that motion could affect how we experience the world around us. For instance, even at small velocities, the Doppler Effect can change the frequency of a sound being heard as a result of relative motion. As an ambulance moves toward an observer, its siren will be higher in pitch. When it passes the observer and begins to move away, the siren will be lower in pitch.

Einstein shows us that in the world of the very fast, relative motion will begin to distort the fabric of both time and space itself.

Time Dilation

Time dilation describes how clocks will behave differently in moving reference frames. Suppose I'm on a train that you are watching travel by you. The speed of the train can be used to calculate a famous factor in relativity called γ (which is the Greek letter "gamma"). The equation to calculate γ isn't particularly important, but you should know that γ must always be equal to or greater than 1, and the faster something travels, the larger γ ends up being. For reference, if something travels at 0.75 c, then γ = 1.5. If something travels at 0.97c, then γ = 4.

Special relativity predicts:

$$(\text{Time at Rest}) = \gamma * (\text{Time in Motion}). \tag{1}$$

So if my train was moving such that γ = 2, this would mean that 1 second for me on the train (Time in Motion) would equal 2 seconds for you on the ground (Time at Rest). Time will tick at different rates depending on the motion; our clocks won't stay in sync with each other. Although this already might seem weird, it gets even weirder!

To explore time dilation further, we will examine what is called the "Twin Paradox". A paradox happens when you would arrive at different conclusions depending on how you think about a situation. There must always be a solution to the paradox, though, since we can always (at least in theory) just perform the experiment to see what actually happens.

For this paradox, let us assume that we have a girl cat named Pippi and a boy dog named Riley that were born on the same day (so they are just like twins). Pippi is on earth, and she watches Riley get on a rocket ship that travels very fast away from the earth for 8 years (as measured by Pippi). The rocket is travelling very fast, such that the factor $\gamma = 4$.

According to Pippi's perspective (she is at rest), she would say that Riley's clocks (which are in motion) would only tick for 2 years using equation (1). If Riley immediately turns the rocket ship around and flies back to the Earth, then another 8 years would pass for Pippi, while only 2 years would pass for Riley. Therefore, Pippi will have aged 16 years old

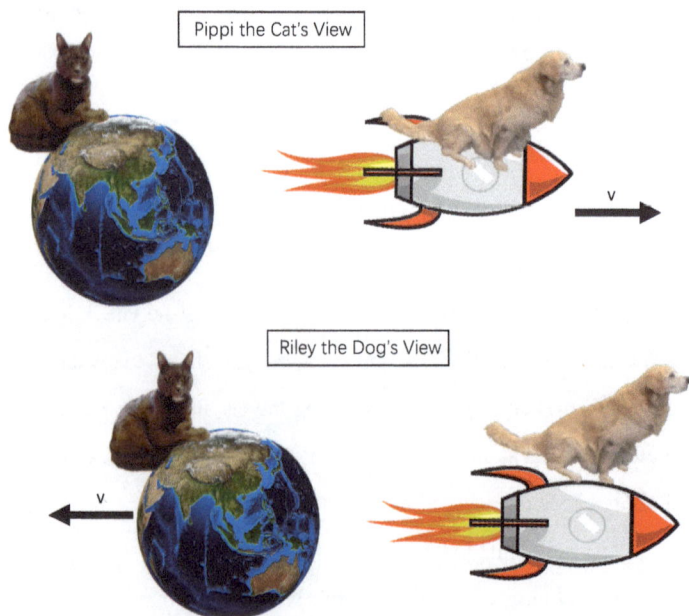

Image 3 Upper Panel: From Pippi the cat's view, Riley the dog is travelling to the right on the spaceship.
Lower Panel: From Riley the dog's view, Pippi the cat is travelling to the left on the Earth

and Riley would have only aged 4 years old.

How would things look from Riley's perspective, though? He would claim that he was the one at rest and Pippi (and the Earth) are moving away from him such that γ = 4. So if Riley were to experience 2 years of time according to his clocks as Pippi hurtles away on Earth, then Pippi's clocks (which are the clocks that he thinks are in motion) would only tick for ½ of a year. Pippi and the Earth would then turn back around, and another 2 years will pass for Riley while only ½ of a year for Pippi. This means that while Riley will have aged 4 years old again, Pippi will only have aged 1 year old (Image 3).

Paradox!

According to Pippi, Riley was in motion, so when they meet on Earth again, Riley will have aged 4 years old while Pippi aged 16 years old (A young dog and an old cat).

According to Riley, Pippi was in motion, so when they meet on Earth again, Riley will have aged 4 while Pippi aged only 1 year old (An old dog and a young cat).

But which animal is actually older when they meet?

You might argue that since we "know" that Riley and the spaceship were "actually moving" that Pippi should be old and Riley should be young. This ends up being the correct answer, but we must ask ourselves a very basic question: "How do you know if you are moving or at rest?"

To answer this, it is useful to imagine that you are in an elevator. If you start at the bottom floor, and when the elevator starts to move up, you will feel heavy (and if you were standing on a scale, the reading would be larger than usual). During the middle of trip, you just feel your regular weight (and a scale reads your usual weight). When the elevator begins to stop, though, you start to feel light (and the scale will read smaller than your usual weight). You can always recognize a physicist when they get in an elevator, because they will be the one who is putting a scale on the floor of the elevator to test this out. (The next time you are in an elevator, you should try it too!)

In the places where you feel (or measure yourself) heavy and light, the elevator is changing its speed. In physics, we call this changing speed an acceleration. Because you can "sense" this acceleration (that is, you could measure it with a scale), then you must have been (or will be) moving if you do. Acceleration can therefore be used to detect who actually was moving!

Back to our twin paradox puzzle, Riley the dog would have to feel an acceleration on his spaceship as it turned around to get back home. He would have to slam on the "brakes" of the rocket ship and then speed back up in the other direction to get back home. This means that Riley knows that he must have been the one moving, because he could feel that acceleration. Because Pippi is just sitting on Earth and never feels an acceleration, she will never feel heavier or lighter. She must have been the one that was at rest. Therefore, we know that Pippi was correct. Sure enough, when Riley gets off the space ship, Pippi will end up being old while Riley is still young. They would no longer really be twins; one is older than the other.

You might argue that this could never really happen, because we could never build a space ship that could go fast enough to actually test this. However, we have actually seen the effects of time dilation with very precise experiments using the most accurate atomic clocks that we have. The experiment is amazingly simple: We take two clocks and synchronize them to each other. We then keep Clock 1 on the ground (so it is at rest) and put Clock 2 on a plane and fly it around the world (so it is moving around the Earth). When the plane lands, we then take a look at both clocks, and we will find that Clock 1 and Clock 2 no longer have the same time on them! At these relatively small speeds (where γ is only very slightly larger than 1), they are only different by hundreds of nanoseconds (~0.000 000 1 sec), but they are still different. Time itself behaved differently for the two different clocks because of the motion.

Another place where we see the effects of time dilation is with the Global Positioning Satellites (GPS) system that we use on a daily basis to help us get directions. These satellites are moving around the Earth, so the clocks on them, required for the system to work properly, have to be continuously adjusted because of the effects of time dilation for the system to work correctly.

Length Contraction

Measured distances will be different depending on relative motion as well.

Special relativity predicts:

$$\text{(Length in Motion)} = \text{(Length at Rest)} / \gamma. \qquad (2)$$

This means that if something is travelling fast enough such that $\gamma = 2$, a long, 2 m pole at rest would actually look like a short, 1 m pole while it is moving. Moving objects are shorter than stationary objects. To think more about this cool effect, we will consider the Pole in the Barn paradox.

Suppose I have a pole that is made of very fragile glass that is 2 m long when measured at rest. On the earth, there is also a barn that is 1 m long when measured at rest with doors on both ends.

We'll also bring back our dog Riley and our cat Pippi to help out with this experiment. Riley will be on the left side of the barn to control the left door and Pippi will be on the right side of the barn to control the right one. You will be standing on the ground along with Riley, Pippi, and the barn to observe this magnificent experiment.

I take the pole (orientated horizontal to the ground) and then run very fast toward the barn. For fun, let's say I can run superfast such that $\gamma = 2$. When I have the pole completely enclosed in the barn, Riley and Pippi will very quickly close the doors of the barn, and then immediately open them back up. Because the pole was moving so fast that it was only 1 m long to you on the ground [using equation (2)], it should be able to just barely fit inside the 1 m long barn.

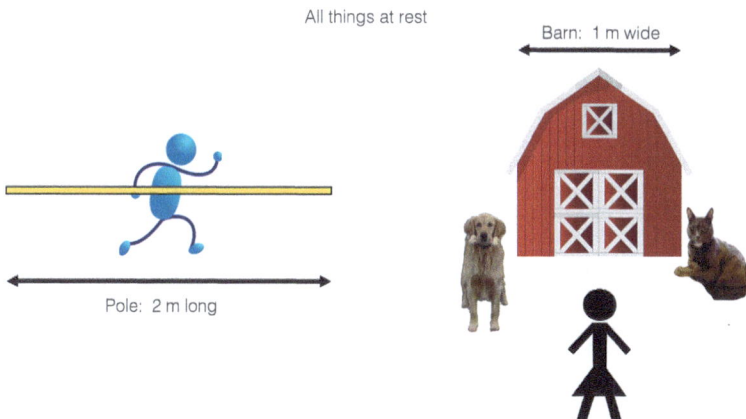

All things at rest

Barn: 1 m wide

Pole: 2 m long

Image 4 When everything is at rest, the pole has a length of 2 m and the barn has a width of 1 m

Therefore, once Riley and Pippi open their doors, I will just continue to run through the barn and out the other side without any issues; the pole will be unbroken (Image 4).

Now, let's shift perspective for this same situation but think about what this looks like to me. I am holding the pole such that it at rest with respect to me, so the pole will still be 2 m long. I see the barn, Riley, Pippi, and you moving very quickly toward me such that $\gamma = 2$. Everything looks very narrow to me (because it is in motion relative to me). Since the length of the barn at rest is 1 m, from my perspective, the barn will look like it is only 0.5 m wide. This makes me very concerned! Since you have told me that Riley and Pippi plan to close the door at the same time, there is no way that my 2 m long pole could fit inside a barn that

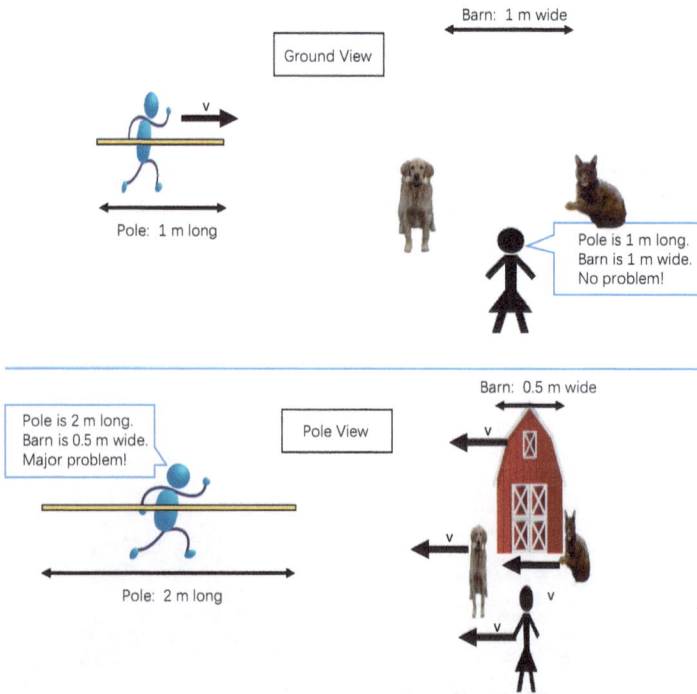

Barn: 1 m wide

Ground View

v

Pole: 1 m long

Pole is 1 m long.
Barn is 1 m wide.
No problem!

Barn: 0.5 m wide

Pole is 2 m long.
Barn is 0.5 m wide.
Major problem!

Pole View

v

Pole: 2 m long

v

v

v

Image 5 Upper Panel: According to those on the ground, the pole is moving and looks to be 1 m long and the barn is still 1 m wide. Riley and Pippi will be able to close and open their doors at the same time, because the pole would "fit" inside the barn. The pole can emerge unbroken.

Lower Panel: According to the person with the pole, the barn is moving and looks to be 0.5 m wide (and the pole is still 2 m long). If Riley and Pippi close and open their doors at the same time, the pole won't be completely in the barn. The pole would have to emerge broken is only 0.5 m wide. This means after I run through the barn, one of the doors will smash against the pole, so the pole would be broken once I came out the other side of the barn (Image 5).

Paradox!

According to you, a 1 m long pole (moving) should fit inside the 1 m wide barn (stationary). Riley and Pippi can quickly close and open the doors at the same time, and I run out the other side with an unbroken pole.

According to me, a 2 m long pole (stationary) will not fit inside the 0.5 m wide barn (moving). If Riley and Pippi quickly close and open the doors at the same time, they will smash my pole and I run out the other side with a broken pole.

How is this possible? Will the pole be broken or will it not be broken?

The solution to this paradox is slightly trickier than the first one. Things that happen

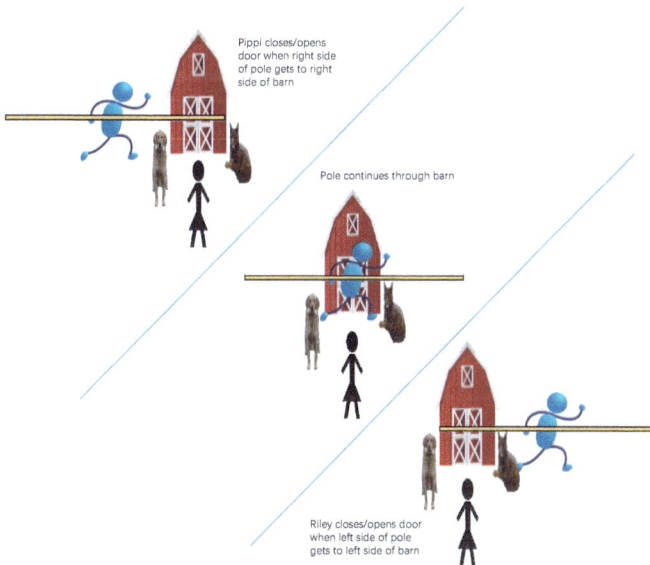

Image 6 The solution to the "pole in the barn" paradox. The pole will be unbroken as it emerges, because according to the person with the pole, Riley and Pippi close and open their doors at different times (even though according to the person on the ground, they close and open their doors at the same time). Simultaneous events in one reference frame won't be simultaneous in another frame. This is the one of the strangest results of special relativity, but nevertheless it must be true!

simultaneously in one frame of reference will not happen simultaneously in a different reference frame.

According to you, Riley and Pippi will close and open the doors at the same time (i.e. simultaneously). However, in my frame of reference, Pippi will actually close and open her door first as the right end of the pole reaches the right end of the barn. Then I will run through the barn until the left end of the pole is at the left end of the barn. Riley will then close and open his door. I was able to run through the 0.5 m wide barn with my 2 m long pole because they actually close and open their doors at different times relative to me, which allows me to run through the barn without any issues (Image 6).

This cool result of special relativity is often referred to as "Simultaneity". Things in one reference frame might happen at the same time, but they will end up happening at different times to observers in another reference frame. This is one of the most difficult things to wrap your brain around in relativity, because we think of time as being an absolute thing. Both descriptions are actually correct: time is just relative!

Bonus Science

Einstein's Theory of Special Relativity was able to show how time and space (often called "spacetime" by physicists) could be affected by the relative motion of objects. He also found that gravity could warp spacetime as well, and he called this effect General Relativity. It is something that scientists are still exploring to this day.

For instance, in the United States there is an experiment called the Laser Interferometer Gravitational-Wave Observatory (LIGO). The basic concept of this experiment is to detect the very small effects that gravitational waves from cosmic sources would have on the apparatus. LIGO has very long (4 km) tunnels with laser beams bouncing back and forth on mirrors located in them. The scientists are able to measure changes in length of one of the arms by 1/10 000 th of the width of a proton due to interactions with these gravity waves. This is a very sophisticated experiment, and China has plans to build a similar one.

Conclusion

Relativity was one of the topics that I learned in school which really made my imagination wonder how the universe actually worked. Because we don't experience time dilation and length contraction on a daily basis, it is hard to imagine a world where time isn't absolute. However, there have been many physics experiments that show that this is indeed the way the world of the superfast behaves. It took someone like Einstein to fundamentally change how we thought about things, and I'm sure that the next big scientific breakthrough will come from a younger generation that isn't afraid to think creatively about how the universe might actually work in ways we haven't even imagined. One of the most important aspects of the scientific experiments that we undertake in the world today is that not only can these lead to great advances in our society (for instance, we wouldn't have working GPS system if we didn't understand relativity), but also that just thinking about them can actually be really, really fun!

(Sun Mengge contributed to this article)

About the Author

Dr. Stephen Parker earned his Ph.D. in Physics from the University of Washington (Seattle, WA, USA) in 2001. He then did his post-doctoral work at the Danish Technical University (Kongens Lyngby, Denmark). Dr. Parker has been teaching physics at the undergraduate level for the past 15 years, and he currently teaches at Saint Martin's University (Lacey, WA, USA). He was the recipient of the Monk's of Saint Martin's Abbey Outstanding Faculty Award in 2012. For the past two summers, he has been co-teaching an introductory physics course at the North China Institute of Aerospace Engineering (Langfang, China).

附　录

Appendix

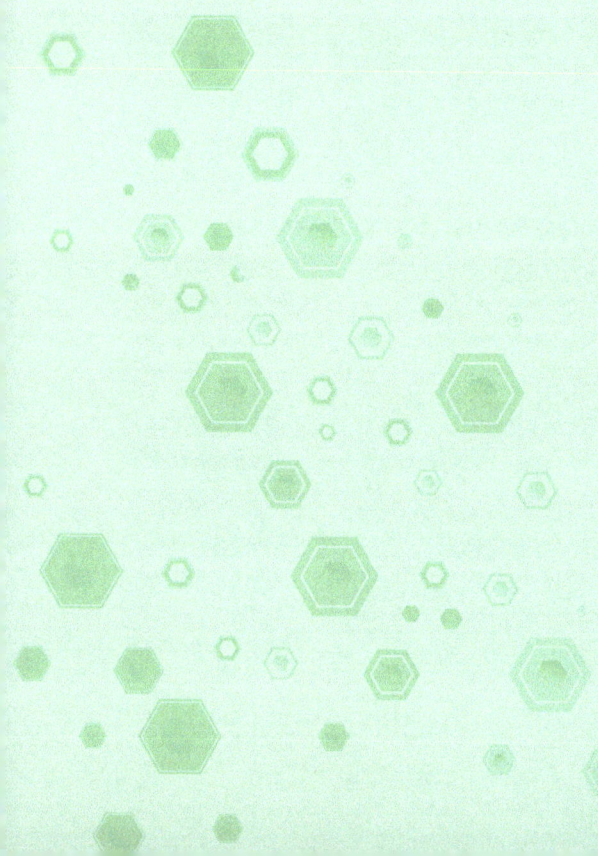

VIPKID 外国专家科普公益课堂
VIPKID Foreign Expert Public Science Classes

日期 Date	专家 Lecturer	国籍 Nationality	课程主题 Theme	授课地点 Place	授课学校 School
2019 年 4 月 29 日 29-Apr-19	阿尔弗雷德·奥托·缪克 Alfred Otto Mueck	德国 Germany	女性的生育能力 Fertility of Women	北京市 Beijing	丰台实验小学 Fengtai Experimental Primary School
2019 年 5 月 20 日 20-May-19	兰尼斯·梅里诺 Lenis Mauricio Meriño	哥伦比亚 Columbia	脑机接口浅谈 Introduction to Brain-Computer Interface	北京市 Beijing	中国人民革命军事博物馆 Military Museum of the Chinese People's Revolution
2019 年 5 月 21 日 21-May-19	谢里 Cyrille Breard	美国 America	声音是我们的朋友吗 Is Sound our Friends	北京市 Beijing	中国人民革命军事博物馆 Military Museum of the Chinese People's Revolution
2019 年 5 月 21 日 21-May-19	储扎克 Zachary J. Smith	美国 America	为人类健康服务的光学技术 Using Light for Human Health	北京市 Beijing	中国人民革命军事博物馆 Military Museum of the Chinese People's Revolution
2019 年 5 月 22 日 22-May-19	加尼·瑞泽普 Ghani Razaqpur	加拿大 Canada	建筑材料的选择标准 Selection Criteria for Construction Materials	北京市 Beijing	中国人民革命军事博物馆 Military Museum of the Chinese People's Revolution

续表

日期 Date	专家 Lecturer	国籍 Nationality	课程主题 Theme	授课地点 Place	授课学校 School
2019 年 5 月 22 日 22-May-19	斯蒂芬·帕克 Stephen Parker	美国 America	狭义相对论：奇妙的时间和空间 Exploring Special Relativity: Fun with Space and Time	北京市 Beijing	中国人民革命军事博物馆 Military Museum of the Chinese People's Revolution
2019 年 5 月 23 日 23-May-19	马吉帝 Majdi Alhmah	叙利亚 Syria	新高铁那么轻，到底用了什么材料 What Materials Are Used to Make the New High Speed Rail So Light	北京市 Beijing	中国人民革命军事博物馆 Military Museum of the Chinese People's Revolution
2019 年 6 月 24 日 24-Jun-19	黄庆荣 HUANG Qingrong	美国 America	玩转食品科学 Acting out Food Science	北京市 Beijing	同心实验小学 Tongxin Experimental Primary School
2019 年 10 月 18 日 18-Oct-19	瑞尼·威尔海姆·思博森 Rainer Wilhelm Spurzem	德国 Germany	天体物理学和黑洞 Astrophysics and Black Holes	天津市 Tianjin	天津第三小学 Tianjin No. 3 Primary School
2019 年 10 月 22 日 22-Oct-19	新井健生 Tatsuo Arai	日本 Japan	机器人的神奇功能 The Magical Function of the Robot	北京市 Beijing	安民学校 Anmin School
2019 年 11 月 22 日 22-Nov-19	布鲁诺·布里斯杰拉 Bruno Briseghella	意大利 Italy	多姿多彩的桥梁 Colorful Bridges	福建省漳州市 Zhangzhou Fujian Province	林仓小学 Lincang Primary School

续表

日期 Date	专家 Lecturer	国籍 Nationality	课程主题 Theme	授课地点 Place	授课学校 School
2019 年 12 月 22 日 22-Dec-19	苏平 Nathan Pelton	美国 America	动物大迁徙 The Great Migration of Animals	上海市 Shanghai	娄塘小学 Loutang Primary School
2019 年 12 月 22 日 22-Dec-19	苏平 Nathan Pelton	美国 America	动物大迁徙 The Great Migration of Animals	江苏省启东市 Qidong Jiangsu Province	聚阳中心小学 Juyang Primrary School
2020 年 3 月 16 日 16-Mar-20	艾米莉 Emilie Carlot	法国 France	人类与病毒：新冠病毒疫情 Humans and Viruses: the COVID-19 Epidemic	线上 Online	公开课 Open Courses
2020 年 5 月 18 日 18-May-20	马克·力文 Mark Levine	美国 America	同心抗疫歌唱希望 Together We Must Take a Stand	线上 Online	公开课 Open Courses
2020 年 6 月 15 日 15-Jun-20	韦恩·曼斯菲尔德 Wayne Mansfield	美国 America	飞机与航空 Aircraft and Aviation	线上 Online	公开课 Open Course
2020 年 8 月 24 日 24-Aug-20	戴伟 David G.Evans	英国 Britain	什么是化学反应 What Is Chemial Reaction	北京市 Beijing	北京天文馆 Beijing Planetarium
2020 年 8 月 24 日 24-Aug-20	戴伟 David G.Evans	英国 Britain	化学无处不在 Chemistry Is Everywhere	北京市 Beijing	北京天文馆 Beijing Planetarium

续表

日期 Date	专家 Lecturer	国籍 Nationality	课程主题 Theme	授课地点 Place	授课学校 School
2020 年 8 月 25 日 25-Aug-20	亨利·阿达姆松 Henry H.Radamson	瑞典 Sweden	纳米科技：从晶体管的发明到纳米技术的兴起 Nanotechnology: from Discovery of Transistor to Emerging of Nanotechnology	北京市 Beijing	北京天文馆 Beijing Planetarium
2020 年 8 月 25 日 25-Aug-20	博江盟 Jean-Marc Bovet	瑞士 Switzerland	科学，我们如何知道我们所知道的? Science, How Do We Know What We Know?	北京市 Beijing	北京天文馆 Beijing Planetarium
2020 年 8 月 26 日 26-Aug-20	萨拉·普拉托 Sara Platto	意大利 Italy	闻声识海豚 How Does It Sound to Be a Dolphin	北京市 Beijing	北京天文馆 Beijing Planetarium
2020 年 8 月 26 日 26-Aug-20	罗杰威 Paolo Vincenzo Genovese	意大利 Italy	建筑空间与技术中的仿生学 Bionic Approach for the Architecture Space and Technology	北京市 Beijing	北京天文馆 Beijing Planetarium
2020 年 9 月 30 日 30-Sep-20	陶益壮 Marie-Jean Thoraval	法国 France	液滴和气泡 Drops and Bubbles	陕西省泾阳县 Jingyang County Shaanxi Province	崔黄小学 Cuihuang Primary School

外国专家讲科普
Science Classes from Foreign Experts

续表

日期 Date	专家 Lecturer	国籍 Nationality	课程主题 Theme	授课地点 Place	授课学校 School
2020 年 10 月 23 日 23-Oct-20	储扎克 Zachary J. Smith	美国 America	"成像"的科学基础 The Science of the Imaging	安徽省岳西县 Yuexi County Anhui Province	柳畈小学 Liufan Primary School
2020 年 11 月 9 日 09-Nov-20	罗杰威 Paolo Vincenzo Genovese	意大利 Italy	构建自己的幸福：生态村战略与适宜技术 Built Your Own Happiness: Eco-Village Strategy and Appropriate Technology	江西省井冈山市 Jinggangshan Jiangxi Province	井冈山小学 Jinggangshan Primary School
2020 年 11 月 9 日 09-Nov-20	西格尔 Jay S. Siegel	美国 America	感官世界的化学 Chemistry in the Realm of Senses	江西省井冈山市 Jinggangshan Jiangxi Province	井冈山小学 Jinggangshan Primary School
2020 年 12 月 1 日 01-Dec-20	萨拉·普拉托 Sara Platto	意大利 Italy	狂犬病防疫与科普课 Family Safety Around Doggy	湖北省武汉市 Wuhan Hubei Province	长岭小学 Changling Primary School
2020 年 12 月 11 日 11-Dec-20	王义汉 WANG Yihan	美国 America	抗癌神药的诞生 The Birth of Anti Cancer Drug	广东省茂名市 Maoming Guangdong Province	河垌小学 Hedong Primary School

后 记

Afterword

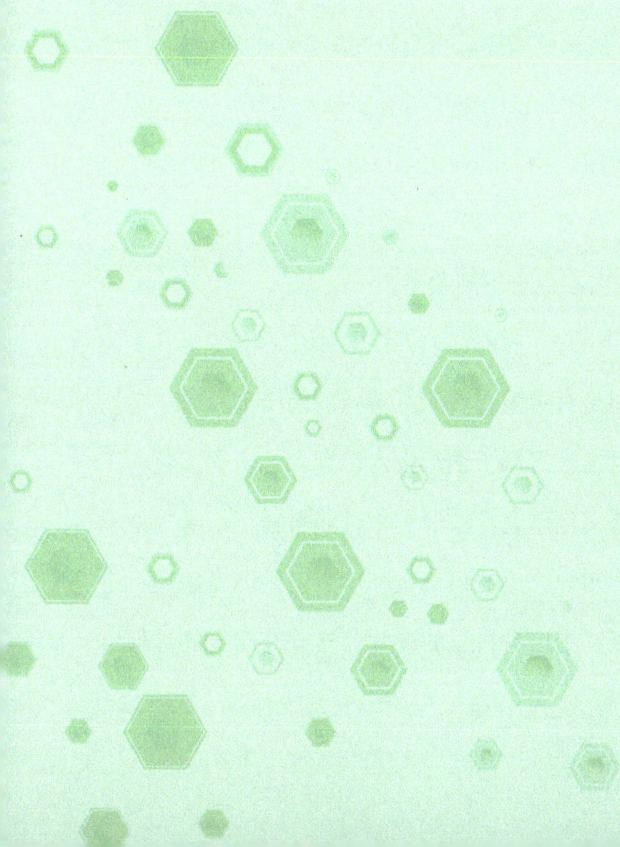

科普启蒙在路上

看到这本书的出版，我感到非常高兴。从国内教育大环境看，资源分布不均衡的情况是客观存在的。随着城镇化的推进，各类优质教育资源越来越向城市集中，城市中的家庭有着丰富的素养启蒙活动，有更多的机会接触专家学者及外国人。但对于偏远乡村地区的孩子来说，不仅缺少拓展视野的场景，连基本的科学课、艺术课，甚至英语课都难以保证。在我们童行学院发起的支教活动中，我们的支教老师在一些地区的学校需要承担全校 6 个年级的科学、艺术、英语课。这里的孩子们对好教师和优质资源的渴望更为真挚和迫切。

当我了解到，科技部国外人才研究中心与 VIPKID 共同打造了外国专家科普公益课堂项目，通过 3 年时间，邀请一流的外国专家到偏远乡村学校、城市务工人员子女学校开展科普讲座，内心由衷感到敬佩。

接近知识源头的信息是最宝贵的。这些外国专家在中国工作多年，多位都曾获得过中国政府友谊奖，他们是对中国有着深厚情感的前沿科学家。他们在不同领域从事研究工作，从相对论、黑洞、纳米技术，到食品工程、化学工程、建筑工程，再到影像技术、跨文化研究，由他们来讲述科普，亲身向处于学业启蒙阶段的乡村孩子解读科学知识，更显得真实和珍贵。外国专家们行走在大别山区、秦岭山区、井冈山区，走进乡村里的课堂，这些在路上的过程本身就是播种科学的故事。

　　无论何时，教育一直是乡村孩子改变命运的最好途径。对多数乡村孩子来说，这是他们第一次见到外国人，第一次见到科学家。用一位外国专家的话来说，鼓励这些孩子们保持好奇、追求学业，只需要一个引子。科普公益课堂上的亲密交流和接触，毫无疑问正在发挥着这样的价值。

　　资源和常识的匮乏使得贫困在代际传递。为乡村地区的孩子们提供良好的教育资源，拓展他们未来的发展方向，我认为这是每一家意愿向上、向善的机构和企业应该具有的担当。让人敬佩的是，外国专家科普课堂不仅走进乡村，还将过程中的每个珍贵时刻都保留下来，通过技术的剪辑处理，作为公益课程资源提供给更多有需要的地区。现在，课堂又以出版物的形式展现在大家面前，未来也会捐赠到更多的乡村学校。

　　可以说科技向善，就体现在这里吧。

　　希望这本书不仅能帮助到更多的乡村学校，也能让更多家庭和孩子打开视野，看到更大的世界！

郝景芳

第 74 届雨果奖得主、童行学院创始人

Technology-Driven Elementary Science Education

I am incredibly pleased to see the publication of this book. The advancement of urbanization has caused quality educational resources to become more and more concentrated in cities. City residents have far greater choices in basic education activities and better access to experts, academics, and foreigners. Children in remote rural areas not only lack opportunities to expand their horizons, but some also do not even have basic science, art, or even English classes. During our Tongxing School Voluntary Education Support Project, some teachers have had to teach science, art, and English to students in every elementary grade. These students need better teachers and quality resources more than anyone else.

I genuinely respect and admire the effort of the Foreign Talent Research Center of the Ministry of Science and Technology of China and VIPKID. These two groups have teamed up to launch the Foreign Expert Public Science Classes Project, a program lasting three years to recruit overseas experts to rural schools and the schools of migrant workers' children.

The closer the information is to the source, the more valuable it is. Most overseas experts have been working in China for many years, and many received the Chinese Government Friendship Award. They are some of the most outstanding scientists and have a deep affection for China. They work in fields as diverse as the theory of relativity, black holes, nanotechnology, food engineering, chemical engineering, construction engineering, imaging technology, and cross-cultural research. It was instrumental and valuable to have them talk and explain science to young children from rural areas. These experts went to the Dabie Mountains, Qinling Mountains, Jinggang Mountains and to enter classrooms in these rural areas, planting the seeds of science. Education has always been and will continue to be the best avenue for children from rural areas to change their fortunes. For most children involved in the program, it is their first encounter with a foreigner and a scientist.

In the words of one overseas expert, "All it takes to encourage these children to stay curious and pursue education is a simple introduction." Undoubtedly, the interaction and contact with these experts provide this critical introduction. A lack of resources and general knowledge allows poverty to pass from generation to generation. I believe it is the responsibility of every organization and company seeking goodwill to find ways to provide children in rural areas with better educational resources and more opportunities to build a better future. The Foreign Expert Public Science Classes Project was particularly admirable because while bringing science into rural classrooms, each class was recorded, edited, and made available as an open resource. These classes have now become something everyone can enjoy.

Furthermore, The Foreign Expert Public Science Classes Project will donate numerous books to many schools in rural areas. This project was a case point of "science and technology for a good cause". I sincerely hope that this book will help rural schools and open doors to the wider world for many families and children!

Hao Jingfang

74th Hugo Award Winner and Founder of Tongxing School

让每个孩子都有机会接受高质量的科普教育

　　启迪和赋能每一个孩子的未来是 VIPKID 一直以来的使命。VIPKID 的公益之路开始于 2017 年，"外教乡村公益课堂"项目从最初的 5 所学校，目前已覆盖了全国 30 个省（区、市）的 1000 多所学校。2019 年 4 月，在科技部国外人才研究中心的指导下，我们启动了"VIPKID 外国专家科普公益课堂"项目，也是这本书的由来。

　　无论是项目本身还是这本书的出版，我们的初衷都是一样的，就是要借助科学家们的精彩演讲，把科学启蒙带给更多学生，让偏远地区的孩子们也有机会去播下科学的种子，让科学思维生根发芽。

　　对科学启蒙的认可。中小学特别是乡村学校，很难接触到专业的、体系化的科普启蒙，学生对高深的科学知识有距离感。专家们用自己对专业和生活的理解，利用生活中的案例为学生们讲解科学原理，使学生们对学习科学知识有了积极的认知和变化。英国皇家化学学会的戴伟教授讲授的化学科普课，通过日常的生活切入、鲜活的实验演示、通俗的科学讲解，让很多孩子在瞬间爱上了化学。

　　对教育公平的赞许。VIPKID 为科普公益课堂专门研发了线上模块，将经过剪辑的课堂视频配以字幕，作为开放的公益资源提供给所有学生学习，用网络填补了教育资源的鸿沟。2020 年新冠肺炎疫情暴发，我们邀请了上海巴斯德病毒研究所助理研究员艾米莉（法）在线做科普讲座，教给小朋友们有关新冠肺炎的防治知识；中国政府友谊奖获得者、中央民族大学马克·力文（美）在线教授他创作的歌曲《团结合作，共同抗击新冠病毒》，帮助在家学习的孩子们建立了信心和勇气。

对中外交流的推动。外国专家走进乡村学校，不仅带去了科学知识，孩子们的表现也给他们留下了深刻的印象，这为外国专家认识一个更加真实、立体的中国提供了平台。记得在北京一所外来务工人员子女学校，日本专家新井建生向孩子们介绍了机器人的发展历史，当新井老师提到中国现在的机器人研发水平居世界领先地位的时候，孩子们的眼中闪烁着光芒和期待，新井老师对他们的未来也给予厚望。

互联网技术的发展和应用为引智工作提供了新的可能，尤其是在疫情常态化的大背景下，来华工作的边界正在逐步扩展至为华工作，"云上引智"也打破了人才引进的时空边界。在这样的大背景下，我坚信，外国专家公益课堂会从一节一节的课，汇成一座世界大课堂。

"VIPKID 外国专家科普公益课堂"项目的开展和本书的出版，离不开科技部国外人才研究中心的各位领导和同事的支持，离不开参与科普课堂的外国专家的智慧，离不开出版社编辑、翻译和校对的贡献，更离不开关心中国科普事业、关爱孩子成长的每一个你的鼓励！

米雯娟

VIPKID 创始人、CEO

Let Every Child Have Access to a High Quality of Popular Science Education

Inspire and Empower Every Child for the Future has always been our mission at VIPKID. Our charity work began in 2017. The Rural Education Project started with five schools and now covers over 1000 in 30 provinces, municipalities directly under the central government, and autonomous regions across China. In April 2019, under the guidance of the Foreign Talent Research Center of the Ministry of Science and Technology of China, we launched the VIPKID Foreign Expert Public Science Classes Project, the fruits of which served to become the basis of this book.

Both the project and the book originated from the same intention: to provide children from rural and remote areas with elementary science education through speeches by scientists worldwide. We hoped to plant the seeds of science in those children and help them embrace a scientific mindset.

This project recognizes the importance of science education at the elementary level. It can be challenging for students in primary and secondary schools, especially those in rural areas, to receive a professional and systematic introduction to science. Too often, students find advanced science to be beyond their grasp. Based on their understanding of their focus subject and life, the experts conveyed scientific knowledge to the students using examples from daily life. This method helps students understand science education better. For example, Professor David G. Evans from the Royal Society of Chemistry presented basic chemistry lessons based on phenomena from everyday life through exciting experiments and straightforward teaching. His classes kindle a passion for chemistry in many children.

This project values educational equity, and VIPKID developed an online module specifically for the project. The module offers edited and subtitled videos of classes as an open resource for the public to use. By ensuring every student to have access to the resource, we can start bridging the gap in educational resources with the help of the Internet.

After the COVID-19 pandemic broke out in 2020, we invited Emilie, an French assistant researcher at the Institute Pasteur of Shanghai, to give an online speech to teach children about the prevention and treatment of COVID-19. The Chinese Government Friendship Award winner Mark Levine, an American expert of the Minzu University of China, gave an online speech about the song "Together We Must Take a Stand to Defeat the Novel Coronavirus", written by himself. This song helped build confidence and courage among students stuck studying at home.

This project also promotes Sino-foreign exchange. Overseas experts traveled to rural schools to teach the children about science. But the children's abilities also impressed the teachers greatly. The experience helped the experts understand a more realistic and lively China. At a school for children of migrant workers in Beijing, Tatsuo Arai, a Japanese expert, talked to students about the history of robotics. When he mentioned that China is now leading the global robotics development, sparkles of hope gleamed in the children's eyes.

The development and application of internet technology have created new possibilities for soliciting talent. Against the backdrop of the global pandemic, more and more people are working "for" China instead of "in" China. Online Talent Recruitment has expanded the temporal and spatial boundaries of recruiting talent. In this context, I am convinced that science classes will grow into something much more significant. It can become an international class for everyone.

Last but not least, the VIPKID Foreign Expert Public Science Classes Project and publication of this book could not have been achieved without support from distinguished senior staff and colleagues at the Foreign Talent Research Center of the Ministry of

Science and Technology of China, the wisdom of the overseas experts who spearheaded the classes, help from editors, translators, and proofreaders at the publishing house, and the encouragement from those who recognize the importance of the cause of science education in China and working for children's futures.

Mi Wenjuan
Founder and CEO of VIPKID

外国专家讲科普　　点燃科学梦想

外国专家讲科普，对于我们《国际人才交流》编辑部来说，这个想法最初来自一位在上海工作的外国专家。当然，最初的想法仅仅是邀请外国专家写科普文章，在《国际人才交流》杂志上双语发表。

2019 年年初，外国专家讲科普这个想法激发了我们与 VIPKID 团队共同的兴趣：我们有大批的高端外国专家资源可以讲科普，VIPKID 之前已经开展了"外教乡村公益课堂"项目，正好合作让外国专家走进各地小学做科普讲座。就这样，外国专家写科普文章升级为外国专家科普讲座。于是，科技部国外人才研究中心和 VIPKID 共同发起了"VIPKID 外国专家科普公益课堂"这个公益项目，邀请科学、技术、工程、艺术和数学等领域的外国专家走进学校，尤其是偏远乡村学校、城市务工人员子女学校，开展科普课堂，传播科学知识，激发科学兴趣。

第一节课来自首都医科大学附属北京妇产医院客座教授、内分泌科名誉主任阿尔弗雷德·奥托·缪克。他是德国图宾根大学的著名妇产科教授，帮助中国建立了首个"卵巢组织冻存库"，2015 年获得中国政府友谊奖。2019 年 4 月，他在北京出席第二届"一带一路"国际合作高峰论坛后，特意安排出时间给孩子们做科普。一边是给各国政要介绍科技的国际合作，一边是给小学五年级的学生介绍生理知识，这个强烈的对比，倒是恰好展现了外国专家科普公益课堂最大的特点，即高端外国专家做科普。

在 2019 年和 2020 年全国科技活动周期间，科普公益课堂升级为外国专家科学讲堂。在中国人民军事革命博物馆、北京天文馆共组织了 12 场讲座，共有约 1000 名中小学生现场聆听了报告。截至 2020 年年底，共有 23 位外国专家参与科普公益课堂，主讲了 28 节科普课。

经过录制、编辑，我们把科普课制作成视频课程，VIPKID 在 APP 中专门研发了科普公开课模块，免费提供给所有注册学员学习；《国际人才交流》杂志微信公众号 WETALENT 也发布了部分视频课程。

高端外国专家深入乡村学校

参加科普课堂的外国专家大都来自我国科研院所和一流高校，科研水平普遍非常高。专家们走进偏远乡村学校、城市务工人员子女学校，如福建省漳浦县林仓小学、陕西省泾阳县兴隆镇崔黄小学等，为当地学校带来了难得的高端资源。

在北京安民学校，北京理工大学日本专家新井健生教授讲解机器人的各种功能，校长也搬来板凳和学生们一起听讲。2020 年 11 月，天津大学西格尔教授和罗杰威教授走进了井冈山小学，校长说两位教授是学校建校以来接待过的最高级别的专家。在大别山区的安徽省岳西县柳畈小学，学生们听中国科技大学储扎克教授讲课，校长激动地说：能见到中科大的教授实在太难得了。

课堂上，外国专家也为孩子们带来了自己最前沿的科研成果。中科院国家天文台德国专家思博森讲解怎样使用超级计算机观测黑洞，中科院微电子研究所瑞典籍研究员亨利·阿达姆松介绍晶体管技术的发明、集成电路技术的突飞猛进和纳米材料。

这些外国专家对科普和公益工作都抱有极大的热情。北京化工大学戴伟教授的课几乎全程展示实验，他讲多长时间，就需要同样的时间准备器皿、药品等，课后他还要清洗、整理所有的实验用具。天津大学药学院院长西格尔教授不仅自己为学生购买小礼物，还联系企业赠送香水小样，为的就是让课上的每一个学生都能亲自体验。

沉浸式的课堂激发科学兴趣

外国专家的科普课堂大多是项目式学习，课程主题的设置紧密围绕现实生活问题，在介绍科学知识的同时，侧重学生的课堂体验。

戴伟教授全程以实验来讲解化学知识，他把一种液体依次倒进一排装有无色液体的烧杯中，只见原本无色的液体变为红、橙、黄、绿、青、蓝、紫……桌上瞬间出现了一道彩虹；把新鲜的玫瑰花、香蕉放入液氮中，瞬间变成冰花、冰香蕉。通过大象牙膏、液体彩虹与鲜花变冰花等物理变化做对比，戴伟教授深入浅出地阐释了化学变化的本质就是将一种或多种材料转换为新的材料的科学知识。

天津大学药学院院长西格尔教授在井冈山小学介绍"感官世界的化学"。干的蝶豆花泡水，水呈蓝色，与柠檬汁混合就变成紫色，这其实就是花青素遇到酸碱物质改变颜色的化学反应。江汉大学外籍专家萨拉的课程主题为"闻声识海豚"，她不仅介绍了海豚独特的发声和回声定位系统，更介绍了自己如何研究海豚，引导学生善待大自然所创造的每一个生命。

这种体验式的教学，让学生们对科学的兴趣大增，更让学生们了解到科学不是人云亦云，而是要通过试验验证的，科学探索的种子就在这一点一滴中生根发芽。

深入乡村的一场探险

通过外国专家科普课堂，在华外国专家走进我国基层学校，了解当地的教育情况、发展情况，有利于他们认识中国、了解中国。

2020 年 11 月，科普公益课堂随"全国优秀科普产（展）品巡展暨流动科技馆进基层"活动走进了革命老区井冈山，更是让外国专家了解了我们的革命历史。在井冈山小学，6 名小学生为西格尔教授和罗杰威教授介绍先辈在井冈山的革命故事：毛泽东同志坚持用仅有一根灯芯的油灯，在井冈山写出了《中国的红色政权为什么能够存在》《井冈山的斗争》。这些革命历史，让外国专家们了解了中华民族的抗争精神与奋斗历史。

福州大学土木工程学院院长布鲁诺教授 2019 年 11 月在福建省漳浦县林仓小学讲课后，用"探险"来形容这次讲课，他已经在福州工作多年，但深入乡镇小学的经历仍然让他觉得像一次探险。

2019 年以来，科技部国外人才研究中心、VIPKID 和各位外国专家，大家通力合作打造了外国专家科普公益课堂这个项目。本书的内容正是基于科普公益课堂活动，我们从课程中挑选了 14 节课，各位外国专家对文字内容又进行了补充、完善。从 2020 年年初开始，本书的文字编写、翻译、校对工作历时约一年。因为新冠肺炎疫情的原因，有几位外国专家没能返回中国，他们在自己的祖国，美国、德国、意大利等，完成了文字的修改完善、内容审核。本书的出版，可以说是外国专家科普公益课堂项目又回归了出版的初心，也拓展了外国专家科普公益课堂项目的生态，学校实体课堂、线上视频课程、图书出版实现了三位一体。

特别感谢科学技术部科技人才与科学普及司对本书出版的资助,感谢本书的编辑出版团队。也借本书的出版,感谢外国专家科普公益课堂项目团队每一个人的辛苦付出。最后只想说,所有的辛苦和付出都是值得的,一切为了孩子!

张 晓

科技部国外人才研究中心《国际人才交流》杂志执行主编

Foreign Experts Science Classes Ignite Science Dream

The Editorial Department of *International Talent*'s initiative to invite foreign experts in China to participate in science popularization was inspired by a foreign expert working in Shanghai. Of course, our original intention was to invite foreign experts to write bilingual science articles and publish them in *International Talent*.

In early 2019, the idea inspired the shared interest between us and VIPKID. We had a batch of high-caliber foreign experts who can popularize science, and VIPKID has carried out the Project of Foreign Teachers into Rural Classrooms before, so we can cooperate in inviting foreign experts to give lectures in primary schools all over China. Thus, we upgraded the science article writing into Foreign Experts Science Classroom. Then, the Foreign Talent Research Center of the Ministry of Science and Technology and VIPKID jointly launched the public welfare project of VIPKID Foreign Expert Public Science Classes.

The project invites foreign experts in science, technology, engineering, art, and mathematics to schools, incredibly remote rural schools, and urban schools for migrant workers' children, giving science classes to promote science knowledge and arouse interest in science. Alfred Otto Mueck, a famous professor of obstetrics and gynecology from the University of Tübingen, had the first class. He is also known as a visiting professor and Honorary Director of the Endocrinology Department of Beijing Obstetrics and Gynecology

Hospital, Capital Medical University. He helped China build the first Ovarian Tissue Cryopreservation Bank and was awarded the Chinese Government Friendship Award in 2015. In April 2019, he arranged time to popularize science among children after attending the 2nd Belt and Road Forum for International Cooperation in Beijing. Such a strong contrast between introducing science and technology development to political leaders. Alfred Otto Mueck was now popularizing physiological knowledge among primary school students. This example manifested the essential characteristic of the project: popularization of science by top-notch foreign experts.

During the National Science Week in 2019 and 2020, the project was upgraded into the Foreign Experts Science Lecture. 12 lectures were given in the Military Museum of the Chinese People's Revolution and in the Beijing Planetarium, and about 1,000 primary students attended. By the end of 2020, the project has invited 23 foreign experts and organized 28 science classes in total.

After recording and editing, the classes have been made into video courses and provided to all registered students to learn for free on the VIPKID app. VIPKID also developed class modules to go alongside the lectures. *International Talent* has also published some video courses on its official WeChat account: WETALENT.

High-caliber Foreign Experts to Rural Schools

Foreign experts joining the project are primarily from research institutes and top universities in China, and all are highly qualified in scientific research. They went to rural and urban schools for migrant workers' children, such as Lincang Primary School in Zhangpu of Fujian Province and Cuihuang Primary School in Xinglong Town of Jingyang County, Shaanxi Province, bringing high-end resources to local schools.

In Anmin School in Beijing, Professor Tatsuo Arai from Beijing Institute of Technology explained various functions of robots, attracting the principal to join in the class with students. In November 2020, Professor Jay S. Siegel and Professor Paolo Vincenzo Genovese from Tianjin University visited Jinggangshan Primary School. The principal said they were the highest-ranking experts they had received since the school was founded. In

Liufan Primary School of Yuexi County in Dabie Mountains in Anhui Province, students attended a lecture given by Professor Zachary Smith from the University of Science and Technology of China. The principal said they were excited to have such a rare opportunity.

In class, foreign experts also brought their cutting-edge achievements in scientific research. Rainer Wilhelm Spurzem, a German expert from the National Astronomical Observatories, Chinese Academy of Wilhelm Sciences (CAS), explained how to observe black holes with a supercomputer. Henry H. Radamson, a Swedish researcher from the Institute of Microelectronics CAS, introduced transistor technology, the rapid advancement of integrated circuit technology and nanometer materials.

These foreign experts all have great enthusiasm for the popularization of science and public welfare. Professor David G. Evans from Beijing University of Chemical Technology demonstrated various experiments all through his classes. He would spend the same amount of time preparing vessels and chemicals as presenting in style, not to mention the time needed to wash and sort out all the laboratory supplies. Professor Jay S. Siegel, Dean of the School of Pharmaceutical Science and Technology, Tianjin University, purchased gifts for students by himself and contacted the company to request perfume samples as gifts, just for every student to gain hands-on experience in class.

Immersed Learning Arouses Interest in Science

Mainly in the form of project learning, Foreign Experts Science Classes Project focuses on real-life problems and emphasizes students' experience in class while introducing science knowledge.

Professor David G. Evans taught chemistry utilizing experiments throughout the course. He poured a liquid successively into a row of beakers with a colorless liquid, turning red, orange, yellow, green, cyan, blue, and purple to create a rainbow on the desk immediately; he also made fresh roses and bananas frozen instantly with liquid nitrogen. By comparing physical changes such as elephant toothpaste, a liquid rainbow, and the frozen fresh flowers, Professor David interpreted, in a simple way, the knowledge of science that chemical changes are the transformation of one or several kinds of materials into new materials.

Professor Jay S. Siegel, Dean of the School of Pharmaceutical Science and Technology, Tianjin University, introduced "Chemistry in the Realm of Senses" in Jinggangshan Primary School. The dry butterfly peas immersed in water make the water blue and turns purple when mixed with lemon juice, which is a chemical reaction of anthocyanin, which changes colors when exposed to acid or alkali substances. Sara Platto, a foreign expert from Jianghan University, gave a class with the theme of Recognizing Dolphins by Their Sounds. She introduced to students how dolphins' unique vocalization and echolocation system works. Then she described how she studied dolphins to guide students in treating every creature of nature kindly.

By attending such classes based on experience, students became more interested in science. They understood that science is not to echo the views of others but to be verified by experiments. Bit by bit, a seed of scientific exploration has rooted and budded.

An Adventure to Rural Areas

Through Foreign Experts Science Classes, foreign experts in China visited grassroots schools, where they learned about local education and development, having a better understanding of China.

In November 2020, with "Mobile Science and Technology Museum to Grassroots", the project went to Jinggangshan, an old revolutionary base, where foreign experts learned about the revolutionary history of China. In Jinggangshan Primary School, six primary students told stories about revolutionaries of the older generation in Jinggangshan to Professor Jay S. Siegel and Professor Paolo Vincenzo Genovese. They told stories about how Comrade Mao Zedong insisted in writing in the light of an oil lamp with just one wick. and completed works like *Why Can China's Red Political Power Exist?* and *The Struggle in the Jinggangshan Mountains*. The revolutionary history helped foreign experts understand the spirit of resistance and the struggling history of the Chinese people.

Professor Bruno Briseghella, Dean of the College of Civil Engineering of Fuzhou University, described it as an adventure after teaching in Lincang Primary School in

Zhangpu of Fujian in November 2019. He has been working in Fuzhou for many years, but the experience of going to a rural primary school still seems like an adventure for him.

Since 2019, the Foreign Talent Research Center of the Ministry of Science and Technology, VIPKID, and foreign experts have made concerted efforts in developing the project. This book is just based on the project, from which we selected 14 classes, the text of which was further supplemented and improved by foreign experts. From the early 2020 on, it takes about a year to compile, translate, and proofread. Due to the COVID-19 outbreak, several foreign experts failed to return to China, but they finished editing and reviewing the book in their home countries, such as the USA, Germany, and Italy. The publication of this book can be regarded as a return of the Foreign Expert Science Classes Project to the original intention of publication, and an expansion of its project ecology, thus achieving the trinity of office classrooms, online video classes, and publication of books.

We want to extend special thanks to the Department of Science and Technology Talent and Popularization, Ministry of Science and Technology of china for supporting the publication of the book and to the editing and publishing team. Taking the opportunity of its publication, we also express our gratitude to everyone in the project of VIPKID Foreign Experts Public Science Classes for their hard work. Last, we want to say all our hard work and efforts are worthwhile, as everything is for the children!

Zhang Xiao
Executive Chiefeditor of International Talent,
Foreign Talent Research Center, Ministry of Science and Technology of China